Globalisation, Economic Reforms and Employment Strategy in India

S.P. Gupta

Academic Foundation
NEW DELHI

Published in 2006 by
ACADEMIC FOUNDATION
4772-73 / 23 Bharat Ram Road, (23 Ansari Road),
Darya Ganj, New Delhi - 110 002 (India).
Phones : 23245001 / 02 / 03 / 04.
Fax : +91-11-23245005.
E-mail : academic@vsnl.com
www.academicfoundation.com

Globalisation, Economic Reforms and
Employment Strategy in India
by S.P. Gupta

ISBN 81-7188-462-8

Printed and bound in India.

CONTENTS

List of Tables and Boxes

Tables

Boxes

List of Annexures

Preface

This book is to be read in tandem with the Special Group Report of May 2002 on "Targeting Ten Million Employment Opportunities per Year," prepared by the Planning Commission, Government of India, (Chairman: Dr. S.P. Gupta, the then-Member of the Planning Commission).

This Report recommends an employment strategy based on the nature of the labour market in India and the labour-intensive character of the unorganised sector of the economy that contributes 60 per cent of the GDP and more than 92 per cent of the employment. This book attempts to monitor the implementation of the Report's recommended employment approach in the field and assesses the effectiveness as well as the limitations of this approach.

Since the release of the Report in 2002, there have been vast and rapid changes in the world scenario and, as a result, changes in the socio-economic fabric of India. It is increasingly realised that in this growing and integrated world it would not be possible to formulate or develop any effective employment strategy in isolation. Indeed, all these new scenarios demand radical changes in the mindset of policymakers and other development agents asking changes in the policy priorities and their sequencing, including the policy on employment generation.

India's growth and development strategy may be broadly separated into four phases since 1947, which one may regard to be rather simplistic. This will, however, provide a perspective to where we stand.

The first phase, just after independence, was marked by heavy emphasis on the development of basic and heavy industries, major physical infrastructures and the industrial base of the country. For this, the public sector was made the dominant player, giving "the commanding heights"—a tenet of socialist ideology, largely influenced by the great success in the fast development of the USSR during this period—unmindful of the cost. Just after independence, India had almost no industrial base, especially in heavy and basic industries. This may partly explain the adoption of the above strategy by the contemporary policymakers.

The second phase was marked by allowing a more liberal entry of the private sector to industrial development in India, by providing them some incentives and removing several existing impediments to the normal functioning of the private sector. The incentives given in many instances were marginal, but implied a big attitudinal change on the part of the Government. This phase reflected a pro-business policy by the Government in contrast to a pro-liberalisation policy to follow in the 1990s.

The second phase also coincided with the Sixth and Seventh Five Year Plans of India over the 1980s that covered the Indira Gandhi and Rajiv Gandhi eras of prime ministership. This period registered the highest acceleration in the growth rate compared to the past several decades, the so-called 'hindu rate of growth' (GDP).

Attitudinal changes and Government policy changes in this second phase may also be considered as a reaction to the existing very low productivity growth, inefficient management of the then dominant public sector, and failure to break away from the very low persistent 'hindu growth trend' of around 3.0-3.5 per cent per annum. According to some economists[1], the former may also be partly due to political calculations and not necessarily due to inefficiency of the economic system. But, the fact remains that this period observed the highest productivity growth, since independence.

The third phase of the strategy centred primarily around liberalisation and globalisation, when the competitive market acted as the sole allocator of resources. To start with, this phase was triggered off by a different reason: to meet the foreign exchange crisis of India in 1991. There are several views as to why this foreign exchange crisis arose, especially after the successful growth achievements of the eighties. Some economists have explained this

---

1. Dani Rodrik and Arvind Subramanian, NBER Working Paper No. 10376, March 2004.

crisis by alluding to India's high external borrowings, resulting from a very high order of fiscal deficit in the central budget (above 9 per cent of GDP). Others explained it as a result of poor management of its external debt portfolios by shifting away significantly from soft and safe loans to hard and volatile capital inflows. This book does not intend to enter into these controversies, but emphasise that this third phase had as its special feature, provision for more consumer benefits in the economy's growth process. It also attempted to bring the Indian economy in tune with global competition, a step not exclusively based on the immediate commercial interests of the private sector in India. This was marked by the slow removal of all prevailing subsidies (not all have gone), explicit and implicit in the economy.

The third phase was also, in essence, a recognition of the inefficiency in the public sector operating in many areas, followed by an emphasis on disinvestment. This phase was initiated in 1991 during Narasimha Rao's Government and has been continued more or less with the same contents by successive non-Congress Governments. The BJP-led Government, in addition, focused on the problem of percolation of benefits of the ongoing development programme to certain backward regions, classes and social groups, hoping also to reduce the observed deficiency in generating sustainable employment and reducing rural poverty, etc. in this phase. Some policy corrections were initiated by them but their full feasibility could not be explored because their term ended in 2004, when the UPA Government came to power. This has ushered in the fourth phase of India's reform strategy.

The fourth phase can be defined as a people-friendly phase, wherein attempts have been made to give the ongoing reform process a human face. This is in response to the feeling, already mentioned, that the growth and reform process initiated in the mid-1980s and 1990s created greater regional inequality, more rural-urban imbalances, more poor people and more unemployment, by leaving out a large part of the informal sector from the mainstream of reform—a sector which provides nearly 92 per cent of employment. This has created in certain regions heavy socio-political disturbances and insecurities.

Often, instances have been found when Government's high-handedness is used to silence protests for large gaps between government promises and performances but given the present worldwide trend towards democracy, decentralisation, easy access to information, and the increasing acceptance of legitimacy of human rights, this occasional harsh approach may prove to be unsustainable.

The endeavour of the present Congress-led Government, trying to make the ongoing growth strategy 'people friendly' (growth with human face), is welcome. This approach promises to remove all visible inequities in the spread of the benefits of the present 'reform led' growth. But the study presented here finds that there is an inherent incompatibility between the basic tenets of this family of reform and the people friendly approach. This is primarily because the ideologies and hypotheses on which the present reform philosophy is built is often far removed from India's grassroot realities[2]; for that matter, the same is true for many other low-income and newly emerging countries.

The present reform strategy basically works under a norm of 'fitness for survival' of any enterprise determined exclusively by the market-led profit maximisation motive. Under this norm, a large number of enterprises in India (contributing 60 per cent of GDP) will turn out to be 'unfit.' It must be recognised, however, that many of these enterprises fulfilled many other key objectives of development like: providing sustainable jobs and livelihood to a large mass of people to redress poverty, helping to reduce regional disparity in development, protecting the environment from excessive use of conventional energy, and giving dignity to people living on earnings from their own enterprise and not on charity.

At the same time, the approach to maximise the size of the GDP (as a 'National Cake') by the fittest in the market and then to transfer some of this increased income to the 'left outs' or 'unfits' as a safety net, has been tried in the past but failed in most cases to provide gainful and sustainable jobs. At best they provided relief to poor

---

2. For example when nearly 60 per cent of GDP and 94 per cent of employment are from informal sector a blanket 'fitness' criteria for survival which immediately asks for an exit of this large numbers is proving to be socio-politically infeasible.

families as income support in slack seasons[3]. And, in no way do they give human dignity to the recipients of Government's basic relief programme. Details are given in the main body of the book.

Furthermore, the composition of the labour force in the developing world is fast changing, with an increasing share of youths in the labour force, particularly those who are educated. Around 80 per cent of the youths currently unemployed are well-educated, and this percentage will increase over time. This development is becoming a socio-political problem since the educated youths come mostly from the increasing number of rich, middle-class families who enjoy growing political and social clout. Until now, most of them used to be absorbed in the organised sector, but today the organised sector is experiencing near-jobless growth and the supply of educated labour is increasing faster because of universalisation of education and large demographic changes in the age composition of population. The gap between the demand for and the supply of educated labour force is ever expanding.

It has roughly been estimated that of the total job opportunities provided by the organised sector nearly 25 per cent comprise supervisory staffs. In 1991-2000 it came to around 5 to 7 million. This is the segment which primarily absorbs educated labour. With increase in capital intensity and use of sophisticated technology the growth of this segment has become much faster (above 2.2 per cent per annum) than the growth of organised workers as a whole, of nearly 0.9 per cent per annum. On this basis in 2003-04 it has been assessed that nearly 7.6 million educated labours might have been absorbed in the organised sector. On the other hand the estimated demand for jobs only for the educated youths in 2003-04 would come to around 70 million and growing approximately at 5.3 per cent per annum in the future (minimum 3 million new entrants in the job market every year coming out of the formal education stream, i.e. from class 8 to class 11 standard). This shows the growing problem of getting jobs in the organised industry for the educated labours. Alternatives have to be found rather than live with the expectation that all educated youths will get high paid corporate jobs in future. This will require, as has already been mentioned, a

3. At times also 'one shot' compensation given to the retrenched labour while downsizing the corporate units.

change in their mindset supported by suitable vocational training to equip them for self employment and availing new opportunities in the Small and Medium Enterprises (SME) including the growing services sector.

At the same time, the expected additional skilled job opportunities in the expanded global market are lagging because of increasing vested interests, arising from political and national interests. The growing resistance at local level is aggravated primarily by the high level of unemployment among nations providing work in the potential job market, especially in the developed countries. There is a strong view that the nation-state and its interests will continue to be the dominant unit of the global order, although economic globalisation and the dispersion of technologies, especially information technology, will place enormous new strains on the nation-state.

All these issues have been covered in this book. This book recommends that unless there is a sea-change in the present mindset among policymakers, bureaucrats, financers, producers and consumers, the present development strategy will create more gaps between the 'haves' and the 'have-nots,' resulting in an unsustainable socio-political condition. And this sea-change in mindsets is not possible because they are the by-product of the basic driving force of the present reform. Way outs have been suggested different from the prevailing policy to change this mindset and address the problem of growing gaps between the 'haves' and the 'have-nots,' those who have decent jobs and those who have no jobs—the prime elements which may derail the sustainability and deprive all the virtues of today's globalisation efforts and appropriate reforms in the economic arena.

In the preparation of this study my indebtedness goes to all my former colleagues in the Planning Commission, State Government officials at the grassroots, NGOs, and many academic and corporate leaders for encouraging and giving the much needed insight in writing this book. Needless to say that I benefited tremendously by many discussions with Mr. K.C. Pant, the then-Deputy Chairman of Planning Commission and Heads of other Ministries, while not necessarily agreeing on all the issues. My special gratitude goes to Mrs. Meenakshi Anand Choudhari, the then-Principal Adviser and

Mr. Shailendra Sharma, Adviser in Planning Commission. I was always assisted by Dr. H. Ramachandran, the then Director I.A.M.R, Professor Amitabh Kundu of JNU, Dr. N.S. Sastry former Director General of NSSO and Dr. Krisnan Lal, Emeritus Professor, University of Saskatchewan, Canada at all stages of the writing of this book. My sincere thanks go to Mr. Sant Lal Arora of I.A.M.R for giving me full support in the preparation of the empirical base of this study, to Mr. Bal Krishna, former Joint Chief, I.A.M.R. for helping the team in Statistical Analysis and designing the report; to Ms. Nandita Khadaria, for helping in editing, to Mr. R.C. Nandwani who moulded the manuscript into its final shape; Mr. Hemant Gaba for his constant involvement at all stages of the preparation of this book, and for overseeing the work of the other members of the secretarial team; and also moulding the manuscript into its final shape. My frequent interactions with the Director General ILO and ASSOCHAM and FICCI have also been a great help to me. I am extremely thankful to my publisher Dr. Uma Kapila of Academic Foundation for bringing out the publication in shortest possible time and to Ms. Patti Madigan for her final editing. Last, but not the least, I could finish this book only because of the continuous encouragement and support of my wife Kamala and my daughter Madhumita from the earliest stage up till the final drafting.

For any error and omission in the text of the book however, the responsibility lies with the author.

— **S.P. Gupta**

New Delhi

1

Changing Employment Strategy and its Rationale

The employment strategy of a country must be cognizant of the ongoing globalisation process and the country's economic reform programme.

In India, the economic reform programme adopted, very closely resembles the 'Washington Consensus Approach' to development. Its objective is defined as the maximisation of growth, its impetus comes from the maximisation of profit by market competition and its main facilitator is liberalisation. The market for competition is the global market which includes all countries of the world. Often by mistake the above definition is accepted as the comprehensive concept of globalisation. However, 'globalisation' as conceived, is not confined exclusively to economic issues and policies but also to many non-economic issues and policies, not always correlated with their economic half. The current reform process in India covers mainly the economic issues.

India's reform programme appears to rest mainly on two sets of neoclassical conditions (1) perfect mobility of labour, capital, technology with infinite substitution between factors of production, and (2) early, uninterrupted information flow within and across country boundaries. Both these are a part of the comprehensive features of globalisation: Growing interrelatedness resulting from expanded flows of information, technology, capital, goods and services, culture and values of life (including human rights), sharing of the common concerns for protection of the environment, free movement of natural persons throughout the world largely triggered by the policy of liberalisation and growth of ICT[1], and the acceptance of democratic values among an increasing number of countries.

---

1. In this book we are not entering into the other non-economic dimension of globalisation and their plus and minus, except when it is extremely difficult to separate the interactions between economic and non-economic forces.

When these two guiding sets of conditions under India's economic reforms are fulfilled, the neoclassical model suggests that the other major social benefits of higher growth will percolate on their own. These include: Improved equity, more employment, better balance of regional development, and removal of poverty. In this scenario the generation of employment becomes a natural end product of a production structure chosen on the basis of global competition. In a world with 'neoclassical labour markets,' the demand and supply of labour are matched by competitive market valuation of labour. Therefore, the problems of unemployment do not arise. But in reality, many of these conditions are absent within and between most countries. In India, as in many other countries, labour markets do not display either neoclassical or classical characters. They are highly fractured by immobility and rigidity in structure between regions and groups. This is evidenced by increasing unemployment in different regions and sectors as the demand-supply gap in labour markets widen. Thus, one of the key challenges facing the policymakers is how to formulate suitable policies to remove the restrictive barriers and revive the neoclassical conditions. But this is not an easy challenge since the policies must take into account the local, national and global conditions. Faster and more comprehensive economic liberalisation can solve part of the problem, but many non-economic policy decisions could stand in the way.

As discussed above, there are several, increasingly influential non-economic forces that are adversely affecting many of the necessary economic conditions needed for desired globalisation. For example, environmental and ethical issues are beginning to question to what extent the new technology will create or resolve the emerging ethical dilemma on the digital divide. Nations' security concerns are creating restrictions on the full flow of goods, services and factors of production, the latter affecting the healthy outsourcing and migration of labour. Although energy supply may appear sufficient on the ground, the 'politics of energy' (which restricts the growth of non-conventional energy) and the impending political instability in oil producing countries with vested interests of the big powers may disrupt this supply. How will the growing power of non-state actors such as the multinational companies, NGOs and the human rights lobby be accommodated by nation-states and international bodies in the future? Finally, how will the unequal level of development in the world compound the problem when transition pains and adjustment problems become severe in many countries, crossing their social and political tolerance levels?

Experiences across the globe now clearly demonstrates that due to the lack of capacity to address many of these economic and non-economic issues, a large number of developing countries, in their growth process, are leaving out a large segment of their labour force from the mainstream of development as 'unemployeds'. This is occurring not only in poor developing countries, but also in several emerging mid-income countries.

The incidence of unemployment has become as high as 5 to 8 per cent on an average in most reforming countries, and much higher at the disaggregated country or sub-country level. Very recently, it has climbed to 9 per cent in Germany and several other European countries. In many of these countries, including developing countries, these high unemployment rates are becoming socio-political as well as security concerns.

According to many analysts, in the 19th century free trade efforts failed because many major, developed countries, faced with high unemployment, were persuaded through social and political pressures to revert to earlier protectionist measures or even attempts to revive old days policies of colonisation in hidden form. To save globalisation and enjoy its benefits, the world community must avoid a repetition of this 19th century scenario. It must identify the changes warranted in the reform programme, especially over the transition period, which will help reforming countries to reap the benefits of globalisation while at the same time helping to save the world from the backlash of emerging unemployment and inequality. To quote Prof. Joseph Stiglitz from his book *Globalization and its Discontents,* (2002) "Opposition to globalisation in many parts of the world is not to globalisation *per se*—to the new sources of funds for growth or to the new export markets—but to the particular set of doctrines, the Washington Consensus policies that the international financial institutions have imposed.... The assumptions underlying market fundamentalism do not hold in developed economies, let alone in developing countries... and it is not just opposition to the policies themselves, but to the notion that there is a single set of policies that is right." The nature of reform, therefore, must be country specific.

Box 1.1

In light of a changing global and domestic socio-political scenario, the approach to employment and equity in India need to be revisited.

A few of the issues which need to be addressed are:

A) Non-Economic: i) Problem of deteriorating environment, increasing pollution, global warming, and related consequentials; ii) ongoing interaction and sometimes conflicting interests between corporate multinationals, corporate domestic, and national electorate compulsions (specially in the democratic countries undergoing evolution of coalition politics); iii) fast growth of information technology with its use often leading to large digital divides that result in growing demand for human rights, more transparency in administration and steps against corruption; iv) ever increasing religious and caste fundamentalism leading to issues of domestic and global security; v) "fair" *versus* "unfair" competitive policies, and lastly; vi) conflicts of interests between domestic economic and international political considerations, For example, decisions appropriate for promoting domestic economic prosperity *versus* decisions appropriate for participating in many international and bi-lateral agreements that are based on non-economic considerations.

B) Economic: i) The reverse redistributing trend in India that is being encouraged by growth with more capital intensive and labour saving production processes, often accompanied by rising inflation. As a result, money is getting transferred from the pockets of the poor to benefit of the rich, with the danger of creating a more inequitable society that leaves out large segments of the labour force from the mainstream of development. This is further nurtured by government subsidies, sometimes implicitly. This is, in contrast to what the World Bank Country Report is asserting "growth can be maximised by more equitable distribution of economic activities with sustainability; ii) increasing gap between the two segments of labour (highly skilled and semi-non-skilled) with respect to income, livelihood and career opportunities, access to health and education, social identity and dignity as a labourer, (i.e., the latter treated as parasites with open and hidden subsidies given by the other segments of the society); iii) the emerging changes in the nature of employment related issues from quantitative to qualitative i.e., moving away from the current definition of unemployment (refer to Report of Special Group on Targeting Ten Million Employment Opportunities Per Year) to one that is based on productivity and not sustained by government subsidies and dole; iv) a large number of unemployment constitutes the educated youth (with many having class 10+ and 12+ formal education); they lack skill mainly as a result of poor government policies that fail to provide opportunities for adequate training facilities. This segment adds around 3 million and above to the labour force each year with a growing trend; v) increasing unrest among the unemployed

Contd...

Contd. ...

> educated youth is fast becoming a recognised political pressure group with many coming from well to do parts of the society—a potential cause of terrorism and other forms of violent activities—a contrast to unemployed among the illiterate who are mute sufferers and have little political clout. Their problem is life below the poverty line.
>
> The lack of R&D for appropriate technology, training facilities and government labour market policy are aggravating the problems further. Added to these are the increasing unequal regional development potentially emerging explosive socio-political and law and order factor; such trends have to be reckoned with an increasing awareness and respect for democratic values and human rights. In India this cannot be suppressed as in many non-democratic economies. The above clearly demonstrates the futility of separating economic issues from many of the non-economic issues as they are complementary and at times competitive.

More or less the same feeling is expressed by the Director General of the World Trade Organization (WTO), one of the key promoters of the globalisation concept through free trade. According to the WTO Director-General Supachai Panitchpakdi, "where there is incontrovertible economic confidence that open market and free trade hold great benefits, it is equally true that trade can create losers. If the global trading system is to continue to progress along the path of trade liberalisation as I believe, the government must take adequate measures to ensure that those who have lost out are looked after... no single system can be applied to all nations. *But every government has a responsibility to implement programmes that ensure that those who are not well prepared for greater competition are looked after often by increasing tariffs or giving domestic subsidies.* Failure to take such actions will not only erode public support in the WTO and in the global trading system, but politically it will not make liberalisation and globalisation sustainable."[2]

India's current reform process clearly demonstrates that under the market-driven growth maximisation path, survival is ensured to those who have the ability to reduce the cost to meet global competition. The focus of the current global technological revolution is primarily on cost-saving devices.

2. *Herald International Tribune*, 21.10.2002.

This technology revolution mostly promotes an automated system of production and, therefore, any cost reduction efforts become synonymous with labour shedding. India's present cost-cutting endeavour, tries to take advantage of its comparatively cheap capital. It overlooks its labour surplus and a capital shortage market while switching over to capital-heavy technology financed by large borrowing both at home and abroad.

The world over, the availability of credit at cheaper terms is increasingly driven by high growth of capital flows (mostly private) between countries (much higher than trade flows) and their fast mobility across countries due to liberalised policies and improved communication and information technology and it makes easy for FIIs to move fast from places of speculative profit and with its potential danger sources for the country concerned.

In contrast, the mobility of labour is still very low within and between countries. India's latest 2001 census shows that the percentage of migrants to population within India is declining both in rural and urban areas, especially on economic and employment considerations (Kundu, 2005). Often, it is argued that under these circumstances, capital should move to labour to ease the unemployment situation. However, given the heavy infrastructure inequality between regions in India, capital (if it wants to maximise profits) is not likely to behave as described above in a significant manner. In developing countries, the expectation is that the changing age profile (i.e. demographic changes) will help ease the unemployment situation through inter-country migration. The growth of the working age population in the developed countries in general will slow down in the future based on an aging population and the trend towards slower population growth. It is hoped that this will make migration of labour from labour surplus to labour shortage economies easy. However, how this will translate into actual numbers in case of India, needs to be analysed.

At the moment, most developed counties are suffering from a high unemployment rate. Based on World Bank data, it is estimated that among the 'high income countries,' assuming an average growth rate of 4 per cent per annum over the next 10 years and given a present (optimistic) employment elasticity of 0.15 and the growth of the labour force at 0.1 per cent per annum, the shortages in labour (after clearing the prevailing back log of unemployment) will come at around 20 to 22 million by end of the 10 year period. On the other hand, assuming that all the 'newly emerging countries' will grow at 6 per cent per annum over the next 10 years and given an employment elasticity of nearly 0.25 and a growth in labour supply of 2 per cent per annum, all these countries together will create a labour surplus of roughly 340 to 350 million over the next 10 years.

This creates a rather dismal scenario: Around 340 million job seekers will compete for 21 million jobs. The share of an individual country obviously can not be very large. Some benefits may come through outsourcing, however, it is anticipated that its growth will also be hindered by many national and sometimes even corporate interests (Chapter 5).

Cheap capital could be procured by the Indian corporate sectors, including large multinationals who have easy access to credit through networking with the world's financial and capital markets; they also have an initial advantage of a larger capital base and better infrastructure. However, at the same time, a large numbers of small and medium industries with their low capital base, inadequate infrastructure and insufficient access to capital (even in the domestic market), may find it difficult to adjust to this changing 'factor market' scenario for their survival and adoption of modern technologies.

Thus, many economists now argue that since the organised sector is providing quality jobs and can survive under emerging global competition; let it replace the informal sector. They unfortunately overlook the fact that the organised sector, of late, has been experiencing almost a jobless growth. In 1990-2000 the organised sector had contributed only around 7 per cent to the country's total employment (28 million jobs); the remaining 309 million jobs (93 percentage approximately) were provided by the unorganised/ informal sector. Even if the employment elasticity of the organised sector (observed over the best period of last decade of around 0.1–0.2) could be maintained, the organised sector will take more than 20 years to compensate for the job loss created by the exit of the informal sector. This is assuming that it grew at more than 80 to 100 per cent per annum in the future; this estimation is based on a labour force growth of 2.0 to 2.4 per cent over the reference period. This demonstrates the infeasibility of such a strategy as a solution to unemployment. The response from these economists is to suggest that if the rigidity of the labour market is reduced by appropriate labour reforms (by making 'firing' easy) then the employment elasticity of this sector will significantly increase, generating more employment to meet the impending higher level of unemployment. But the experiences of the 90s do not show that the Industrial Dispute Act (IDA) and its restricted provisions on firing of workers in any way inhibited the significant downsizing of labour in many corporate units, both in private and public, nor has it impaired the decisions of the corporate managers in restructuring their workforce according to their requirements. During this period, substantial reconstruction of workforce took place to meet the requirements of 'high capital intensive technology' by reducing the ratio of regular workers to supervisory staffs and temporary contract labour. But its effect came as a jobless growth. It proves that (IDA) has not posed much of a hindrance in restructuring of the corporate sector.

The following Table in brief explains the above scenario:

Table 1.1

Growth Rates Per Annum (1991-92–2000-01)

GDP Organised Manufacturing	*Total Work Force*	*Real Wage Workers (90s)*	*Real Wage Supervisors (90s)*	*No. of Workers 1980-81 to 2000-01*	*No. of Supervisors 1980-81 to 2000-01*	*Industrial Disputes*	*Mandates Lost*
5.8 [1]	-0.4[1]	0.0[2]	6.5[2]	0.2[2]	1.6[2]	-11.2[3]	-5.5[3]

Based on: 1. *Economic Survey*–2000-03.
2. R. Nagaraj : *EPW* 24.7.2004.
3. IIPA Chronic Poverty Research Centre Working Paper No. 7.

The restructuring of manufacturing was also influenced often by the changes in its management, and by the nature of the joint venture agreements and other global commitments it fulfilled. Therefore, any change in the IDA is not likely to make the corporate sector more labour intensive. Further, a rough calculation shows that even if the employment elasticity could be raised above 0.5 (historically, the highest ever reached) still the organised sector will need more than two decades to cover the growing unemployment by attaining a 30 per cent plus growth over this period. Besides, one should remember that this organised sector is maintaining its technological competitive edge, (primarily to survive in the global competition), by adopting 'high-tech' capital intensive production. Thus, this much of increase in its labour intensity in production will be a contradiction. The answer: There is no alternative but to adopt a 'labour use' and 'capital saving' appropriate technologies, by reviving many of the prevailing indigenous technologies in the small and medium sectors and a healthy ancillarisation between large and small units to create more employment opportunities as has been tried in certain areas of China. This growing gap between demand for and supply of labour is becoming wider, with nearly 41 per cent of unemployed constitute the educated labour force, of which, 82 per cent are from educated youth. For details, see Chapter 3.

Domestic research and development on appropriate technology that could offer alternative 'capital savings' and 'employment intensive' production (i.e., appropriate technology) is almost absent in India and in most developing countries. For India, the resources spent on such R&D is 1/60th of the R&D budget of South Korea's.

This means that many new areas of employment opportunities will remain untapped in India given the expense of such R&D and the limited and declining allocation of GDP to such research. In fact, there is no unique or universal technology for direct application to such a situation. Such technology, more often than not, has to evolve over time in a particular context of learning, often by inter-country experiences, as to how to cater to multiple objectives including sustainable livelihood options.

Some traditional, labour-intensive sectors like agriculture, construction, trade, and small and medium industries are becoming increasingly capital intensive. For example, according to a report in the *Hindustan Times*, (dated 5.1.05) planners are exploring ways to construct flyovers in Delhi that can be built within 36 hours by using imported, fabricated bridges—a form of "reverse out-sourcing"—threatening the construction sector with the loss of jobs and its labour intensive character.

Quite often, these high-technologies and automated systems are not necessarily cost effective, but their selections reflect the mindset of decision makers, politicians and even technocrats, who find it easier to deal with machines than labour. There are plenty of case studies to support this view. Research and Development represents one area where India can learn how to make modern technology useful in labour-intensive production by protecting their labour-intensive character, as being done in China.

As a result, production agents at the lower end of the margin, deprived of many of the above opportunities, are slowly getting sick and facing closures. Several countries like China managed to save, for the time-being, their labour-intensive sectors in the global competition, often by reducing unit labour costs through reducing wage bills by increasing the hours of work or by reducing other benefits traditionally provided to labour. This has been practiced in the coastal regions of China by multinationals, with the help of *hukou* system, producing labour-intensive goods for exports. They ignore the socio-political and humanitarian implications of these endeavours, though, these can be very high at times.

The Chinese so-called 'Hukou system'[3] or the household legislation system, was initiated to prevent and control rural urban influx of population. This system overtime became more and more liberal and retained and changed its form from time to time. Now, in this system, the city authorities mainly in coastal cities can shift back the workers to the countryside because without a job, a migrant has no right to stay in a harbour area. The migrant workers generate local tax revenues by providing government with a cheap labour, but because of the *hukou* system, the local government has no regulation to pay anything for the welfare of these temporary workers.

In a democratic country like India, with the strong value placed on human rights, this practice is neither possible nor desirable. Ironically, many of the ardent proponents of this 'exclusive market-driven reform' like to conclude that the consequent 'left-outs,' as production agents, justifiably should die as unfits, because they believe only in the survival of the fittest according to how 'fittest' is defined by them. For this school of thought, no employment strategy is needed to re-examine the patterns of growth which can help survival of the left-outs as production agents. To them, the government can at best, innovate policies for relief by transferring some wealth generated by the fittest to the not-so-fittest to reduce their pains and soften the

3. *Hukou* System: If a person/s wants to migrate from rural areas to urban areas for employment they have to obtain a licence from migration depositing a prescribed fee. If they fail to get a job within the stipulated time they have to return to their home and in addition their licence money is forfeited. This makes them very susceptible to exploitation in the job markets.

bite of the socio-political instabilities. This is, in essence, the often quoted promise of protecting the human face of reform.

However, the above approach does not provide a human face and dignity to recipients who remain depended on the subsidy, open or hidden by the public sector; a close similarity with Russia under the reform process. For example, to quote Mr. Goyal,[4] "A focus on reform (in Russia) of the biggest enterprises and large corporations brings more misery to people who remain ill-equipped to deal with the changes being imposed on them from the top. The Government's response, then, is to throw a few more *kopeks* into pensions or support for the poor driving them further into dependence. The rich are not willing to give, the government is unable to collect and bureaucrats are not willing to let go. The money cannot reach the poor through the inch-thick steel sieves of the Russian system. It just keeps moving along the top to those holding the reins of power. Real poverty relief should focus on enabling people in wealth creation, helping them get away from state support and benefits... poor countries should focus on basic healthcare, literacy, education, communication and transport infrastructure, small and medium scale business and self employment, which affect the poorest people in society."

The Indian Perspective and the Dimension of the Problem

Nearly 92 per cent of India's employment and 60 per cent of GDP are generated by the so-called informal or unorganised sector (comprising tiny, small and medium enterprises). A large number of these enterprises function as healthy, viable production units in the market, contributing a major share to output and employment.

The robustness of the SSI sector and its competitive efficiency is demonstrated by its export performance. In 2000-2001, SSI sector exports accounted for 34.5 per cent of India's total export of which, export of non-traditional products was 94 per cent. Other than in leather, rayon and synthetic products, almost in all other sectors, the percentage share of SSI exports has increased between 1995-2000. Until very recently, for example, their growth of output in relative

---

4. *Russian Journal*, June 2003.

terms was 20 per cent higher than that of the corporate or the so-called organised sector (Table 2.1).[5]

Besides, although the corporate sector is still producing more than 42 per cent of GDP growing at 7 per cent plus, it has contributed hardly 7 per cent to employment and, moreover, its contribution to incremental employment has, over time, become zero and even negative.[6] This clearly demonstrates that the organised sector has failed to contribute incrementally to employment generation.

Much more alarming is the fact that the organised sector's indirect contribution to employment is also dwindling. The generation of indirect employment happened in the past primarily due to a healthy 'ancillarisation' process between large, small and medium enterprises (SMEs). But, for reasons cited later in this book, this process is slowing down.

This slow down in 'ancillarisation' is partly due to growing import contents in the production process of the organised sector, and partly to insufficient capacity of the SME's to pick up the 'high technology'-based needs for inputs of the large industries. Further, the capacity building and sustenance of the small industries in many instances, given their low working capital base often get handicapped by the practice of delayed payments of their dues by the large contracting establishments. Finally, the 'ancillarisation' process to a significant extent has also slowed down as large enterprises to cut costs have adopted the reverse outsourcing practices to neighbouring countries with cheap labour.

According to the Deputy Director of ILO India office, the outsourcing (something called reverse outsourcing) from India is touching more than 11 billion dollars (nearly 2 per cent of GDP), much higher than the USA, Germany, U.K. and even China in terms of outsourcing as a percentage of GDP.

---

5. Between 1993-1994 to 1999-2000 the relative growth of GDP in the organised sector was higher by 54 per cent but since 1999-2000 and 2002 the relative growth in organised sector has fallen to 29 per cent.

6. Understandably the Public Corporate Sector is carrying excess labour, accommodated in the past as social obligation. Hence, this joblessness can be explained. But accordingly to the Economic Survey, even private corporate sector is showing, a negative growth in employment. Separate study shows they are also jobless in many greenfield projects.

"Indeed, the 'net' outsourcing benefits for India, while not always positive, reduce employment initially, [however] pay off adequately in the long run as the labour market has tremendous scope from adjusting."[7] But when India's existing unemployment and under-employment are so high and labour market flexibility very low, the so-called adjustment mechanism is likely to be slow and inefficient.

The above apprehensions were substantiated in the late 90s (1994 to 2000), when a comparatively high growth of GDP could not sustain the growth in employment; employment declined to around one per cent per annum compared to more than two per cent in the pre-reform period of the 80s. The magnitude of unemployment over the same period (1994 to 2000) went up from 37 million to 44 million.[8] Given the increasing growth of the labour force, unemployment may increase further.

This problem of growing unemployment and resultant poverty is becoming a socio-political and security concern. This is more acute within some regions or groups, where unemployment and poverty touched as high as 50-60 per cent of the labour force and the population, respectively. One glaring example is the heavy social unrest in recent years followed by many underground activities in the North-Eastern states of India. The socio-political dimension of unemployment is further aggravated by the fast changes in the composition of the unemployed.

At present, nearly 80 per cent of the unemployed youths are educated. Given the increasing literacy trend and the growth in skilled workers, the jobless growth of the organised sector (which mostly absorbs high skilled workers) will instigate the problem further. Total labour force of educated youth currently stands at 56 million. This labour force is growing at 5.5 per cent per annum. The organised sector currently absorbs 7–8 million educated persons, growing at 2.2 per cent per annum. The result is a widening supply-demand gap. The aspiration of India's educated youth is looking for a high-salaried job in the private/public corporate sector. Unless the mindset is changed and appropriate vocational training is provided

---

7. Business and Final Supplement; *Statesman*; December 04, 2004.
8. Annexure VIA and the Preface of this book.

to promote self-employment or jobs with SMEs, the gap will widen further with possible heavy socio-political repercussions.

In this context, I am reminded of a quote from Prof. J.E. Stiglitz (2002) who was the Chairman of the Economic Advisory Council of the US Government and Chief Economist at the World Bank. Prof. Stiglitz wrote, "I believe, it is important to view problems of choice of alternative development strategy in a dispassionate way, to put aside ideology and to look at the evidence before making a decision about what is the best course of action. Unfortunately, though hardly surprisingly, in my time I saw that decisions were often taken because of ideology and politics. As a result many wrong-headed actions were taken. I believe governments need to and can adopt policy that help countries grow but that also ensures that growth is shared more equitably."

The new employment policy that was recommended by the Special Group in Planning Commission took a pragmatic approach and kept all the grassroot realities uppermost in mind. Indeed, in developing any employment strategy, it is important to keep the nature of the labour market in mind, covering both the macro and the micro (i.e., at the grassroots) levels. The fundamentals of this approach are two: (i) macro growth, *per se*, is not the answer to employment when the nature of the market and its failures differ at both the micro and regional level, and (ii) the left-out or abandoned labour force in the reform process cannot be relieved through budgetary instruments or through transferring of funds *via* financial intermediaries (i.e. domestic and foreign saving) by the Government.

The magnitude of the labour force that is left-out is too large to provide income and job security by government alone, particularly when keeping the health of the present Indian fiscal situation at Centre and States in mind. Further, the surplus funds are generated primarily with profit maximisation 'mindset' and cannot easily be directed to areas of no immediate profits. Therefore, transferring of surplus funds by the existing institutions (like Banks, Financial Institutions and the Government bureaucracy) has not proven easy. A change in the 'present mindset' is therefore required for major transfer of funds on social ground, direct or *via* the government to the informal sector and is only beginning to happen now.[9] The NDA government also tried to transfer the surplus fund of the financial and banking sector in a similar way, but as the following table will show, they were not very successful.

The status of credit flow to SSI sector from Public Sector Banks since 1998 is as under:

(Rs. in crore)

	As at the end of March						
	1998	*1999*	*2000*	*2001*	*2002*	*2003*	*2004 (P)*
NET Bank Credit (NBC)	2,18,219	2,46,203	2,92,943	3,40,887	3,96,954	4,77,899	5,58,608
Credit to SSI	38,109	42,674	45,788	48,445	49,743	52,988	58,277
% to NBC	17.5	17.3	15.6	14.2	12.5	11.1	10.1

Source: RBI.
(P): Provisional.

The NSSO's report on the survey of the informal sector and the second and third census of small scale enterprises clearly demonstrate that any increase in the allocation of funds to small and medium enterprises will help increase their productivity and thereby contribute to higher growth and employment. The reports and census highlight that with a higher allocation of funds to units in the SSI sector, their capital intensity has increased, reflecting modernisation by use of better technology and resulting in an increase in labour productivity, capital productivity and, accordingly, the total factor productivity.[10] However, as mentioned above, the present strategy of transfer of funds by banking channels has not worked very well.

Good physical and social infrastructure is also a prerequisite for improving efficiency and marketing of the informal SME sector. However, most infrastructure development is guided by profit motivation. It will not percolate to backward areas or handicapped

9. For example banks taking directions on the overall reform of objectives of profit maximisation find it extremely difficult to channel the surplus to less profit investment areas or the backward areas where they have not immediate prospects of profit. The same is the case when they find that the viability of a project can only be justified on environmental ground or on other social considerations other than the immediate profit. This has been made possible, because in any project appraisal, in most cases, the concept of shadow price has been given up.
10. Arora and Saxena, 2003 and the Third All India Censes on Small Scale Industries.

people, which are obviously not the most secure and high profit investments.

Thus, India's infrastructure development, when guided exclusively by market profit, cannot provide the infrastructure needed for development, at the grassroots level, in the backward areas. This is equally true in the case of FDI. No one can force FDI to move to low profit areas, unless some incentives are provided based on 'social cost' concept; alternatively, like in China and other countries, it will concentrate around the Metropolitan or high growth areas already having good infrastructure and connectivity. It therefore become increasingly apparent that a development strategy that focuses exclusively on growth with some attempt to give *ad hoc* relief to the left-outs will not work.

But instead of dealing with the root cause of the present mindset i.e. profit maximisation motivation as defined by the market, the government tries to solve this problem primarily by budgetary transfer routes, i.e., relief measures. One such programme is the National Rural Employment Guarantee Scheme recently passed by the Parliament (For comments see Section III of Chapter 7).

It is an ambitious bill. It promises "income support" and "gainful sustainable employment." There is a detailed discussion of this in Chapter 7. A review of the provisions of this scheme clearly demonstrate that, on its own, it cannot generate any 'sustainable employment.' It has potential as a social security measure for the unorganised rural sector (as a welfare dimension of employment policy), but it is not fit for generating new employment on sustainable and gainful basis.

To promote gainful employment on a sustainable basis, it will take a detailed, holistic, livelihood programme at the grassroot level to make a significant difference. Such a programme must include an entrepreneurship programme; skill development especially for the youths as new entrants to the labour force through vocational trainings, technology support and research and development.

Recommended Alternative Employment Strategy

- Ideally, an approach should be developed where every able-bodied worker has the opportunity to become a partner in the growth maximisation process. Only then will the induction of social obligation in the use of the surplus funds be possible. Therefore, we have to search for a participatory growth process where the contribution to the growth of the National Cake (maximised GDP) is by all, and not primarily by one section of the society, i.e., by the large, corporate-organised sectors. The 'left-out' workers who normally justify their survival on considerations—such as 'employment', environments, development of backward regions and classes, and security concerns—must be included.

- Development goals must be multi-dimensional and include all other considerations as against only maximisation of GDP driven by profit.
- Then, and only then, will the transfer of surplus become easy, and a change in the 'mindset' of the banks and financial institutions will occur. In a democratic country like India, with a large, decentralised political decision process, only mass participation in development will result in gainful, sustainable employment.
- In this approach, the market will be a facilitator and not the supreme allocator of the economy's resources, based on 'market profit.' This awareness must be disseminated not only among the private producers but also among government servants and planners.
- During my tenure as a Member of the Planning Commission between 1999 and 2004, I have rarely come across an evaluation and monitoring report on projects or schemes of the central or state ministries where the success and shortfall of employment targets are to be reported. Instead, the ministry and implementing agency are only concerned with approval, disbursement and the speed with which a project is completed. This is in spite of the fact that many of these schemes are primarily meant for employment generation.

Operational Methodology

This study essentially suggests a revival of the use of some proxy concept of 'shadow prices' (or similar weighting diagram) as social cost while selecting projects to meet the multifaceted needs of development and to avoid the growing gap between the 'haves' and the 'have-nots' in the ongoing reform process in India, as in many other developing countries. As defined by Adam Smith, the wealth of a nation is to be regarded as the key indicator of social well-being and more recently to quote Prof. Partha Das Gupta of the University of Cambridge, " ... since wealth comprises manufactured, human and natural capital, the public policies that recommend themselves are those that would lead to the accumulation of an appropriate mix of those capital assets. Identifying an appropriate mix requires knowledge of shadow prices.... This means that markets on their own cannot be relied upon to select the right projects" (Gupta, 2003).

The precise formulation and use of shadow prices however have their own problems. Therefore, some near proxy to this as a measurement of the social cost (as against the private cost), should be attempted as a broad guide for better allocation of a country's resources. Some of the key, but neglected objectives of development, in the ongoing reform process should be kept in mind, such as the regional spread of reform benefits, avoidance of an unbearable rate of unemployment and non-use of manpower, protection of the environment and the fulfillment of the needs for basic social expenditure. Such valuation system should be used primarily by the public sector in its key infrastructural programmes. Also, as a broad guide, the private sector and financial institutions must use similar social cost considerations for funding projects with large externalities in order to fulfill the needs of the neglected sectors. As a result of the non-use of some explicit concept like 'shadow prices,' or social costs project choices, in many cases, have been made by implicit 'weighting systems' especially in global transactions (such as 'non-tariff barriers,' 'official restrictions on legitimate immigration,' etc.) thereby distorting the rational allocation of resources between and within many countries. This approach has further promoted lack of transparency guided by narrow shortsighted vested interests and encouraging corruption in bureaucracy and private corporates.

This revised approach would avoid the gesture of a favour or charity or relief in the allocation of funds to the selected projects. It will only ask for a level playing field for all players in the domestic and international market.

Instead, the ministry and the implementing agency are only concerned with approval disbursed and the speed of completion for a project. This is in spite of the fact that many of these schemes are primarily meant for employment generation. Any awareness and accountability for monitoring employment—even in employment oriented projects launched by the government—were almost absent.

Just as the forefathers of US Constitution gave a call for a democracy "by the people and for the people," similarly any growth strategy will be sustainable only when the call is for growth 'by the people and for the people' and 'not by few, for the few.'

The Planning Commission Special Group Report on "Employment Generating Growth" tried to spell this strategy out. The 'job-seekers' in this case need be converted to 'job-givers' by proper entrepreneurial policy and bringing out the potential job creating capability mainly among the large, unorganised labour force. This approach attempts to generate employment from the production end, i.e., by helping to create viable production units through developing entrepreneurship, providing opportunities for basic education, and skill development in the unorganised sector, thereby facilitating change within the private sectors, financial institutions and the bureaucracy.

To change the 'risk aversion' mindset in the decision-making process, specialised institutions catering to 'venture capital' need to be constituted. In this way, the trap of a shortsighted quick and easy profit motivation can be avoided, replaced by a 'self reliant', sustainable, long-term growth and employment strategy.

Under this scenario, the government should act as a facilitator and not as a job-giver by virtue of an income transfer programme through a budgetary process. The number of underemployed and unemployed labour is too large for this purpose conservatively estimated at a 100 million. Given the present poor financial position of both central and states, any such attempt will be unfulfilled.

The private sector and the people will be the main actors in partnership with the Government. To execute this approach, the following measures are recommended:

- The Public sectors' responsibility is to see that all have equal opportunity to generate the surplus; the generated surplus then can be transferred to the 'very needy' with less resistance and with dignity.

- It should also be understood that any programme providing wage employment in slack seasons (which is the main thrust of the present Government's employment programme) may not solve the problem of providing sustainable employment status to such a large labour force; the major sectors of the workforce left-out of the mainstream are the tiny, small and medium enterprises, which comprise 92 per cent of the total workforce. Most of them (nearly 51 per cent), in the year 2000, were self-employed (NSSO, 2001: 73).
- Cost cutting should happen by improving the quality of service through proper skill, and providing appropriate infrastructure support, etc. This will increase the productivity of labour and reduce the percentage of wage bill to total costs; the commonly proposed "employment intensive growth" strategy to make labour cheaper and more competitive by reducing wage rates along with other facilities (e.g., increasing working hours to reduce the unit cost of production doesn't work).
- These units should improve their "technology and capital base" by having easy access to credit, at a competitive price (level playing field) *vis-à-vis* other competitors. Only then can the viability of employment intensive enterprises be achieved. But care should be taken to ensure that, in the absence of readily available 'appropriate technology' on the shelve, they would not transform themselves into miniature capital intensive units, with less use of labour, and more use of capital, as is happening now.
- In many economies the above suggested approach has worked well; proper government support along with appropriate public–private partnership, has created small and medium enterprise sectors that provide sustainable employment and help bring better regional benefits and growth to the global capital market. Infact, signs of recovery through GDP growth and employment from the present global recessionary conditions, have come mainly from small and medium enterprises. They are providing more employment per output,

less consumption of capital and are mostly financed by banks. Further, the domestic banks provide more insulation from the volatilities of the global capital market. Most developed and large emerging economies share this experience.

In November 2002 the *Financial Times* carried an article titled "Employment Data: A Tale of Two Economies" that clearly shows that, in the US economy (based on its employers' survey) over the past 12 months, there has been a decrease in the payrolls of large corporate units by more than 0.7 per cent. At the same time, its household survey (which covers both large and small units) showed an employment growth of 0.13 per cent (for the same period). This reflects more than 0.2 per cent employment growth in small and medium sectors. Such scenarios and case studies have been elaborated in the book.

At the end, we must stress that the above strategy does not stop large corporate growth. They have their own valuable role. But for the informal or unorganised sector, a positive development programme will be needed with proper government supports and community endeavours, especially in the near future to create gainful employment in the future on a sustainable basis. The details of this have been spelled out in the Special Group Report on Targeting Ten million employment opportunities per year. A brief summary of the report is given in the Annexure XII.

The present book tries to trace the impacts and implications of this new strategy along with some of the key emerging issues which India is now facing or will shortly face and, accordingly, will need to prioritise the country's future manpower development programme.

To translate this new development strategy, following are the key measures recommendations for immediate operational purposes,[11] i.e., until the concepts and practical use of social cost, in specific areas in project selection are operationalised.

1. Creating specialised agencies for venture capital and revival of many of the development banks at the State levels.

11. Details are provided in the Report of the Study Group on Development of Small Scale Enterprises, under the Chairmanship of Dr. S.P. Gupta, Member Planning Commission 2001, pages 4-8. Many of these recommendations have been implemented by the NDA Government (Annexure-XIII).

2. The avoidance of commercial banking by some of the major development banks, which have been initiated from time to time.
3. Use of some specific weightage formula and rating procedure in project selections in the small and medium enterprises to protect other development goals like employment, regional balances, environment, technology adoption programme, etc. Innovate alternative collateral to replace the conventional one for tiny and small industries to explore. The managers of bank branches should be trained accordingly.
4. Given that the NPA is as low as 10 to 15 per cent in small industries, the very cautious approach to lending in this sector should be avoided; indeed, the government must be more liberal in dealing with the NPA issues and implementation of the 'penalty clauses' and must initiate revival programmes in all special cases, where defaults in repayment are not deliberate.
5. Large scale skill development and vocational training programmes are recommended by restructuring the existing training institutions both in the 'government and non-government' sectors, compelling these institutes to be more flexible and autonomous in their decision making.
6. Encourage the corporate sectors to help technology transfer to SMEs *via* ancillarisation, with financial and technical support. In a recent survey (2005), it is noted that for developing healthy ancillarisation, the following are the priority requirements: (1) technical support; (2) prompt payments by large firms (it is currently received after considerable time lag); (3) reduce paper works and so-called 'inspector raj'; (4) helping in the raw material supply; and (5) marketing and branding—of SME product, to mention some of the key requirements.
7. To improve the accountability and flexibility of the training agencies by strict monitoring of their 'placement records' and making their training programme demand-oriented (i.e. close to the emerging demand patterns). Most of the curriculum of these institutes have become backdated, partly due to the skill

background of the existing trainers and an almost absence of any programme for training or updating of their skills.

8. Try to adopt cluster development approach (both vertical and horizontal) among SMEs to benefit from scale in marketing, research, branding and finance.
9. Develop new, innovative agencies based on public-private partnerships to help assess the changing demands with realistic projections of the demand supply situation. At the moment, they are largely influenced by vested interest groups when the estimates by different agencies widely differ.
10. Employment exchanges should be computerised. Special types of employment agencies should facilitate adapting workers for jobs in markets outside India.
11. To take care of the transition problems in many areas, selective programmes on trade, industry and finance should be formulated and addressed in the international forum. Over the transition period, a subsidy is needed to make the production system viable, especially in the unorganised sector during the liberalisation process. To quote WTO Director-General Supachai Panitchpakdi, again "Indeed, this strategy (opening up) is thoroughly compatible with special support to small enterprises by having the right mix of policies in a manner which is fully consistent with the market principles and WTO rules."[12] In the long run, that may prove more economical than sustaining a large unemployed and under-employed labour force in poverty, and to cover the necessary cost of peace and security, arising from possible social unrest from these unemployed groups.[13]

12. *Herald International Tribune*, 21.10.2002.

13. See the recommended transition measures in Annexure XIII.

2

Changing Employment Scenario: Emerging New Issues

Overview

The Planning Commission, in its Tenth Plan Document, chalked out an employment strategy largely based on its Special Group Report of the feasibility of 50 million sustainable employment opportunities over the five years of the Plan.

In the present book, an attempt is made to assess and monitor the impact of this employment strategy during the Tenth Plan period, and to identify many new, emerging issues which might have a bearing on India's employment strategy, *vis-á-vis* domestic restructuring and increasing global interaction. In brief, they are the following: (i) accelerating growth of the young labour force; (ii) a growing percentage of the educated in labour force; (iii) a mismatch between the nature of demand for skilled labour and their available supply; (iv) the deteriorating quality of labour standard, impinging more on poverty; (v) the growing need for skilled and entrepreneurship development for the left-outs (unemployed and under-employed) in the growth process; (vi) the issue of technology and problems related to increasing automation; (vii) the impact of growth over regions, groups and genders from the failure of reasonable percolations; and (viii) the impact of opening of the economy and the growth of BPO and other outsourcing both from within and outside of India.

All these changes are influencing the global, socio-political and social security dimensions of the country's employment policy. Of course all of them are not new features. But, some threaten to become more conspicuous and are appearing on the surface, because of the advent of increased transparency and the spread of knowledge and information *via* new Technology, which results in more public awareness.

The Search for Alternatives: The Basic Rationale for the Chosen Employment Strategy in the Plan

Among several alternative employment strategies, three major ones have been examined. They are:

(i) The absorption of the labour force is subservient to the production process, motivated by the principle of growth maximisation under the profit maximisation principle of the market. In this scheme, the market is 'the supreme allocator' of resources. The pattern of employment is the outcome of a chosen production structure. No specific policy is warranted to operate on the unemployeds i.e., those who are not employed in the production process. The welfare of these sections is hypothesised to be taken care of by the 'automatic percolation process' of the market.

(ii) Basically, it is the same as above: the by-product of the exclusive growth oriented strategy. But, it may include some positive policies to accelerate the percolation process (which proved to be extremely feeble in most cases). These positive policies constitute different redistributive policies to provide employment support primarily by the public sector, often in an *ad hoc* manner, to cope with the seasonal and cyclical disturbance in employment.

(iii) The third approach is based on the inference that growth is necessary but not a sufficient condition for employment generation. This is supported by the prevalence of 'growing jobless growth' in many countries. In this approach, the 'growth with equity and generation of employment' is attempted by policies operating on selecting the patterns of growth. In this scheme, the market is a facilitator but not the supreme allocator of resources. The key message of this approach is to identify sectors of growth which are employment intensive, and make them sustainable not on the basis of perennial subsidy policy, but by providing a level playing field along with reasonable transition incentives. Accordingly, any employment generation must be gainful and sustainable by providing finance, improving the skill/productivity of labour, choosing suitable technology on the supply side, and, improving the marketability by proper information infrastructure entrepreneurship on the demand side.

The rationale choice of the last policy is spelled out as follows:

Over a major part of the 1990s (1993-1994 to 1999-2000), the employment growth slowed significantly and fell below the growth of labour force, resulting in an increase in unemployment both in absolute terms and also as a percentage of the total labour force.

Over that period, the organised sector of the economy comprising large units exhibited an almost jobless growth, which resulted in a significant absolute decline in employment, especially in the public sector. The employment generation in the organised private sector has hardly been able to compensate for the decline in employment in the public sector.

Most of the growth in employment during the late nineties came primarily from the unorganised sector which, although exhibiting a relatively low GDP growth as compared to that of the organised sector, contributed significantly to employment due to its high employment intensity in production. Around 92 per cent of total employment was contributed by this sector. The level of unemployment by Daily Status had become significantly high: 7.4 per cent as compared to the past. Added to the under-employment, the estimate came to as high a figure as 23 per cent of the labour force (NSSO, 2001: 129).

Against this scenario, the Special Group (SG) Report observed that the public sector was already carrying an excess of labour. Furthermore, given the recent reform policy with its emphasis on the need for a shift from public to the private sector, one cannot expect any contribution from the public sector towards growth of employment in the near future.

Similarly, although the organised private sector is likely to grow faster in the future, its main focus has been on increasing productivity (i.e., reduced unit cost) to face domestic and external competition, and to adjust production to the changing world pattern of demand. In this endeavour, the reduction of unit cost has almost been made synonymous with replacement of labour by capital, that is, by automation. This has further been motivated by some of the existing rigid labour laws, mainly in the organised industrial sector, where 'hiring' and 'firing' has been made very difficult.

But even if some changes in the labour laws were to be initiated, the potential ability of this sector to contribute to generation of employment is not likely to improve significantly, especially because of its very low contribution to employment (hardly 5 to 6 per cent of total employment) in the economy. Therefore, policy changes for generating employment in this area are not given high priority (Chapter 1 for details).

Employment growth, in the past, came primarily from the labour intensive sub-sectors operating in the unorganised segments of the economy. Because of its very large base, even a small increase in the GDP growth of this sector was found to have a significant impact on employment in the country.

The magnitude of the challenge is to accelerate the growth and efficiency of the unorganised sector. However, it can be assessed properly only when placed against the urgent need to absorb the very high, projected growth of the labour force in the economy. This high growth is projected to come from changes in the age structure of the population, and through the addition of youths in the labour force.

This large, unorganised sector exists with a low margin of profit and is often supported by different forms of subsidies. With the ushering in of the globalisation process, there will be a reduction in many subsidies in the future.

Their viability in the face of a global competition may be at stake. Therefore, to meet this challenge, a large number of new measures are to be undertaken. They endeavour to provide a level playing field in fiscal and monetary policies *vis-à-vis* the organised one and their global competitors (mostly of the nature of market corrections).

To make this transition smooth, a gradual reduction in all the non-core subsidies is recommended to avoid a sudden shock to this sector. This gradualist approach in fiscal and monetary adjustments is practiced in many developed and emerging economies. It asks for a change in the mindset of the financial sector and reduction in their risk aversion attitude. In general, an awareness in this sector for taking some social responsibility in their investment policy will be much needed. It places some social responsibility on this sector and reduces their risk aversion attitude.

The practice of a special dispensation for small and medium sectors has been adopted in order to protect employment in many economies (both in DC's and LDC's). The Small Business Administration of the US is one such glaring example (Planning Commission, 2001).

There is also a need to improve the skill and vocational training of the labour force, along with domestic research and development, especially in the vast unorganised sector, so that they can gear up with the modern technology for diversifying the products and maintaining quality in order to take advantages of the emerging global demand.

The Special Group Report recommended that the employment problem should not be handled only by macro policies, and that it needs specific policies and programmes with active government involvement at the regional and local levels. This is because the incidence of unemployment very much varies between regions, genders, and between different sections of the society, and their causes are different. It should be realised that unemployment has no single common cause, and it differs between groups and regions.

Lastly, workers in the informal sector, at the moment, lack legal protection in many areas, compared to employees in the organised sector. Further, the informal sector has no significant lobby, and is, therefore, likely to be exploited. This exploitation may continue even when the productivity and efficiency of this sector improve with higher 'value addition.' Because of the lack of pressure in the labour market, and its resultant large unemployment, the higher productivity may not always be translated into higher remuneration.

The report, therefore, recommended that open unemployment be tackled first, with highest priority, before moving to consider the quality of employment. Indeed, it is only when the unemployment level in the labour market is reduced that the bargain for better real wages will become easy and, accordingly, the quality aspect can be improved.

The Assessment of the Plan Strategy: Its Achievements

This section presents in a tabular form the status and achievements, until recently, of the Tenth Plan's employment strategy, which has been detailed by the Special Group (SG) Report of the Planning Commission (2002). As has been explained latter in the chapter and Annexure VII, it is based on whatever limited data and information is now best available, constrained by several shortcomings. It will be reviewed as and when more information and with greater reliability is available. This is expected to come primarily from the NSSO's large quinquennial survey on employment and unemployment in India from the 61st round.

Emerging Issues

This section covers some of the emerging areas of concern in the field of employment, and the appropriate policy changes required.

Technology

India, along with many other developed and developing countries, is quickly integrating with the global economy. In the process, many new and common problems are appearing among most countries in the area of employment and related issues. It is observed that the driving force of the present day globalisation comes mainly from the technology end.

These technologies are mainly emerging from the developed countries (who could afford the high cost of research and development) and they are appropriately geared to the endowment of those countries which are of capital-surplus and labour-shortage nature. This so-called appropriate technology is helping them in the global competition by reducing the 'unit cost' of production with the help of relatively cheap capital and substituting their comparatively expensive labour.

The less developed countries (LDCs), in facing the challenge to meet global competition, are adopting mainly labour-replacing technology with high capital intensity. This is due to the absence of 'appropriate' labour intensive technology on their shelves, especially in the new, emerging areas under global demand.

Indeed, the expenditures on research and development in technology, in most of the LDCs, have been rather negligible in the past. The global, hi-tech labour-displacing technologies have now started invading even traditional labour intensive areas like

Box 2.1

Strategy and Achievements: Tenth Five Year Plan

No.	*Plan Employment Strategy*	*Achievements (on UPSS Basis)*
1.	Given the perspective of slow growth of employment in the nineties, the key recommendation of the Special Group (SG) Report (Planning Commission, 2002) was to adopt all necessary strategies that will increase the growth of employment. Several of these recommendations have been incorporated in the Plan.	The employment growth in the aggregate since the year 2000 has nearly doubled. See Tables 2.3 & 2.4, 2.9 & 2.10. This holds good also for Rural and Urban, Males and Females and age breakup.
2.	The growth rate of employment must increase to the extent at least so that all new entrants to the labour force are provided with employment opportunities.	Most of the new entrants to the labour force since the year 2000 have been provided with employment opportunities when the rates of unemployment in the aggregate has been reduced although not necessarily in the case of new entrants.
3.	No significant contribution on employment can be visualised from the organised sector, as in the late-nineties it exhibited almost a jobless growth. The Special Group Report projected zero growth rate over the Tenth Plan in this sector. This assessment was based on (i) the pace of privatisation (ii) the technology trend of capital substituting labour.	The GDP growth of the organised sector indeed has proved to be not only a 'jobless' one, but also a 'job-loss' one. The net loss of jobs from the organised sector over this period added to nearly 4 lakh persons; (Table 2.1) Adding another year according to latest Economic Survey the decline since 1999-2000 is around 9 lakh. This is in spite of the fact that growth rate of this sector was above 6-7 per cent suggesting zero labour intensity and more capital intensity in production.
4.	Since 92 per cent of employment in 1999-2000 came from the unorganised/informal sector and its employment elasticity is higher (0.200) as against the very low elasticity (0.066) of the organised sector, the key recommendation was to increase the relative growth of the labour intensive activities mainly in the unorganised sector. (Table 2.1)	Relative GDP growth (unorganised sector to organised sector) has increased by 20 per cent in period II (2000-02) as compared to period I (1994-2000) (Table 2.1). For manufacturing, the growth of organised sector was consistently two percentage points below the unorganised manufacturing. Now post-2000 this gap is further increasing. The growth of the unorganised sector, however,

Contd...

Contd. ...

No.	*Plan Employment Strategy*	*Achievements (on UPSS Basis)*
		is accompanied not so much by productivity increase but with large increase in underemployment.
5.	It was further recommended that to absorb all the new entrants to the labour force and to reduce the backlog of unemployment, the employment intensity of the unorganised sector needs to be increased so that both by a relatively increased output in the unorganised sector and by increase in the labour intensity of this sector, the aggregate employment increase can be achieved.	The employment intensity of the unorganised sector by usual status has increased from 0.200 during the period 1994-2000 to 0.478 during the period 2000-02 (the corresponding decline in the labour intensity in the organised sector is from 0.016 to –0.085). In the Tenth Plan, the target for employment elasticity is at 0.338. The employment intensity of the unorganised sector has been increased partly, compensating the decline in employment in the organised sector (Table 2.1).
6.	For increasing the employment elasticity in the different sub-sectors of the unorganised segments of the economy, many policy prescriptions have been recommended.	Many policies have so far been accepted but only some of them have been implemented in this Plan. Some details are given in the main text.
7.	The Tenth Plan expressed major concern on a slower growth in youth employment between the years 1994 and 2000, defined as period I. The youth labour force constitutes more than one-third of the total labour force (Annexures V-A and V-B) and is projected to grow faster in the future given the age distribution of the population. The slower growth of youth employment and faster growth of youth labour force (Table 2.9) was taken to be a serious concern leading to a heavy increase in the youth unemployment rate. Indeed, in period I, the unemployment rate among the youth is seen to be already much higher than the 'all age'.	In period II (2000-2002), as compared to period I (1994-2000), it is gratifying to note that the rate of growth of youth employment went up by nearly four times as against the growth of the labour force by two times. Unemployment rate among the youth has come down also. A large number of programmes pertaining to youth employment both in the public and private sectors have been initiated or reinforced in period II. The following provides an illustration:

Contd. ...

Contd. ...

No.	*Plan Employment Strategy*	*Achievements (on UPSS Basis)*			
		Employment Generation Programmes			
		Rural Programmes		*Urban Programmes*	
		Wage Employment Programmes	*Self-employment Programmes*	*Wage Employment Programmes*	*Self-employment Programmes*
	labour force (Table 2.9). It has been accordingly recommended that all necessary measures should be taken as appropriate policies and programmes for generating higher employment growth for the youth and to reduce their unemployment rate in future.	Jawahar Gram Samridhi Yojana (erstwhile JRY)	Swarna-jayanti Gram Swarozgar Yojana (SGSY)	20-Point Programme	Swarna Jayanti Sahari Rozgar Yojana (Urban Self-Employment Programme)
		Pradhan Mantri Gram Sadak Yojana		National Slum Development Programme	Prime Minister's Rozgar Yojana (PMRY)
		Rural Housing		Swarna Jayanti Sahari Rozgar Yojana (Urban Wage Employment Programme)	
		Employment Assurance Scheme (EAS)			
		State	*Type of Assistance*		
		Andhra Pradesh	Provides revolving fund, technical skills and financial skills		
		Karnataka	Training in quasi-engineering skills		
		West Bengal	Marketing support during fairs and exhibition		
		Tamil Nadu	Setting up micro enterprises		
		Tripura	Skill upgradation, backward and forward linkages with existing schemes		
		Jammu & Kashmir	Loan for land purchase and equipment		

Contd. ...

Contd. ...

No.	*Plan Employment Strategy*	*Achievements (on UPSS Basis)*
8.	Identification and exploration of the emerging areas of employment opportunities, arising from the opening up of the economy, is another recommendation of this Report. But at the same time, the apprehension of facing a lack of reciprocity from the other major trade partners in terms of liberalised policies in many sectors in movement of natural persons and outsourcing has also been expressed. Besides, there is the felt need for allowing a gradual adjustment process over the transition period to the local industries in a holistic fashion for avoiding transfer or adoption of technology from other systems completely in deference to the local conditions and the existing tested indigenous technology, mainly in rural India.	The pace of globalisation and India's integration has increased significantly as captured by the percentage increase in the external sector to the total GDP. Many new opportunities of employment are now being identified in the area of BPO and other forms of outsourcing. At the same time, teething troubles have surfaced in terms of non-reciprocity from many of the trading partners often on the basis of their short-sightedness, immediate domestic problems and other associated vested interests. Indeed, in recent WTO negotiations, the lack of consensus among the global partners, for reciprocity in the trade, capital and technology flows, and subsidies has been acutely felt. Similarly, the awareness for choice of technology *vis-à-vis* labour intensiveness in production has increasingly been created. For example, many traditionally labour intensive areas (as shown below in the sector-wise employment elasticity) like construction, financial services, retail trade, tourism, health and small enterprises are losing their labour intensity with more automation and use of capital in the unorganised sector as practiced in the organised segment of the economy.

Sectors	*Employment Elasticity vis-à-vis NDP 1993-94 to 1999-00*	
	Organised Sector	*Unorganised Sector*
Agriculture	-0.61	0.01
Mining & Quarrying	-0.25	-0.58
Manufacturing	0.165	0.43
Electricity, Gas and Water Supply	0.056	-3.30

Contd. ...

Contd. ...

No.	*Plan Employment Strategy*	*Achievements (on UPSS Basis)*

Sectors	*Employment Elasticity vis-à-vis NDP 1993-94 to 1999-00*	
	Organised Sector	*Unorganised Sector*
Construction	-0.136	0.72
Trade, hotels and restaurant	0.069	0.79
Transport, storage and communication	0.024	0.58
Financing, insurance, real estates and business services	0.358	2.09
Community, social and personal services	0.081	-0.52
Total	**0.066**	**0.22**

		But one must be careful in analysing the increase in labour intensity in the unorganised sector *vis-à-vis* their loss in factor productivity. Major domestic research and development programmes have to be initiated to identify and evolve appropriate technologies to conform to the factor endowment of each sector both ensuring viability and labour intensity in production. The Planning Commission under NDA Government constituted a high level task force to recommend the appropriate rural technology. The Task Force is now discontinued.
9.	It has been emphasised that there is a need for formulation of macro and micro policies on employment generation—sector-wise, region-wise and for different classes differentiated between ages and genders. The problem of employment and unemployment seemed to be different in different regions and groups (Table 2.10 and 2.11). Hence, they need different policy prescriptions.	Since the year 2000, although the aggregate unemployment situation has improved, their incidence have diverged increasingly between regions and groups. The macro economic policies are showing decreasing effectiveness. The Government had instituted, accordingly, a number of programmes/schemes at the Central and State levels to develop an appropriate approach to the different groups. To assess their precise impacts, we need detailed information and data. A large part of it will be available when the comparatively large survey of NSSO on quinquennial basis is made accessible from the NSSO. (Table 2.13 and 2.14).

Contd. ...

Contd. ...

No.	*Plan Employment Strategy*	*Achievements (on UPSS Basis)*
10.	(i) Diversification of agricultural activities is likely to increase its employment intensity of growth as happened in the past, and contributed to more value addition. (ii) Rural GDP and employment will get a booster from faster non-farm growth. (iii) It has also been, recommended that employment be increased mainly in primary and secondary sectors, (i.e., goods sector) when in the late-nineties the employment growth, came mainly from the services. This recommendation is based on the experience that the service sector led growth can be sustained only by proper support by the growth of the secondary sector.	A number of policies and programmes have been initiated for diversifying agriculture and higher growth in animal husbandry, fisheries, social forestry, poultry, horticulture, floriculture, medicinal plants, bamboo development, etc. Indeed, post-2000, in all these sectors taken together, the employment growth increased nearly by 11 times, compared to late-nineties with significant increase in their employment elasticities. Percentage contribution of the primary and secondary sectors to employment increased from 39.4 per cent in period I, to 54.8 per cent in period II. Indeed, the higher growth of employment since 2000, as compared to late-nineties, came mainly from agriculture and the secondary sector like manufacturing, construction and electricity & mining (Table 2.2). This trend should be encouraged.
11.	To get the benefit 'of scale' in credit, marketing and technology operations, and skill development, which are the handicaps in small scale operations a cluster approach in the small and medium enterprises needs to be adopted.	Already, the Reserve Bank of India has selected more than 50 natural clusters. The Ministry of Small Scale Industries has initiated implementation in collaboration with the UNDP and other agencies in nearly 26 clusters. Apart from the natural clusters, several new clusters for export promotion are also being evolved.
12.	The need for revival and a healthy set up of ancillarisation relationship between large and small industries, as well as increasing outsourcing activities have been emphasised. It has also been pointed out that where there are certain grey areas emerging in exploring the opportunities in globalisation, immediate action will be needed.	Several programmes have been adopted and initiatives taken in these areas, along with changes in government regulations to ease the ancillarisation process. Details of these issues have been presented and discussed in the *Report on Development of Small Scale Enterprises in India* by a Committee set up by the Planning Commission on May 20, 1999. Outsourcing is an area where indeed large opportunities are appearing in the global market. However, as expected, several hindrances are also coming on the way.

Contd. ...

Contd. ...

No.	*Plan Employment Strategy*	*Achievements (on UPSS Basis)*
		Consequent to the increasing trend in automation, a large unused unemployed labour force is appearing in almost all the economies, ironically even in the developed countries. As a result, the developed countries are becoming more protective explicitly or at times implicitly and depriving the less developed countries of the great opportunities of generating more employment through trade in labour intensive production, both in goods and services (including BPO activities), and movement of 'natural persons'. Dialogue in WTO should start earnestly to resist the protection tendency in the global transactions.
13.	The Plan recommended special measures to improve the quality of employment in the large unorganised sector of the economy, e.g., child labour, bonded labour, migrant and casual labour, construction workers, landless agricultural workers etc., and a comprehensive Social Security Scheme (Chapter 7).	Some of these recommendations have been implemented, especially those pertaining to small enterprises. The latest announcement is in the area of comprehensive social security measures for a large section of unorganised workers (Chapter 7).
14.	A large section of the employeds in the unorganised sector are of foot loose type, with high degree of underemployment and having earnings below the poverty line. An improvement of the quality of employment of this category, by improving their productivity through proper vocational training and skill development, is therefore very necessary. Thus, the focus needs to be shifted gradually from the quantity of employment to quality of employment over time.	To address this problem, a large number of programmes on vocational training, skill development and measures for self-certification have been instituted. Further, now urgent need for detailed programmes and policy changes have been spelt out in the main text of this book. This may be regarded as the second phase of India's employment strategy. The post-2000 scenario stresses its urgency of such programmes as there are a number of indications that in many areas, under-employment is increasing because of. being engaged in low level unskilled jobs.
15.	Finally, special vocational education and training programmes for educated youth, who exhibit a much higher rate of unemployment than the average, must be integrated in our general education system.	An elaborate integrated scheme of vocational education has been recommended in this book, details of which are given in the main text.

Table 2.1

The Macro Economic Indicators on NDP, Employment and Unemployment—Organised and Unorganised Sectors, 1993-94 to 2001-02 (on Usual Status)*

(NDP in crore and employment in million)

Year	Organised Sector	Unorganised Sector	Gross Total	% Comparison: Organised as % of Total	% Comparison: Unorganised as % of Total
	NDP Growth				
1993-1994	256849	441143	697992	36.80	63.20
1999-2000	420005	609703	1029708	40.78	59.22
Growth Rate Per Annum (1994-2000)	8.5	5.5	6.7		
2000-01	444888	633975	1078964	41.2	58.8
Growth Rate Per Annum (2000-2001)	5.9	4.0	4.8		
2001-02	473805	669896	1143701	41.4	58.6
Growth Rate Per Annum (2001-02)	6.5	5.7	6.0		
Growth Rate Per Annum (2000-02)	6.2	4.8	5.4		
	Employment Growth				
1993-94	27.18	346.97	374.15	7.8	92.2
1999-2000	28.11	369.77	397.88	7.1	92.9
Growth Rate Per Annum (1994-2000)	(0.56)	(1.1)	(1.03)		
2001-02#	27.7	393.26	420.96	6.5	93.5
Growth Rate (2000-02)	-0.053	2.27	2.07		
	Employment Elasticity				
1993-94 to 1999-2000	0.066	0.2	0.154		
1999-2000 to 2001-2002	-0.085	0.478	0.383		

Note: * Updated Table-A pg. 6 of "Special Group Report on Targeting Ten Million Employment Opportunities," Planning Commission.

Up to October

Table 2.2

Sector-wise Growth of Employment from 50th to 55th Round and 55th to 58th Round of NSSO (Usual Status)

	Employment (in '000s)			*AAGR*		*Employment (in '000s)*			*AAGR*	
	50th Rd.	*55th Rd.*	*58th Rd.*	*50th to 55th*	*55th to 58th*	*50th Rd.*	*55th Rd.*	*58th Rd.*	*50th to 55th*	*55th to 58th*
	Rural Males					*Rural Females*				
Primary	139118	141808	146881	0.32	1.29	90285	90257	88345	-0.01	-0.78
Secondary	21027	25025	29462	2.94	6.11	8693	9406	9053	1.32	-1.38
Tertiary	27598	31778	37147	2.38	5.84	5761	6024	6764	0.75	4.30
Total	187744	198610	213490	0.94	2.66	104739	105687	104058	0.15	-0.56
	Urban Males					*Urban Females*				
Primary	5801	4975	5855	-2.53	6.10	4251	3222	3381	-4.51	1.77
Secondary	21206	24725	28187	2.59	4.88	5008	5333	6228	1.05	5.81
Tertiary	37449	45681	49599	3.37	3.04	7951	9629	10144	3.24	1.91
Total	64456	75382	83640	2.64	3.85	17209	18202	19773	0.94	3.06
	Rural					*Urban*				
Primary	229403	232064	235226	0.19	0.49	10052	8197	9236	-3.34	4.44
Secondary	29721	34431	38515	2.48	4.16	26214	30058	34415	2.31	5.05
Tertiary	33359	37802	43911	2.11	5.60	45399	55310	59742	3.35	2.84
Total	292483	304297	317548	0.66	1.56	81665	93584	103413	2.30	3.70
	All Areas Males					*All Areas Females*				
Primary	144919	146783	152736	0.21	1.46	94536	93478	91726	-0.19	-0.69
Secondary	42233	49750	57648	2.77	5.50	13701	14739	15282	1.22	1.32
Tertiary	65047	77459	86746	2.95	4.20	13711	15653	16907	2.23	2.84
Total	252200	273992	297130	1.39	2.99	121948	123889	123831	0.26	-0.02
	All Areas (Males and Females)									
Primary	239455	240261	244462	0.06	0.63					
Secondary	55935	64489	72930	2.40	4.57					
Tertiary	78759	93112	103653	2.83	3.98					
Total	374148	397881	420961	1.03	2.07					

Note: AAGR stands for Average Annual Growth Rate.
Source: NSSO.

Table 2.3*

Aggregate Employment Growth (Overall and Sectoral): Usual Status

	Period-I 1993-94 to 1999-2000	*Period-II 1999-2000 to October 2002*
All India	1.03	2.07
Rural	0.66	1.56
Urban	2.3	3.7
Males	1.39	2.99
Females	0.26	-0.02
Youth	0.36	1.48

Note: * See Annexures IV-A, V-A, VI-A and VI-B.
Source: *NSSO* data for Relevant Years.

Table 2.4

Number of Unemployed and Percentage to Corresponding Labour Force

	1999-2000	*2000 to October 2002*
All India	2.20 (8967)	2.04 (8773)
Rural	1.43 (4427)	1.20 (3869)
Urban	4.63 (4540)	4.53 (4904)
Males	2.44 (6859)	2.31 (7044)
Females	1.67 (2108)	1.38 (1730)
Youth	5.55 (8031)	5.01 (7502)

Note: Parentheses give the number of unemployed in '000s.
* See Annexures as in Table 1.3.
Source: *NSSO* data for relevant years.

construction of roads, flyovers, houses, bridges, dams, and, in many of the financial sectors, tourism, agriculture and many other small industries and trade.

Competitiveness and reduction in unit cost have now become synonymous with replacement of labour by capital. Along with this, the large industry is also becoming more and more capital-intensive and less labour-intensive. As a result, a large and grossly unutilised labour force is appearing in almost all the LDCs, and, ironically, even in the developed countries, in spite of the fact that the rate of their labour force's growth has started declining fast.

For the latter, this may be for a short and medium period. In future, by more automation (which has already started) and changing the pattern of education and skill development, the problem of unemployment largely may be taken care of.

This growing unemployment in developed countries is now pushing LDCs to increase the types of protective measures (often implicit) required to save their industries and reduce unemployment from global competition. This practice is taking away many of the new opportunities arising from globalisation either by freer movement of the 'natural persons' across national boundaries or by availing the BPO facilities from the developed countries.

Indeed, developed countries, due to their present large unemployment, are under many socio-political pressures and discouraging a significant outsourcing or allowing movement of natural persons from the LDCs. In the long run, the high expectation of a large demand for labour from the developed countries may not materialise, if the present trend of technology replacing labour continues. In the future, no policy of employment and unemployment could be looked at in deference to the corresponding policies of technological innovations and their adaptations.

In an article by Kim Jung Min (2004), this phenomenon is explored from the South Korean experience. To quote, "In South Korea, millions of 20-somethings are out of work, thanks mainly to more use of technology, outsourcing and a weak economy.... A weak economy, the allure of cheap outsourcing, off shore and the embrace of technology are all contributing to the fact that there are unenamoured jobs to go around.... They have all turned into technology, which are all labour replacing. In the retail industry alone, the technology is taking the place of thousands of hundred job-seekers. Take for example, Lottee Departmental Store, which has just built a counter system that replaces sales staff with personal digital assistance."

Nationwide, it is planning to introduce automated system in its stores. The company expects, the system will reduce the number of sales people, by 70 per cent."

Organisation

There are a large number of tiny, small and medium units spread over a large area in the unorganised private sector. Therefore, it has to be borne in mind that when India wants to explore the possibilities of increased employment generation in the large unorganised/ informal sector, some integration or networking among the large number of actors operating in this sector will need to be explored.

For this, indeed, a different type of organisational approach will be needed. For example, a close relationship between government and non-government agencies is imperative. It would be wrong to try to improve the productivity and growth of this sector only through public sector agencies. The experiments must be done by creating 'best practice' cases and networking between different units, so that the scale-economy benefits can be enjoyed both in the area of physical and human infrastructure development. Only then, by demonstration effect, can the success cases be replicated. This book, accordingly, recommends a cluster approach to achieve this objective, as given in the main text. Its implementation has recently been started by the Ministry of Small Scale Industries and several other non-government organisations. Also a healthy process of ancillarisation between large and small industries is to be accelerated.

Outsourcing

To avail of the increased opportunities, the growing global demand for jobs would be possible both at the global and national levels only through a free flow of labour, capital, technology and information. In reality, although the capital is becoming more mobile (often too volatile), labour is still suffering from restrictions in their movements, e.g. movements of natural persons are affected by many national laws, triggered by short-sighted interests and the interests of vested groups. The same is the problem in many areas for technology transfer.

A part of the employment opportunities have been availed by their movements by outsourcing in the services sector and avoiding immigration rules. But here, also, national interests, at times, are acting as constraints. All these will ask for a thorough discussion on the issue of outsourcing and the future development of the capital market *vis-à-vis* the domestic and local. A chapter on outsourcing has been included in this book (Chapter 5).

Underemployment and Poverty

In a poor country like India, a large section of the labour force is pushed to a low value, often working part-time and seasonal jobs as highly under-employeds. This is primarily because of a lack of alternative, gainful employment available to them. Further aggravating the issue is the fact that most of the labour force has no holding capacity, and cannot remain unemployed for a long period in anticipation of better jobs in future.

Indeed, this has been the root cause of poverty among a large section of the low-income population. Admittedly, the precise measurement of under-employment is a difficult task. But, in any employment policy, if these under-employed workers go unidentified and unattended, then the economy runs the risk of getting stuck in a low equilibrium growth and poverty trap.

The estimate of measurement of employment by the usual, with subsidiary status of NSSO (UPSS), therefore, has great limitations; because it categorises a large number of underemployed workers—particularly seasonal workers—as already employed. This explains the finding that while unemployment among the well-off sections of society—including educated ones—is increasing by UPSS method, unemployment among the poor is decreasing.

To achieve an alternative measurement of employment, including only workers having decent and gainful employment (free from under-employment), the estimates of employment under current daily status given by the NSSO have been recommended by the Special Group on Employment, constituted by the Planning Commission, and adopted in the Tenth Plan of the Government as against the measurement by UPSS, as was done in earlier Plans. The differences between the two concepts of employment provide some idea of under-employment.

Using the cross tabulation of NSSO 55th round, Table 8.1 page 155, an estimate of 'underemployment' of nearly 15.4 per cent of the total workforce in 1999-2000 has been calculated. As no measurement of employment on CDS (Current Daily Status) basis is available for the year 2002 (October), estimates on the basis of weekly status, which includes, at best, part of the under-unemployment, have been used.

This measurement is treated as proxy of CDS base, although it still gives an inflated figure of employment by including some significant under-employment. Our findings show that the "under-employment" has increased significantly post-1999-2000, e.g., has increased to 8.2 per cent on the basis of weekly status in 2002 (October) compared to 6.8 per cent in 2000.[1] From this, poverty may also be adversely affected.

As a result, the Tenth Plan document adopted the CDS-based estimates of employment, which are largely free from under-employment and give a better picture of sustainable employment (often called gainful employment, which, hopefully, will keep the relevant households above the poverty line).

Table 2.5

Workforce, Underemployment and Employment Elasticity under UPSS, WS & CDS

	UPSS			*Weekly Status*			*Current Daily Status*	
	1993-1994	*1999-2000*	*2000-2002 (Oct)*	*1993-1994*	*1999-2000*	*2000-2002 (Oct)*	*1993-1994*	*1999-2000*
Total Workforce (m)	374.148	397.881	420.962	344.308	371.017	386.525	315.84	336.750
Growth Per Annum		1.03	2.07		(1.25)	(1.50)		(1.07)
Under Employment (%)				8.0	6.8	8.2	15.6	15.4
Average Per Annum Additional Employment (m)		3.95	8.39		4.45	5.64		3.49
Elasticity		0.154	0.383		0.187	0.278		0.160
NDP Growth		**6.7**	**5.4**		**6.7**	**5.4**		**6.7**

Source: Estimates based on NSSO Employment rounds, For Current Daily Status, see Special Group Report on "Targeting Ten Million Employment Opportunities per year, Planning Commission.

It estimates the absolute average of employment increase per annum between '1999 to 2000' and 2002 (October) as 5.64 million

1. Table 2.5.

compared to 8.4 million estimated by UPSS, on weekly status. The total under-employment for the year 1999 to 2000 on CDS basis comes to 61.3 million, which explains a large part of the poor of 260 million observed in 1999 to 2000; assuming the dependency ratio of the lower income households as given in the NSSO report, at 3.3 per worker, (the estimate seems to be on the lower side).

As to the composition of total increase in employment between 1999 to 2000 and 2000 to 2002 (October) by UPSS estimates, nearly 33 per cent can be explained by including acute under-employed according to weekly status basis. On CDS base no estimate for 2002 (October) is available, but on rough estimate this percentage goes up to 48 to 50 per cent. Thus, a large part of overall employment growth by both the methods is explained by increased under-employment in the economy—a matter of great concern.

To analyse further, the total employment in the year 1999 to 2000, estimated by UPSS, can be disaggregated into 33 per cent from casual labour—of which 20 per cent are under-utilised—52.9 per cent from self-employed—of which 8 per cent are under-utilised—and of the roughly 13.9 per cent from the salaried wage earners, 5 per cent of which are under-utilised.[2]

This gives the total number of under-employment as 46 million. The total number of unemployed during this period on the CDS basis comes to 7.0 million. Hence, total number of under-employed and unemployed in this year comes to around 53 million. This corroborates closely to the macro estimates of under-employed for the whole economy to around 61 million.

Most of the under-employed are coming from casual labourers. Total casual labourer together with the unemployeds add 34.4 million which is nearly 63 per cent of all unemployed and under-employed estimated. The wages of the casual labourers have been estimated for the year 1999 to 2000 at Rs. 39.64 per day for the rural area and Rs. 56.96 for the urban area. Hence, over a month, they have been roughly calculated at Rs. 1189.20 for rural area and Rs. 1709 for the urban area. From NSSO estimates the average dependency ratio for the below poverty families has been calculated at 3.3 (3.2 for rural area and 3.6 for urban area) and for casual labourers slightly higher, at around 4.

2. Table 8.4 page 157, NSSO 1999-2000.

On this basis, the per capita income of casual labour families comes to Rs. 297.3 per rural and Rs. 427 per urban. The corresponding poverty line for this year, given by the Planning Commission, is Rs. 327.6 for rural and Rs. 454.1 for urban.

From this, one can observe that only if the casual labourers are in a full-time job, throughout the year, will their remuneration keep their family above the poverty line. But if they are under-utilised, as about 20 per cent of them are, then most of these casual labourers and their families will remain below the poverty line. This explains more than 50 per cent of the total people under poverty in 1999 to 2000. For policy purposes, it should be remembered that if they are given wages less than the casual labour wages, and even less than the minimum wage and with only 100 working days a year, by implication they all will be driven into a chronic poverty trap. The implications of the poverty trap has been explained recently by the DFID paper by Dr. Raghav Gaiha.[3]

This is precisely the reason why the author of this book has given high priority to improving the productivity and wages of casual labour by vocational training, skill development programme and improved health services (Any scheme otherwise will boil down to giving unemployment allowances or subsidy in Public Works programme, both resulting in a big drainage for the government exchequer). In the second phase of India's employment strategy, emphasis must be given to improving the quality of labour in the unorganised sector in particular, to enable workers to fit into quality jobs, sustainable under a globally competitive environment. This is the only sustainable way to reduce under-employment and unemployment and reduce poverty in the country.

Vulnerable Groups

There are broadly five groups of labourers where the unemployment and underemployment problems are more acute compared to the average and are aggravating over time. These groups are: (a) the female labour force and workforce; (b) the youth in the

3. Gaiha, Raghav, Raghbendra Jha and Anurag Sharma (2004). *Poverty Nutrition Trap in Rural India*, UK Department for Industrial Development (DFID), December.

labour force and workforce; (c) the educated labour force and specially the female educated ones; (d) the scheduled caste and scheduled tribes; and (e) the inter-regional disparities in employment situation in the development process.

Female Labour Force and the Workforce

Annexure IV (A) presents the growth of the workforce, labour force and the incidences of unemployment among female labourers between 1993-94, 1999-2000 and 2002. Growth in the female labour force compared to the total growth in labour force is seen to be significantly lower and the gaps in the growth of female and male labour forces and workforces are increasing over time (Period-I: 1993-94 to 1999-2000 and Period II: 1999-2000 to 2002). Indeed the growth of female labour force and the workforce post-2002 have been negative (absolute decline), although the male labour force picked up significantly from 0.98 per cent in the first period to 2.64 per cent post-2000. However, the level of unemployment (as per cent to labour force) is lower among the female labour force in the latter period. This is because the growth of female labour force is lower than the growth of the workforce, i.e., employment in the latter period. The NSSO 1999-2000 report shows that the female-headed households give better gender ratios (i.e. number of females are more than number of males), more consumption per capita both among their lower and upper income groups and lower poverty ratios in general with the single exception of destitute (very poor) households. In that light the welfare implication of this decline in the number of female workers is of great concern. Does it mean that the female-headed household do take better care of the female members of the household by showing less discrimination against the female child? The one reason for the higher per capita consumption of these households is their lesser household size than the male headed houses. To give an example, in 1999-2000 the male headed households have a size 5 whereas the female-headed ones have around 3.5; (As a contrast, over the same period, female-headed households in the urban areas are showing a declining per capita consumption than in the male headed ones. Further their consumption inequalities were increasing and their poverty ratios were marginally higher. As for gender ratios they are less favourable than in the rural areas; although they are improving over time). All these have a strong policy implication on the welfare of the rural females. But at the same time the NSSO report shows that in the rural sector the numbers of female-headed households as percentage to the total, have increased between 1993-94 to 1999-2000. It has increased to 10.4 per cent of the rural households in 1999-2000· from 9.7 per cent in 1993-94; This trend may reduce the negative welfare effects of this declining employment trend among rural females.

Why there is such heavy decline in the female labour force and workforce has become a big question. Are females going out of the job market for lack of their capabilities or skill? The female labour force is declining partly because without the prospect of a job, it is presumed that many females are opting out of labour force. Going into detailed breakdowns between rural and urban sectors, it is seen that the scenario can be exclusively explained by the heavy decline in the need for employment in the farm sector.

At the same time, females in the rural sector are not finding enough opportunities for non-farm jobs in the non-agriculture sector. In contrast, female labour force growth in the urban sector and workforce growth has increased in the second period, as compared to the first period. It shows that because of the job opportunities in the urban sector, females are migrating to cities, exceeding the capacity of available jobs for women in that sector.

The question, then, is whether this trend of female migration is sustainable over a long period, given the heavy bottleneck in the infrastructure and their high development cost in the urban areas? The policy thrust will therefore be to look for alternative jobs for females in the rural sector, away from the farm sector.

There is some apprehension that, with fast move in mechanisation and advance technology, women have not been able to adjust by changing their skills. This demands high priority training and education for rural females to work with machines and find suitable jobs in the non-farm sector, and in many of the new, 'extended farm sectors' like Animal Husbandry, Horticulture, Fishing, Social Forestry, etc.

Table 2.6

Number of Female-headed Households; Household Size and Sex-ratio for the Female-headed Households during 1993-94 and 1999-2000

Characteristics of the Female Headed Households	*Rural*		*Urban*	
	1993-94	*1999-2000*	*1993-94*	*1999-2000*
No. of Female-headed hhs per 1000 hhs	97	104	106	94
Household-size	3.2	3.5	3.2	3.5
Sex-ratio	1861	1820	1706	1721

Source: NSSO Report of 1999-2000 (Employment & Unemployment Situation in India).

Table 2.7

Average Household Size (0.0) and Sex-ratio (Female per 1000 Males) over the different NSS Surveys

NSS Survey Periods	*Rural*		*Urban*	
	Household Size	*Sex-ratio*	*Household Size*	*Sex-ratio*
1977-78 (32nd)	5.2	959	4.9	904
1983 (38th)	5.1	963	4.7	905
1987-88 (43rd)	5.1	948	4.7	912
1993-94 (50th)	4.9	944	4.4	905
1999-2000 (55th)	5.0	959	4.5	915

Source: Same as Table 2.6.

Table 2.8

Consumption and Poverty by Gender Groups

	Male Headed Households	*Female Headed Households*	*All Households*
I. Rural Areas			
1. *Per Capita Monthly Consumption (Rs.)*			
(a) Bottom 30 per cent	149.69	148.65	149.52
(b) Middle 40 per cent	238.77	250.83	239.96
(c) Top 30 per cent	465.87	511.38	468.53
(d) All Population	280.18	298.34	281.40
2. *Inequality (Lorenz Ratio)*	0.2802	0.3039	0.2816
3. *Poverty*			
(a) Very Poor	15.25	15.46	15.27
(b) Moderately Poor	22.12	20.00	21.98
(c) Poor	37.37	35.46	37.23
(d) Lower Non-Poor	34.32	32.03	34.18
(e) Upper Non-Poor	28.30	32.51	28.57
(f) Non-Poor	62.63	64.54	62.75

Source: Same as Table 2.6.

Youth Labour Force and Workforce

Table 2.9 consistently rates the unemployment among youths as higher compared to the total. Youths constitute 37 per cent of the labour force in 1994 (Annexure V-A and V-B) and the growth of the youth population in the labour force is accelerating more than that of the total labour force (Table 2.9). This suggests that the total weightage of youths to the all age labour force is increasing over time.

In this context, the higher unemployment rate among the youths should be regarded as an emerging problem for the future. This is despite the growth of employment among youths that was higher than the past, but that is more than compensated for by the very large growth of the youths reflecting the younger age composition of the population.

Table 2.9

Youth Unemployment in Contrast to All Age Unemployment

(i) Youth *versus* All Age

	1994-2000		*2000-2002*	
	Youth	*All Age*	*Youth*	*All Age*
Employment Growth	0.36	1.03	1.48	2.07
Unemployment Rate (at the end of the period)	5.55	2.2	5.01	2.04
Labour Force Growth	0.51	1.07	1.27	2.04

Source: Annexure V-A and V-B.

(ii) Female Youth *versus* All Age Female

	1994-2000		*2000-2002*	
	Female Youth	*All Age Female*	*Female Youth*	*All Age Female*
Employment Growth	-0.58	0.26	-3.46	-0.02
Unemployment Rate (at the end of the period)	4.36	1.67	3.55	1.38
Labour Force	-0.48	0.26	-3.77	-0.13

Source: Annexure V-A and V-B.

(iii) Male Youth *versus* All Age Male

	1994-2000		*2000-2002*	
	Male Youth	*All Age Male*	*Male Youth*	*All Age Male*
Employment Growth	0.8	1.39	3.54	2.99
Unemployment Rate (at the end of the period)	6.08	2.44	5.53	2.31
Labour Force	0.96	1.45	3.34	2.99

Source: Annexure V-A and V-B.

(iv) Female Youths (Rural *versus* Urban)

	1994-2000		*2000-2002*	
	Rural	*Urban*	*Rural*	*Urban*
Employment Growth	-0.67	0.04	-5.12	6.3
Unemployment Rate (at the end of the period)	2.68	13.93	1.67	11.6
Labour Force	-0.53	-0.21	-5.52	5.35

Source: Annexure IV-B and V-B.

The next concern is the comparatively slower growth among female youths in employment, compared to male youths. The labour force growth of female youths is also declining in a sharper way than the males. The latter may be as a response to the lesser opportunities for the females.[4] The big question is why female employment, even in absolute terms, is declining. This trend has to be stopped by giving more employment opportunities to young women and developing more capabilities among this group. The declining trend in job opportunities for female youths in the rural sector is of even more concern.

The negative growth in employment and labour force among the total female youths is largely explained by the heavy negative growth among the youths of the rural females. Indeed, the urban area exhibited a substantial, higher growth of females. Interestingly, however, the unemployment rate in urban areas among female youths is considerably higher.

4. Partly because the school enrolment among girls is increasing but the estimates show that it can explain very marginally the decline in the youth female labour.

All these show that growth of job opportunities for female youths are mainly in the urban areas, which, in turn, has attracted a further increase and higher participation rates in the urban areas, resulting in more job-seekers than jobs. This is reflected by comparatively higher unemployment rates among females in the urban areas, which happen to be as high as 14 per cent in the year 2000. The lesson we gain, is that, to solve this unpleasant situation and crowding out of female youths, attempts should be made in the rural areas to create jobs for the female youths—presumably not so much in the farm sector as in the non-farm sector.

Table 2.10

Educated Unemployment in the Rural and Urban Sectors: 1987-88, 1993-94 and 1999-2000

	Percentage of Educated Unemployed to Total Educated LF		Percentage of All Unemployed to Total LF		Percentage of Unemployed among Non-educated LF		Percentage of Educated Unemployed to Total Unemployed		Percentage of Educated LF to Total LF	
Years	Rural	Urban	Rural	Urban	Rural	Urban	Rural	Urban	Rural	Urban
1987-1988	6.6	7.4	2.0	5.3	1.2	2.5	52.1	73.5	16.2	45.6
1993-1994	5.1	7.3	1.3	4.5	0.3	1.5	83.5	84.0	20.8	52.2
1999-2000	4.6	6.6	1.5	4.6	0.4	1.7	80.5	84.2	26.0	58.6

Note: NB: Labour Force = 15+ years. Educated = Middle and above

Source: NSSO Report of 1999-2000 (Employment & Unemployment Situation in India).

Table 2.11

Female Educated Unemployed 1987-88, 1993-94 and 1999-2000

	Percentage of Female Educated to Total Female Educated LF		Percentage of Female Unemployed to Total Female LF		Percentage of Unemployed among Non-Educated		Percentage of Female Educated Unemployed to Total Female Unemployed		Percentage of Female Educated LF to Total Female LF	
Years	Rural	Urban	Rural	Urban	LF in Rural	LF in Urban	Rural	Urban	1999	2000
1987-1988	14.7	16.8	2.4	6.2	1.7	2.3	34.0	79.5	5.6	29.2
1993-1994	10.0	15.7	0.9	6.2	0.2	1.0	84.0	88.9	7.8	35.1
1999-2000	8.1	12.0	1.0	5.5	0.2	0.9	86.4	90.4	11.2	41.4

Source: Same as Table 2.10.

The Educated Labour Force with Special Reference to Females

Table 2.10 shows that the percentage of unemployed (on usual status) among educated job-seekers in general is much higher than among non-educated. In the rural sector, it was 5.5 times in 1988, while in 2000 it was 11.5 times greater. In urban areas, the educated unemployed are 3 times greater in the first year, rising to 3.9 times in the second year.

This increasing incidence of unemployment in both rural and urban sectors and among the educated is of great concern. Indeed, nearly 80 per cent in rural areas and 84.2 per cent in urban areas of all unemployed are educated. This problem is seen in the context of increase in the proportion of educated to the labour force, both in rural and urban areas.

One of the main reasons for lower unemployment among the uneducated is that non-educated job-seekers have less capacity to wait to look for a better quality job than educated job-seekers. The result is that under-employment and low-salaried employment is increasing fast among the non-educated, compared to the educated. Thus, it is becoming the problem of poverty and deprivation for most of the non-educated. This problem is further aggravated by the trend of jobless growth in the organised sector, which, mostly in the past, has provided high salaried, better quality jobs to the educated.

Growing Elderly Population–Emerging Problems

The percentage of the elderly in the total population is projected to rise faster in the future. This is to come about primarily due to the demographic developments and for reasons of increased longevity of the population resulting from better health and hygiene. Over the next 20 years, it is expected to increase from around 2.7 per cent in 2001 to nearly 3.8 per cent of the total population in 2021, i.e., an increase of 40 per cent over this period.[5] In this increase of the elderly people the female population is estimated to be higher than that of the elderly males. But, unfortunately, unlike in the developed countries, India has no major social security schemes. The existing old age pension schemes of all states and union territories cover hardly 9 to 10 per cent of the elderly population (Rajan, 2004). Without

5. UN (2002). UN Report on Demography.

supplementary financial support from other sources the average pension around Rs. 75 to 80 per month per elderly person is too low to keep them even above the abject poverty line. In spite of the increased longevity of the population the retirement age in the formal sector is retained at 60 to 65 years. The majority of the elderly population, to support itself, will either be working in the informal sector or be asking for help from relatives. However, because of the low literacy rate among the elderly population, it is getting opportunities to work mostly in low paid, low value activities and is always subject to exploitation; Nearly 70 per cent of them are self employed which is much above the national average. Indeed the elderly have become the major victims of improved technology which needs more skilled labour along with capital. They have no opportunity to receive vocational training or reorientation to new skill –worth mentioning. With the shrinking of the traditional family size in India, the present high rate of dependency of the elderly on family support, which is 45.2 per cent among males and 60 per cent among females, may soon become non-sustainable (Rajan, 2004). The highest dependency rate is found among urban females. As a result of these developments, most of the elderly people are driven into poverty. The desperate need for life support is so heavy that even those above 70 years in age are seeking jobs in the labour market in large numbers. Among the elderly, 37.3 per cent of the males and 29.7 per cent of the females find themselves in the labour market which is close to the average labour force participation rate in the total population in the country. This is in sharp contrast to the fact that in developed countries only 2 per cent of the total elderly population is found to be seeking jobs. The NSSO survey further shows that nearly 28 per cent of elderly males and 58 per cent of elderly women have no financial assets or regular place to live (Rajan, 2004). In the elderly population, females face more problems than males and their share of such problems continues to increase with a declining work opportunity among females, as in the rural sector recorded in the recent NSSO report and the percentage of the elderly female in the labour force is increasing. The financial strains among the elderly females will be further compounded. In the 1991 population census, widows among the elderly were already 67.2 per cent. As has already been mentioned, the existing social security schemes for the elderly are very inadequate. While there are some schemes for the organised sector and for specific groups like mine workers, *bidi* workers, cine workers and building workers, there are very few schemes for the unorganised sector. For example, in Kerala we see that the welfare fund of the Kerala Government is providing old age benefits to some workers in the unorganised sector, such as handloom, coir and cashewnut workers. But all such welfare programmes put together touch only a fringe of the problem. With the traditional family support receding and shrinking job availability for the largely unskilled elderly, it is only a matter of time before they are driven into abject poverty and insecurity. Even their physical security has become a concern. There is no comprehensive safety net policy for the old people both at the Centre and the States.[6]

Weaker Sections of the Society:
Scheduled Caste and Scheduled Tribes

With reference to the Table 2.12, unemployment among scheduled caste and scheduled tribes, together, is much higher than the aggregate, but the scheduled tribes, separately, have a comparatively lower unemployment rate. This is precisely because, compared to the usual status estimates, it is clearly shown that the male of the scheduled castes are the maximum sufferers on employment, both in rural and urban areas.

As far as females in the scheduled castes are concerned, they are comparatively better off in an urban area, *vis-à-vis* the total female labour force in urban areas (in terms of level of the unemployment). Among scheduled tribes, the comparatively lower unemployment rates are mainly based on doing very low paid jobs, which are defined as employment.

Therefore, the employment policy of scheduled tribes must be approached from the angles of poverty and deprivation, whereas the scheduled castes have genuine problems of getting jobs, especially among the males. This is corroborated in a recent study by Professors Sundaram and Tendulkar (2003), showing consistently higher poverty ratios among Scheduled Tribes than Scheduled Castes. Further, it is of importance to note that the small scale industries sector is dominated primarily by management of the backward class entrepreneurs (nearly 52 to 55 per cent) as given in the 3rd Census of Small Scale Industries 2001 to 2002. Therefore, in any policy to reduce the

6. For details, refer to S. Mahendra Dev's work on the safety net for the chronically poor in India.

inequality of income and employment between social groups, the healthy growth of this small enterprise and informal sector should be given high priority.

Table 2.12

Unemployment Rates 1993-94 and 1999-2000

(i) Rural (Usual Status)

Years	*Scheduled Tribe*		*Scheduled Caste*		*All*	
	Male	*Female*	*Male*	*Female*	*Male*	*Female*
1993-1994	0.8 (4.3)	0.3 (3.8)	1.2 (8.1)	0.4 (8.1)	1.4 (5.6)	0.8 (5.6)
1999-2000	1.1 (5.6)	0.5 (4.5)	1.8 (9.8)	0.6 (9.0)	1.8 (7.2)	1.0 (6.0)

(ii) Urban (Usual Status)

Years	*Scheduled Tribe*		*Scheduled Caste*		*All*	
	Male	*Female*	*Male*	*Female*	*Male*	*Female*
1993-1994	4.7 (8.5)	1.7 (4.5)	4.6 (9.6)	4.4 (9.9)	4.0 (6.7)	6.2 (10.5)
1999-2000	4.4 (7.6)	2.8 (6.2)	5.1 (10.2)	3.1 (7.9)	4.6 (7.4)	5.4 (9.8)

Rural + Urban (M+F)

Years	*Scheduled Tribe*	*Scheduled Caste*	*All*
1993-1994	(4.32)	(8.34)	(5.99)
1999-2000	(5.30)	(9.60)	(7.32)

Note: Parentheses gives at CDS.

Inequalities in the Unemployment Rates

Table 2.13 presents the unemployment rates between different states over time between 1994-2002.

This period is covered by two large sample surveys of NSSO from 1993 to 1994, 1999 to 2000, and a thin sample survey from 2002 (October). It shows that Kerala suffered from very high unemployment, especially in the urban areas, whereas in Rajasthan unemployment was lowest during this period. The gap between the the highest and the lowest unemployment rates between 16 major states increased in 1999 to 2000 by 9.6 percentage as compared with

1993 to 1994. From 1993 to 1994, the gap in unemployment rates was 7.3 points, which increased in 1999 to 2000 by 8.0 per cent.

Table 2.13

Unemployment Rates: Selected States (on Usual Status)

	1994			*2000*			*2002*		
	Rural	*Urban*	*Total*	*Rural*	*Urban*	*Total*	*Rural*	*Urban*	*Total*
Andhra Pradesh	0.4	3.0	0.9	0.7	3.9	1.4	0.4	4.7	1.4
Assam	1.0	8.9	1.9	3.9	9.8	4.6	1.4	3.0	1.6
Bihar*	1.6	7.1	2.2	1.7	7.3	2.4	1.8	6.5	2.3
Gujarat	0.9	3.3	1.6	0.4	2.0	0.9	0.4	1.8	0.9
Haryana	1.1	2.6	1.5	0.9	2.8	1.4	0.9	2.6	1.3
Jammu & Kashmir	0.7	6.6	1.8	1.1	5.1	1.8	1.8	3.9	2.2
Karnataka	0.7	3.6	1.4	0.8	3.4	1.5	0.6	4.0	1.6
Kerala	6.9	10.3	7.8	8.3	10.1	8.8	5.8	3.1	5.2
Madhya Pradesh*	0.5	5.0	1.3	0.4	3.6	1.0	0.2	7.5	1.7
Maharashtra	0.8	4.4	2.0	1.4	5.7	2.9	1.0	2.4	1.5
Orissa	1.4	6.5	2.0	1.9	6.8	2.4	1.7	9.0	2.7
Punjab	1.3	3.4	1.9	1.9	2.8	2.2	1.7	1.1	1.5
Rajasthan	0.3	1.4	0.5	0.4	2.4	0.8	0.9	5.3	1.8
Tamil Nadu	1.3	5.0	2.5	1.9	3.9	2.7	2.3	12.1	6.4
Uttar Pradesh*	0.7	2.9	1.1	0.9	4.1	1.5	0.6	4.0	1.2
West Bengal	1.8	7.9	3.5	2.8	7.7	4.2	2.1	5.8	3.2

*: Undivided, before the formation of new states.

Source: NSSO Report of 1999-2000 (Employment & Unemployment Situation in India).

Table 2.14

Variation of Employment Rates among States for the Years 1994, 2000 and 2002

Year	*Rural*	*Urban*	*Total*
1994	0.79	2.07	0.94
2000	1.19	2.11	1.31
2002	0.86	2.17	1.05

Source: Same as Table 2.13.

An attempt is made by the simple calculation of 'coefficients of variation' as to the extent of interstate unemployment gaps between 1993 to 1994 and 1999 to 2000 (Table 2.14). The unemployment gaps increased significantly both in the rural and urban areas over this period. Even by changing the method of estimation of employment and unemployment, from usual status to current daily status, these high increases in disparity have not changed. The highest to lowest gap in coefficient of variations changed from 14.2 per cent to 18.0 per cent, i.e., nearly 27 per cent by CDS, much more than the estimates based on usual status. Thus, on CDS basis also we find similar results of increasing regional disparity of unemployment. The details of this have been discussed in the Special Group Report of the Planning Commission (2002: 31).

If we use the small sample results of October 2002, this trend in inequality continues, especially in the urban sector, but we find some reduction in this inequality in the rural sector. However, we know many economists do not want to use the small sample results, as their sample size renders them not very authentic.

This increasing gap in the rate of unemployment between states is creating social, cultural and sometimes political problems. It reflects the failure of the market system in terms of perfect mobility of labour and capital to equalise the gaps between regions. It also reflects a lack of proper infrastructure policy over regions, both in the public and private sector.

In many instances, the movement of entrepreneurship and investment in the private sector is deterred by the non-availability of suitable infrastructure in certain regions, which even now primarily comes from the states. In such cases, one should seriously think of a policy to encourage and give incentive to small and medium industries and services in these states, which are labour intensive and less of an infrastructure nature, at least for the immediate future.

At the same time, in regions where unemployment is very high, labour intensive non-farm activities and domestic tourism, to mention a few, should be encouraged to reduce the rate of migration from one state to another. It should be remembered that migration is a rational measure for equalising the inequalities of economic activities, but, in reality, there are many economic socio-political problems in fast migration to over-crowded urban areas of states. Positive policy in this aspect will be needed in the future to deal with 'this emerging' problem of interstate development disparity as part of the country's future employment policy.

Empirical Findings of the Growth of Employment and Unemployment Indicators (1993-94 to October 2002)

The following findings covering a period between 1993-1994 to 1999-2000 (defined as period I) and 1999-2000 to October, 2002 (as period II) are based primarily on the NSSO reports of Employment and Unemployment in India (EU). For the year 1999 to 2000, the NSSO's last quinquennial survey on large sample basis has been used. For the year 2002 (till October), in the absence of a comparable large sample, NSSO's annual surveys on EU, based on a small size sample (although regarded by many economists and statisticians to be quite large compared to any other sample based study in India and abroad for drawing broad macro conclusions) has been used.

It is expected that by 2005, comparable large quinquennial sample survey results will be made available to provide more detailed and disaggregated results for our analysis. Because the annual survey on EU did not provide employment estimates on a current daily status (CDS) basis (which have been adopted in the Tenth Plan document), the usual and weekly status basis estimates have been used in this analysis for inter-temporal comparisons. It is well admitted that measurement of employment on usual status basis includes considerable under-employment and therefore, give some inflated picture of employment generation. CDS basis measurement excludes a large part of these under-employeds for measuring employment.

The overall NDP growth of the economy in the late nineties (period I) was 6.7 per cent per annum (period I) Table 2.1. Compared to 2000 and 2002 (October) (period II), the annual growth declined to 5.4 per cent per annum. The organised sector growth slowed down from 8.5 per cent to 6.2 per cent, and the unorganised sector from 5.5 per cent to 4.8 per cent.

Under the circumstances, one would have expected slower employment growth of the economy in period II. Fortunately, it has not happened. The overall employment growth increased from 1.03 per cent in period I to 2.01 per cent per annum in period II, implying that the adverse effect of slower growth in period II has been more than compensated by an increase in the employment elasticity of the unorganised sector (from 0.2 to 0.478), along with its relative growth *vis-à-vis* the organised sector increasing nearly by 20 per cent.

It is to be noted, however, that this scenario is based on the 'usual status criteria,' which includes in the estimate a large number of under-employed. Indeed, the percentage of under-employment is observed to have increased in period II. Besides, whole of this increase in period II compared to period I can be explained by the increase of labour intensity in production in the unorganised sector in period II; since the organised industry in this period contributed to jobless growth, therefore, the unorganised sectors must be generating a large number of under-employed.

The average employment growth in this period (2000 to October, 2002) is still less than the Tenth Plan's target growth, although its elasticity of employment has risen much higher than the Plan's target (0.372 as against the target of 0.338). The overall shortfall of the employment target from the Tenth Plan, however, is primarily due to the shortfall of GDP from the targeted 8 per cent to 5.4 per cent per annum, realised between 2000 and October, 2002.

In all the sectors and groups, the employment growth on UPSS basis has been significant since the year 2000, much higher than in the late-nineties, with one exception. The growth of female employment in the aggregate has come down to a negative, i.e., a decline in absolute numbers since the year 2000. (Table 2.2) Female employment in the rural sector has gone down significantly, from 0.15 per cent in period I to 0.56 in period II (Table 2.2). This is in contrast to a significant rise in the urban employment between these two periods, from 0.94 per cent to 2.66 per cent.

It is interesting to note that this decline has not adversely affected the unemployment rate of females since the labour force growth during period II went down faster than in the past (Table 2.6). Part of the decline in the rural female labour force can be ascribed to the increasing attendance of this group at educational institutions (5.66 per cent in UPSS in period II, the highest among all other groups and higher than that in period I, at 5.18 per cent), (Annexure X) partly due to the scarcity of jobs in the market.

In general, urban unemployment has been seen to be higher than rural (Table 2.4). This is in spite of very high employment growth in the urban sector, and can be explained by faster growth in the labour force in the urban sector, mainly from large scale migration from the rural sector in expectation of better jobs.

Lastly, although the unemployment rate is declining in the urban sector as compared to the past, the rate of unemployment is still very high among urban females. This is in spite of the fact that the growth in employment among the urban females is very high (Annexure V-A). This again is explained by very high growth in available urban females looking for jobs.

The major area of increase in employment growth during the period II came from the secondary sector (4.57 per cent per annum), followed by the tertiary sector (3.98 per cent per annum), and, lastly, from the primary sector, i.e., agriculture (0.63 per cent per annum, Table 2.2). Although the last mentioned sector reflects comparatively low growth in employment in period II, it is very high in contrast to period I, when it was as low as 0.06 per cent per annum. Moving to further disaggregation, the highest employment growth came from the rural tertiary sector (5.6 per cent)—mostly covering rural non-farm activities.

The urban sector's comparatively high growth came from its secondary activities (5.1 per cent), comprising mining and quarrying, manufacturing, electricity, water, and construction. When we compare these growth rates with the growth rates of the nineties (1993-1994 to 1999-2000), we find that the increase in employment growth is as high as 90 per cent in the secondary sector, 41 per cent in the tertiary sector, and nearly 11 times more in the agriculture sector.

Compared to the 1.3 lakh additional persons employed per annum in period I in agriculture, employment of 15.3 lakh per annum was achieved in period II. Finally, it is observed that out of the annual increase in employment of 3.96 million in period I, 60 per cent comes from services, whereas out of the 8.39 million in period II, 45.7 per cent comes from services and the major part (54.3 per cent) from the primary and secondary goods producing sector (Table 2.2). This comparatively high growth in the primary and secondary sector was as per the recommendations of the Special Group of the Planning Commission.

3

Vocational Training and Skill Development[1]

Introduction

The recommended employment strategy emphasises the need for high growth as a necessary condition for increase in employment. This can be achieved primarily by increasing the demand for domestic products at home and abroad, mainly by reducing the unit cost and improving the quality of products. This, in turn, requires quality consciousness and price competitiveness across all activities in the economy. It also requires appropriate, qualified manpower with improved skills competent to interact with better technologies necessary to reduce cost and improve the quality of products. Recent data has shown that our education system and vocational training programmes have not provided the necessary skilled manpower. In fact, hardly 5 per cent of the workforce is skilled.

At the same time, experience shows there is no guarantee that higher growth with better-skilled manpower will always generate higher employment. The case in sight is the presence of jobless growth in many of the high growth organised sectors of the Indian economy. For generating growth along with additional employment opportunities, one must search for sufficient conditions of growth with employment. The answer is an appropriate sector composition of growth. There are sectors in many Less Developed Countries (LDCs) where a choice of technology has a wide range, and the majority of them have used the labour intensive production technology in spite of present changes in 'technology conditions' that favour machine. The use of improved labour intensive technologies, still make production viable. This is true for some developed countries as well. In India, many such sectors are located in the

1. Based largely on a study by Dr. H. Ramachandran, Director, I.A.M.R, New Delhi.

unorganised segment of the economy. Therefore, the growth in these sectors may provide more employment and still be viable in global competition.

This book, therefore, recommends that unorganised sectors—which according to NSS survey conducted in the year 1999-2000 accounted for nearly 92 per cent of employment—be targeted for higher, sustainable growth with employment. Thus, the first priority of vocational training is skills development of the labour force in these sectors. However, it should be emphasised that vocational training and skills development cannot solve the problem of unemployment unless the products satisfy the changing demand pattern of the marketplace, workers are flexible in adapting their skills, and the infrastructure exists to transform goods into high quality, price-competitive products.

But in India, in most cases, the lack of demand orientation in vocational training and skill development projects often resulted in unemployment, while at the same time a large number of activities could not grow because of the lack of availability of appropriate types of skilled personnels. This mismatch is further aggravated by a lack of physical infrastructure such as electricity, roads, availability of an appropriate credit delivery system, lack of proper market infrastructure, technology know-how, etc. The quality of vocational training emerged as the most critical ingredient, as often the quality is so poor that the placement ratio (PR) of vocationally trained personnel becomes extremely low (on an average the PR is not more than 30 per cent in most ITIs). This means a demand-oriented approach to vocational training needs to be adopted along with general development activities.

In an economy where a very large part of the economic activities relevant for employment generation (loosely mentioned as unorganised sector) are all in the private domain, any formulation and implementation of an efficient vocational training programme should explore how the government can act as a facilitator and trigger the process of skill development by public-private partnership. Government alone cannot solve this gigantic and primarily grassroot or local-based problem, nor does the private sector have sufficient knowledge, experience, capability or organisation to solve this alone. The dimensions of the challenge in this sector are appreciated upon recognising that less than 20 per cent of the labour force in India has marketable skills (NSSO, 1993-94 Survey), and only around 5 per cent of those with so-called marketable skills received training from formal channels. In the case of rural males, approximately 10 per cent of males and 6 per cent of rural females possess any skill. In many cases, these skills are traditional in nature, such as weaving, cutting, tailoring, construction activities, and motor vehicle driving. Only urban males exhibited some diversity in skill endowment. Moreover, most of these major skills are acquired from informal sources and only 5 per cent of the population in the age-group between 20 and 24 is vocationally trained through formal channels.

The skills training level in India contrasts sharply with other emerging high growth economy countries: 96 per cent in South Korea; 20 per cent in Mexico; 22 per cent in Botswana; 36 per cent in Mauritius. Given low literacy rates and technical abilities, it is not surprising that both the productivity and incomes of the Indian labour force are so low. If the objective is to create employment that is gainful (with benefits accruing to labour), then it should be remembered that increasing the productivity of labour does not necessarily increase its remuneration, especially in a labour market where there is a large informal sector with high unemployment, under-employment, low bargaining power, and labourers often looking desperately for some jobs. This requires a different set of policies for protecting the labour interests, as discussed later in this book, particularly in view of the opening up of the economy and the consequent new demand for goods and services at home and abroad.

Dimensions on the Need for Vocational Training

The mismatch between the quality of labour demanded and its availability needs to be analysed and quantified. This will ultimately require reorientation of India's educational system, particularly existing vocational education and training programmes, as well as enhancing their capabilities. It has been observed that vocational training and skill development can be imparted better among persons with basic education rather than to non-literates. Therefore, the present drive for literacy and basic education should continue, along with more vocational education and training programmes. For India to grow at 8 per cent per annum (as stipulated in the Tenth Plan) and to rank as a developed country by the year 2020, the capacity of the appropriate formal vocational training programmes needs to be expanded significantly.

Vocational education and training primarily refer to the education and training required to help job-seekers in the labour force achieve gainful employment other than foot loose as wage-earners or as self-employed individuals. It also includes increasing the productivity of those who, although employed, are largely under-employed and in low productivity low valued jobs.

In India, the implications of this task are huge when one considers unemployment on Daily Status basis in 1999-2000 was as high as 26.5 million (i.e. 7.4 per cent of the total labour force), 10.8 million of whom were educated (i.e. 41 per cent of the unemployed). Compared to this large, unemployed labour force, the existing, available training and skill development facilities in formal training institutions and agencies throughout India number around one to one-and-a-half million.

Of India's 10.8 million educated unemployed, the educated youth unemployed number 8.83 million (i.e. 82 per cent of the total educated unemployed) and as many as 80 per cent of whom are males. This clearly shows the need for imparting vocational training to these educated youth on priority basis.

Further, of the 104 to 114 million educated and employed workers, nearly 50 to 55 per cent are self-employed. Hence, special vocational training and entrepreneurship development for the self-employed need to be developed. Indeed, educated youth are the primary source of future potential entrepreneurs. As to semi-educated youth (upto primary class), there have also been a large number of unemployed or under-employed (although the unemployment rate is lower here compared to the educated) and they need a different type of educational and vocational training.

There is a vast area where formal and informal vocational training is called for: the large section of the workforce engaged in low productivity and low earning jobs (i.e., largely under-employed). The earnings of this group in most cases are well below the norm for a decent living.

To help this sector entering new areas and discover new opportunities currently available within present technology and knowledge, suitable programmes for vocational training and skill development will be needed, some on a part time basis, so that the enhanced training programme will not cause a disruption in their running sources of earnings. Here, again, a different nature of skill development programme is needed. In this programme even the skill imbibed from informal training should be utilised by proper certification. The magnitude of this largely under-employed workforce is as high as 60 to 63 million.

All of these statistics give a sense of the magnitude of need for large scale vocational education and training programmes, particularly as the existing capacities in the formal sources are very little and often very imperfect (e.g., not demand driven). Besides ITIs there are (a) around 3000 positions for undergoing training in seven IITs, (b) 3.5 lakh in the 1208 engineering colleges, (c) 2.3 lakh in 1220 technical institutions, and (d) 2.9 lakh in the apprenticeship training programme for trained graduates and technicians. Aggregating, they come to around 1.0 million. One can easily see the big demand-supply gap here. This meagre capacity is also over estimated because many are running as overlapping schemes spread over different agencies and government departments, and many are also of poor qualities and not demand-driven.

All these obstacles demand a thorough re-examination of the educational and vocational training programmes and policies in India. The public sector alone will not be able to tackle these obstacles, forcing appropriate NGOs, private corporate sectors and universities to join in.

Prioritisation of Skill Building and Vocational Training

This study found an urgent need to identify the priority areas in selected sections of the labour force to render appropriate training and skill at the earliest. In this context, the study refers to Table 3.1

which separates labour force into unemployed and largely under-employed categories. While it is difficult to estimate the exact number of under-employed in a given period, an attempt has been made to do so on the basis of NSSO 1999-2000 Survey.[2] The estimates show that of the total rural and urban workforce employed (on usual status), nearly 90 per cent and 94 per cent are utilised on gainful basis[3] among the rural and urban males, and 68 per cent and 79 per cent among the rural and urban females, respectively. This makes the total under-utilised workforce 15.7 per cent. The present Report interpreted this proportion as an estimate of 'under-employment,' meaning that nearly 62.5 million persons had been 'under-employed' in 1999-2000. Further examination shows that these "under-employed persons" do not satisfy the criteria for gainful employment. This group mostly comes from casual labourers[4] in agriculture: marginal farmers and a large number of footloose, self employed in the services sector. To bring them to a viable and sustainable growth path, they need appropriate vocational training. A large part of this group is illiterate or semi-literate.

Besides analysing the present status of employment, unemployment, and under-employment in the year 1999-2000, we need an assessment as to the future trends in these variables. Only then may appropriate policies be developed to create an infrastructure with vocational training and skill building. To start with, India must estimate the likely addition to labour force and its educated component annually, to have some idea of the vocational training needs for the Tenth Plan period. Table 3.2, based primarily on the HRD Ministry's information, provides approximate estimates of children leaving classes VIII and IX and class X and XI at 3.80 million and 4.31 million respectively, adding to a total of 8.11 million, and growing around 5 per cent per annum, according to a study group in the Planning Commission.

2. SG Committee Report of the Planning Commission, 2002, Table E, Page 22.

3. As per current Daily Status Basis.

4. See Chapter I

Table 3.1

Ranking of Priority Areas for Vocational Training and Skill Development

(Dimensions based on NSSO Survey of EU, on CDS Basis)

Sl. No.	*Unemployed*		*Priority Ranking in Decreasing Order*	*Percentage Unemployment to Respective Labour Force*	*Under-employed*		*Priority*	*Percentage Under-employed*
	Category	*In million*			*Category*	*In million*		
	1	2	3	4	1	2	3	4
1.	Total	26.5		7.3	Under-employed Workforce	62.5	IV	15.7
2.	Youth	15.6		12.1	(a) Male	24.9		9.1
2A	Educated	8.83	II	15.6	(b) Female	37.6		30.4
2A (i)	Female Educated	1.92	II	22.5				
3.	New Entrants from Class VIII, IX, X & XI	3.0	I	100				
4.	Uneducated Youth	6.77	III	9.3				

Note: Based on NSSO Survey on (EU) 1999-2000.

Table 3.2

Estimated Number of Children Leaving School (2001-02)

(in '000)

States and Union Territories	Estimated Number of Children Leaving Schools after Completing Class VIII & IX	Estimated Number of Children Leaving Schools after Completing Class X & XI	Total
Andhra Pradesh	186.45	82.09	268.54
Arunachal Pradesh	5.87	4.17	10.04
Assam	78.82	125.45	204.26
Bihar	163.55	263.32	426.87
Jharkhand	85.35	136.19	221.53
Goa	8.28	5.99	14.26
Gujarat	180.94	205.08	386.02
Haryana	54.83	103.58	158.42
Himachal Pradesh	18.22	58.38	76.60
Jammu & Kashmir	48.15	54.73	102.88
Karnataka	160.00	303.61	463.62
Kerala	128.65	284.71	413.36
Madhya Pradesh	339.36	197.56	536.92
Chhattisgarh	124.75	58.95	183.70
Maharashtra	440.36	477.63	917.99
Manipur	9.76	23.42	33.18
Meghalaya	7.62	7.57	15.19
Mizoram	3.23	8.22	11.45
Nagaland	5.02	9.14	14.16
Orissa	150.00	55.40	205.40
Punjab	26.63	136.66	163.29
Rajasthan	538.03	218.62	756.65
Sikkim	4.26	1.15	5.41
Tamil Nadu	351.37	357.36	708.73
Tripura	13.33	18.33	31.66
Uttar Pradesh	251.27	650.83	902.10
Uttaranchal	5.81	85.64	91.45
West Bengal	295.01	329.16	624.16
A & N Islands	2.15	2.17	4.32
Chandigarh	1.82	2.70	4.52
Dadra & N. Haveli	1.43	0.67	2.10
Daman & Diu	0.81	0.58	1.39
Delhi	97.93	34.20	132.12
Lakshadweep	0.49	0.40	0.89
Pondicherry	5.71	7.02	12.74
India	**3795.24**	**4310.66**	**8105.90**

Source: Based on *Selected Educational Statistics (2001-02)*, Ministry of Human Resource Development.

Note: Total may not tally because of rounding off. The values are derived on the basis of the difference between enrolment figures of classes VIII, IX, X, XI and XII.

As to 8.1 million youths coming out from the education system those joining the labour force could be estimated by using the existing group-specific participation rates and comes to around 3.2 million in the year 2001-2002. Among those, going by past experiences some are likely to get jobs without vocational training. Assuming that we want to impart vocational training to all the educated youth in the labour force in future, then the above estimate is realistic. Our study finds that the group, comprised school leavers after classes VIII and XI, should be the first priority target for vocational training and skill development. Out of around 1 million seats in school providing vocational training at 10+2 level, 0.4 million remain unutilised. Only 0.6 million students have some vocational training while leaving the school.

In identifying the next priority group, the study feels that the 'incremental educated youth' (totalling 8.83 million in 1999-2000 and will be more in 2001-2002) with a high unemployment rate, i.e., 12.1 (against the national average of 7.3 per cent) should be first targeted (Table 3.3). In this group, educated, unemployed females adds to 1.9 million and their unemployment rate is as high as 22.5 per cent. The study recommends that this sub-group among the educated youth should be given special focus.

The third priority goes to all other youths who are in the labour force, whether illiterate or semi-literate.

Then comes the large number of 'under-employeds.' Adding all the sectoral estimates together, they approximate 62.5 million. By the end of the Tenth Plan they will total about 75-80 million. Indeed, over time, the magnitude of these targets will grow as the present age distribution of the total population grows. Further, given Government's universal elementary education programme, the educated part of the youth will increase still faster.

Assuming we have to reach a target of around 90-100 million of all unemployed and 'under-employed' by the end of the Tenth Plan period, a proper prioritisation of the work programme will be needed. This will mean an additional target for skill development and vocational training as a percentage of the total workforce to rise to around 30 per cent. This should be reckoned, in addition to the percentage of vocationally trained persons, at around 5 per cent of the workforce already achieved on a formal basis and 20 per cent on an informal basis. All together, it will take the total vocationally trained workforce reaching around 55 per cent—a respectable figure when compared with many of the advanced economies.

The nature/composition of vocational training and skill development differs between the target groups and sub-groups. The selection of skill and nature of vocational training in each target group should take into account the pattern of emerging demands and labour market composition for each separately. For example, the nature of skill and training needed for males and females in rural and urban sectors will be very different. Further, they may belong to different regions like arid, hilly or susceptible to floods. Individuals also belong to different social classes. The definition of youth (ages 15 to 29) needs to be re-qualified in many cases. Many females aspiring to work as entrepreneurs, for example, may not come into the labour force in the age group of 15 to 29 years. Many housewives join the labour force as self-employed and entrepreneurs after 30, when their family obligations are mostly met. Finally, there is a need for matching these targets with existing vocational training and skill capacities in the country, both in the formal and informal sectors. Roughly, in the formal sectors, which are mostly confined to the educated group and are offering courses for one year or more, the total capacity is estimated at 1.72 million (Details will follow in the next Chapter). Any other training in the formal sector is provided for a duration of 'less than one year'; the two formal sectors together equal a capacity of near 2.78 million. Even this capacity is mostly outdated and the training and skill curricula not geared to the emerging demand pattern. As a result, this sector has a very low placement rate, sometimes below 30 per cent. On the other hand, there is a large pool of informal training institutions which can be revived. This is where the role of public-private partnership, NGOs and civil societies come in. In the next chapter we will look into these issues.

In taking stock of existing capacities for training and skill development, the state of demand orientation, quality, and flexibility to change over time must be examined. For example, it is mentioned several times in this study that the vocational training should be made demand-oriented, so that the Placement Ratio (PR) can be improved from its current very low level (around 30 per cent).

But the operative question is how to assess the demand for any vocation that is likely to emerge over the short and medium term period. One school of thought suggests that vocational institutions should develop their curriculum structure according to the student's choice when they opt for admission. But in a fast changing market economy, where so many national and international forces interact, this way of measuring potential demand may turn out to be very short-sighted, especially in areas where the gestation lag of skill development is rather high, and their demand changes very frequent. In addition, there is a glamorous connotation associated with working in the high-tech industry that attracts more labourers than needed. The experience with fast automation shows that, over time, the demand for high-tech workers will fast decline. All this suggests well-developed, market research bodies will be needed, keeping the overall development strategy and available resource base in mind. Accordingly, this present report reiterates that any vocational training course must be accompanied by research in technology and proper information flow on the changes in market demand.

To conclude, simply offering vocational training and skills without providing proper physical and social infrastructure will create more problems than currently exist today. As an illustration, a large number of IT-trained personnel (in response to growing potential demands in this area) may prove to remain unutilised (i.e., unemployed) if a stable power supply is not available in their work places. Hence, training programmes and their size should be developed by taking a holistic view of the availability of infrastructure directly or indirectly related to the needs of the sectors, which generate IT demands.

An Outline of the Existing Vocational System

In India, skill acquisition takes place through two basic structural streams—a small formal one and a large informal one. The formal structure includes a) higher technical education, imparted through professional colleges, b) vocational education in schools at the post-secondary stage, c) technical training in specialised institutions, and d) apprenticeship training. A number of agencies, such as the Ministry of Human Resource Development, the Ministry of Labour,

Table 3.3

Demography of Labour Force, Youth and Employment

(Dimensions based on NSS Survey of EU, on CDS Basis)

Col.1	*Percentage Unemployed to Total Labour Force*	*Col.2*	*Percentage Unemployed to Respective Educated Labour Force*	*Percentage to Total Col.1*
A. Total Labour Force and its Structure		**A. Educated Labour Force and its Structure**		
1. Total Labour Force = 363.33 m		1. Educated Labour Force = 125.0 m		(34.4)
2. Youth Labour Force = 129.4 m (i.e., 35.6 per cent of Total)		2. Youth Educated Labour Force = 56.6 m		(43.7)
(i) Youth Labour Force (Male) = 95.77 m		(i) Youth Educated Labour Force (Male) = 47.97 m		(49.8)
(ii) Youth Labour Force (Female) = 33.63 m		(ii) Youth Educated Labour Force (Female) = 8.63 m		(26.8)
B. Unemployed (in million)		**B. Unemployed (in million)**		
1. Total (Unemployed) = 26.5 m	7.3	1. Total Educated (Unemployed) = 10.8	8.6	(41.0)
2. Total Youth = 15.6 m	12.1	2. Total Youth Educated = 8.83	15.6	(56.6)
(i) Youth (Male) =11.6 m	12.0	(i) Youth Educated (Male) = 6.91	14.3	(59.5)
(ii) Youth (Female) = 4.0 m	12.1	(ii) Youth Educated (Female) = 1.92	22.2	(45.5)

Summary inferences:

1. 81 per cent of the educated unemployed are youth.
2. Highest unemployed among educated youth (women) = 22.5 per cent (class VIII and above)
3. Above graduate unemployed in educated youth (women) = 35.9 per cent (above graduates)
4. Only 8.6 per cent of total educated labour force is unemployed and it is 15.6 per cent among educated youths.
5. Among youth, unemployment is higher among the educated; 15.6 per cent and among non-youth 9.3 per cent.
6. Among non-youths, unemployment is higher among illiterates than educated; 5.6 per cent and 3.8 per cent.
7. Higher the level of education, higher is the unemployment rate and in all educated category unemployment among female youth is higher than male.
8. Higher the basic education, higher is the level of skill.
9. Of the educated labour force of 125.0 m only around 7 m i.e. 5.6 per cent of total are absorbed in the organised sector.

the Ministry of Rural Development, the Ministry of Urban Affairs and Employment, the Khadi and Village Industries Commission, the Development Commissioner of Small Scale Industries, and the Indian Council for Agricultural Research each with a network of its own impart vocational education/training at various levels. Some of these are short-term programmes to augment productivity and to diversify sources to earn supplementary income.

Higher professional and technical education, primarily in the areas of agriculture, education, engineering and technology, and medicine, is imparted through various professional institutions. Expansion of these institutions is often supply-driven and lopsided as, for instance, the growth of engineering degree colleges *vis-à-vis* polytechnics, or the neglect of nursing education. Nevertheless, such shortages as have developed in these higher technical and professional fields are generally lapses of quality, and have not posed any major quantitative constraints in the process of meeting the manpower needs of the unorganised or informal sector. Suffice to say, there is a need to redress the balance in the growth pattern of various levels of technical education and room for substantial qualitative improvement. The rest of this section will be confined to low-end skills that require at best 10+2 years of schooling as entry qualification in the prevailing vocational education system, and the need to develop systems that could impart skill training to those who leave after the elementary level of schooling.

The major low-end skill building activity is confined to two major systems—at the 10+2 level of school education operated by the Ministry of Human Resources Development through its counterpart departments in the states and the Craftsmen Training Scheme and Apprentices Training Scheme run by the Ministry of Labour with its counterpart departments in the states. Vocationalisation of education at secondary level was introduced in 1988 under the Ministry of Human Resource Development with a view to enhancing individual employability and providing an alternative to those who did not want to or could not pursue higher general education. A scheme of pre-vocational education at lower secondary level was also started from 1993-94 to impart training in simple marketable skills and to develop vocational interests. There are now about 6,800 schools offering about 150 vocational courses of two years duration in the broad areas of agriculture, business and commerce, engineering and technology, health and paramedical, home science, and science and technology at the +2 stage with a sanctioned capacity of 9.73 lakh (Annexure X). Those passing out of this vocational stream are eligible to undergo apprenticeship training up to one year under the Apprentices Act. About 20 thousand apprenticeship positions have been located for such apprentices.[5]

There are over 1,200 polytechnics with an annual intake capacity of about 2.16 lakh, approved by the All India Council of Technical Education (AICTE), offering three-year diploma courses in various branches of engineering. Those who successfully complete 10 years of schooling may seek admission to the polytechnics. State-wise intake capacity is given in Annexure X.

There are also 675 community polytechnics, which are attached to the regular polytechnics and share the infrastructure, performing functions like rural technical manpower development, transfer of technology, and technical support services to the community.

The Ministry of Labour is responsible for vocational training. Under the Craftsmen Training Scheme, training in 49 engineering and 49 non-engineering trades is imparted through a network of about 4,877 Industrial Training Institutes (ITIs) and Industrial Training Centres (ITCs) run both by the respective State governments and those in the private sector affiliated with the scheme for recognition and certification. These courses are open to those who have passed any class between 8th and 12th class depending on the trade chosen and are of six months to three years duration, again depending on the trade. The Ministry of Labour also runs Advanced Training Institutes for training instructors and National and Regional Vocational Training Centres for Women. The Apprenticeship Training Scheme provides on-the-job training in industrial establishments and the programme is dovetailed to some extent with the institutional training in ITIs. State-wise information on the Craftsmen Training Scheme is also shown in Annexure X.

Skill training, currently being offered by the formal system, can be viewed from two broad categories—(a) those which are more

5. Excluding positions for graduate and technician apprentices requiring higher entry qualifications.

stable and ubiquitously distributed across the country relating to carpentry, baking, and the repair of televisions, refrigerators and air conditioners, etc. in the trade service sector, as well as vocations in the manufacturing sector such as turner, fitter, machinist, etc., and (b) emerging areas that could peak and fluctuate before stabilising, such as biotechnology, information technology, business processing, etc. A significant part of the latter appears to be addressed by the private sector.

The training programmes for the development of manpower in information technology present another model of vocational training. The training is imparted by grassroot level institutions, with the Ministry of Information Technology and the Computer Society of India setting standards, testing and certifying skills. There are a number of other government departments that are imparting formal and informal training in a wide variety of areas, such as hotel management (Ministry of Tourism), self-employment schemes (Department of Rural Development, Department of Social Justice and Empowerment, Department of Tribal Welfare, Department of Urban Employment and Poverty Alleviation, etc.). The Department of Science and Technology, Export Promotion Councils, various commodity boards, KVIC, universities (nearly 281), ICAR, NGOs, professional bodies, private institutions, etc. also conduct a large number of formal and informal training programmes. As indicated in Table 3.4, which presents a summary of various vocational training programmes, the total intake capacity is about 1.3 million in courses of one or more years duration and about 1.5 million in short duration courses.

These formal streams of skill formation cater only to a small segment of the population. By and large, skill formation takes place through informal channels like family occupations and on-the-job training under master craftsmen with no linkages to formal education, training and certification. Even though some of them are highly skilled, their skills are not recognised for employment purposes. The large workforce in the unorganised sector also has hardly any structured system of acquiring or upgrading skills.

Thus, agriculture and allied sectors, though characterised by under-employment, low productivity and seasonal unemployment, would continue to absorb a substantial proportion of the labour force. Employment and productivity issues in agriculture will have to be addressed through crop diversification, increased value addition, improved post-harvest technology and creation of off-farm employment opportunities. In all this, skill building and dissemination of emerging technologies among the vast rural labour force will be needed. Among the providers of vocational training relating to agricultural and allied sectors is the Indian Council of Agricultural Research (ICAR). The research set up of ICAR includes 47 central institutes, 5 national bureaus, 12 project directorates, 33 national research centres, and 82 all-India coordinated research projects.

ICAR promotes and coordinates research, education and the application of technology in agriculture, animal husbandry, fisheries, natural resource management, home science and allied sciences. In this task it is supported by a large number of centres of research, agricultural universities and a network of *Krishi Vigyan Kendra* (KVK) spread across the country (approved 276). The Government of India has approved establishment of one KVK in each of the 578 rural districts of the country by the end of the Tenth Plan period.

KVK imparts training for farmers and farm women through work experience, yet without any uniform syllabus. Training content is tailored according to felt needs and local resource base. The duration of training is flexible and does not prescribe any educational qualifications for the entering trainees. During 2003-04, about 4.78 lakh farmers underwent such training through about 20,000 programmes in areas like crop production, plant protection, horticulture, livestock production and management, fisheries, soil fertility, agricultural engineering, agro forestry, home science, agricultural extension, mush production, sericulture, bee keeping, etc. Such programmes address issues relating to productivity in agriculture, diversification of the agricultural sector, and skill development. In order to increase the reach of these programmes, over 60,000 extension personnel, who constitute the bulk of the trainers, were trained during 2003-2004.

The KVK also organise vocational training for rural youth to promote self-employment and off-farm employment. The duration of the courses vary from one day to one year, depending on the skills needed. During the year 2003-04, about 1.10 lakh youth were trained in various skills related to agriculture and allied sectors. The number of beneficiaries of various types of training provided by KVK during 2003-04 can be summarised as follows:

Farmers and Farm Women	4,77,780
Rural Youth	1,10,210
In Service Extension Personnel	60,911
Extension Activity Beneficiaries	11,87,209

As there is no precise information on intake capacities for vocational training through the ICAR network, it is not clear whether the number of beneficiaries represent full utilisation of capacities. There is also some overlap in some of the courses offered by ICAR related institutions, and institutions from other ministries.

Besides these, the KVK also organise extension activities for technology dissemination, annually reaching more than a million farmers. The production and productivity of Indian agriculture depend on 103 million farm families cultivating 140 million hectares spread over 600,000 villages. Clearly, an individual approach through training and demonstration can hardly reach these numbers. Group approach, distance learning, and dissemination of information through electronic media are being extensively used to attain a reach on that scale.

There is sufficient empirical evidence to show that the farming community is willing to meet reasonable costs for efficient and timely diagnostic services and some farmers associations, as in Maharashtra, have established their own service and training centres. There is, therefore, a need to strengthen the KVK network, regularly monitor the impact of the training and extension services provided and constantly update and expand training programmes in emerging technologies in agricultural and allied sectors.

Quantitative Deficiencies in Skill Development

The capacities created for various types of vocational education and training must be viewed in relation to the number of persons that need such training. As mentioned earlier, the formal system of vocational training is confined to those who have completed 10 and 12 years of schooling, and to some extent, those who leave the educational stream after completing 8 years of elementary education. In the year 2001-02, about 3.8 million children left school after completing class VIII and IX (Table 3.2). The number of departures

Table 3.4

Vocational Training Programmes Conducted by Departments/Institutions

Sl. No.	*Ministry/Department*	*Estimated Training Capacity/Persons Trained (Annually—in Lakh)*
1.	M/o Health & Family Welfare	0.20
2.	M/o Human Resource Development	
	Vocationalisation of Secondary Education	4.9
	Apprenticeship Training	0.19
	National Open School	0.067
3.	D/o Information Technology DOEAC 'O' Level	0.75
4.	M/o Labour DGE&T	
	Craftsmen Training Scheme	About 5
	Apprenticeship Training Scheme	About 1.5
	Other Long Term Training Programmes	0.07
5.	D/o Small Scale Industries	0.02
6.	D/o Tourism (Food Crafts Institutes)	0.011
	Total	**12.708**
	Skill Upgradation of Existing Workers	
1.	HUDCO & Others in Construction Sector	0.18
2.	Khadi & Village Industries Corporation	0.08
3.	M/o Agriculture	2.00
4.	M/o Food Processing Industries	0.025
5.	M/o Health & Family Welfare	0.16
6.	M/o Heavy Industries and Public Enterprises	0.10
7.	D/o Information Technology	0.025
8.	M/o Labour DGE&T	
	Short Term Training Programme Under DGE&T	0.23
9.	D/o Small Scale Industries	0.14
10.	M/o Textiles	0.425
	Total	**3.365**
	Skill Training Imparted under Poverty Alleviation Programmes or Programmes for Employment of Specific Target Groups	
1.	M/o Human Resource Development	4.50
	Community Polytechnic *Jan Shiksha Sansthan*	1.80
2.	M/o Rural Development (SGSY)	2.00
3.	M/o Social Justice & Empowerment	0.15
4.	M/o Tribal Affairs	0.19
5.	M/o Urban Development & Poverty Alleviation	0.59
6.	D/o Women & Child Development	2.50
	Total	**11.73**

Note: The data has been compiled by DGE&T and Ministry of Labour based on information collected from various ministries, their annual reports, websites, reports of the working group constituted by the Planning Commission for finalisation of Tenth Plan proposals etc. It includes both less than one year and one year or more courses.

from school at these levels is expected to increase sharply with the progressive impact of Sarva Shiksha Abhyiyan, through increased enrolment rates at the entry level of schooling and increased retention rates. A large proportion of these students subsequently enter the labour market. Vocational training for this group is extremely limited in the formal system—of the total intake capacity in vocational training of about 1.7 million, available in the ITIs, Polytechnics and in +2 stage schooling, only about 0.1 million seats are available for those who complete the VIII class.

In addition to those who leave the educational stream after completing eight years, more than four million did not continue their education after completing 10/11 years of schooling. The labour force participation rates for the general population as per NSS 55th Round for the age groups of 15-19 for males and females were 48.5 per cent and 26.0 per cent respectively. Labour force participation rates would be higher for those who do not continue their education beyond VIII or X class. Thus, a large proportion of about eight million youth (who discontinued education) would enter labour market without acquiring any formal vocational training.

Of the 8.1 million estimated school leavers, 3.24 million are girls and 4.86 million are boys. Using the age and gender specific labour force participation rates of the relevant age group (15 to 19 years of age, and 26 and 48.5 per cent respectively for girls and boys), we find that 3.20 million joined the labour force from this group in 2002 without any formal vocational training. The corresponding figure for the year 2007 (assuming the labour force participation rate of 1999-2000) works out to 4.16 million. The values would be proportionately higher since labour force participation of school leavers in this age group would be higher than in the population in this age group.

Besides this group, a large number drop out before completing eight years of schooling.[6] While estimates are available, they reflect the increase of youth entry into the labour force who are not necessarily educated (education defined as Middle and Secondary level).

The estimated vocational training capacity (Table 3.4) does not include intake capacity of other unregulated training providers in the

6. Enrolment in Class VIII in 2001 was about 54 per cent of the enrolment in Class I in 1994.

informal sector, NGOs and private sector. Evidence of considerable regional variations that are currently found in formal vocational education/training is illustrated by the fact that the four Southern States of Andhra Pradesh, Kerala, Karnataka and Tamil Nadu account for about 45 per cent of the total capacity of the Craftsmen Training Scheme. If the two Western States of Maharashtra and Gujarat were also taken into account, this proportion would go beyond two-thirds of the country's total capacity under the scheme. The situation is only slightly better in the case of vocational education in schools, with the Southern States accounting for one-third, and together with the two Western States for about 55 per cent of the total sanctioned capacity. The expansion of vocational training in these six States is primarily due to enhanced private sector participation (Annexure X).

Skill Mismatches

Installation of facilities to the required degree, by itself, does not ensure that skill mismatches do not occur. These skill shortages and surpluses arise for various reasons, like values attached by society to various lines of learning, inadequate quality of training, absence of an efficient labour market signalling system and an absence of the training system to respond quickly to changes in demand patterns. Creation of training capacities is one thing and it is quite another to ensure that school-leavers pursue vocational courses instead of general education streams. With the pattern of social demand being what it is, the accent is primarily on higher education and there are relatively few takers of vocational education in schools. Students go in for vocational training only when all attempts for higher education fail. The effect of this social value system on demand for vocational education is brought out in the ILO's *World Employment Review* (1998-99). Commenting on the training needs of the leather industry, the Report observes that, "The sector faces acute shortage of trained manpower and especially lacks trained managers, supervisors and design operators. The stigma attached to leather trade, lack of modern teaching infrastructure and outdated courses have all contributed to skill shortages in the sector." In 1995, only 635 candidates underwent formal training courses in leather-work out of a total capacity in all courses of 4,20,000 in the Industrial Training Institutes. In the ITIs, the 10 top trades in terms of intake capacity account for about 80 per cent of the total capacity as illustrated by figures in Table 3.5, whereas the rest of over 60 trades account for about 20 per cent of the intake capacity. Labour market demand in the urban informal sector for trades such as carpentry and plumbing, that are more ubiquitously distributed, account for a very small proportion of annual intake capacity.

Table 3.5

Intake Capacity in the ITIs by Trade (2002)

Sl. No.	*Trade Engineering*	*Sanctioned Intake* Total (in lakh)	Per Cent	Cumulative
1.	Fitter	1.39	20.75	20.75
2.	Electrician	1.21	17.98	38.73
3.	Mechanic Motor Vehicle	0.43	6.38	45.11
4.	Wireman	0.38	5.65	50.76
5.	Electronic Mechanic	0.38	5.62	56.38
6.	Turner	0.38	5.59	61.97
7.	D/Man Civil	0.36	5.29	67.26
8.	Welder	0.33	4.94	72.20
9.	Mechanic Diesel	0.31	4.62	76.82
10.	Machinist	0.25	3.66	80.48
	Total of above	5.42	80.48	–
	Total of all Trades	**6.73**	**100.00**	**100.00**

Source: Based on different sources as explained in the following write-up.

As per the information (March 2004) from the Ministry of Labour, there were 1.62 lakh trade apprentices undergoing training against a total capacity of 2.32 lakh. A special drive was launched by the Directorate General of Employment and Training (DGE&T) during June 2000, to expand apprenticeship training in industry in which 32,000 smaller establishments, which were not covered so far by the states, had been identified as warranting coverage by the Apprentices Act.

In schools, too, vocational streams attract few students. In spite of the created capacity for 11.5 per cent of the secondary pass students, only 4.8 per cent of the students could be diverted to vocational streams as against a target of 25 per cent (Planning Commission, 1997-2000).

While mismatches of this type lead to shortages, there are a number of areas where the pattern of skill development has led to surpluses and unemployment among trained persons. According to the 55th Round of NSSO (1999-2000), 31 per cent of the educated unemployed are those who do possess professional and technical skills. A case in point is the expansion of facilities for engineering education at the degree level over the years, in absolute terms and in relation to the development of diploma-level education, leading to a situation where there are as many degree-holders as diploma-holders, or even more, against a general norm of one degree-holder for two or three diploma-holders. As a result there is considerable unemployment and underemployment among engineering graduates.

Available data from the National Technical Manpower Information System indicates that absorption of degree-holders within two years of completing their education is less than 70 per cent. Reports for Andhra Pradesh, which has seen substantial expansion of engineering education in recent years, suggest that the graduates have little choice but to accept low paid jobs. Availability of graduate engineers at low salaries has affected the demand for diploma-holders and their rate of employment is below 50 per cent (within two years of successfully obtaining a diploma). At the craftsmen level, the situation seems to be somewhat better. A recent sample survey in Delhi indicated that 80 per cent of the civil and mechanical draughtsmen trained in ITIs were absorbed in the trade within three years, most of them within the first year after training. However, in other trades, such as instrument mechanics, machinists, plumbers, and maintenance mechanics of refrigerators and air-conditioners, the absorption rate was about 55 per cent only. In some trades, the lower rate of employment is because wage employment is generally sought, rather than the option of self-employment.

Another area in the lopsided development of technical education is the relative neglect of nursing education. In spite of the shortage of qualified nurses at home and the steadily growing demand from overseas, training facilities have not been expanded. Successive Five Year Plans have lamented the lopsided development of medical education. The Eighth Plan, for example, pointed out that, "While states have been more than anxious to start new medical colleges, their efforts to develop institutions for training of paramedical staff have been entirely sub-optimal." As a result, the number of available doctors in the early-nineties, which should ideally have been one-third that of the nurses, exceeded the latter by a sizeable margin. The Eighth Plan, therefore, proposed vocational courses at the +2 stage of general education to bridge the gap between demand and supply of paramedical personnel. The situation has gradually been remedied and by 1998-99, the ratio of doctors to nurses, though nowhere near the ideal 1:3, nevertheless improved to about 1:1.5.

Structural Deficiencies

The problems with vocational education and training, to a substantial degree, are the result of structural deficiencies in the training system. The vocational training system in the country as it evolved, for historical reasons, has generally been geared to the needs of the organised sector, though for reasons of inadequate absorption in that sector, the trainees have sometimes been forced to find employment in the unorganised or self-employment segments of the economy. Programmes in ITIs were straight jacketed, without strong linkages with industries, polytechnics or with informal streams of skill development. Rigid entry qualifications prescribed do not allow persons from informal streams to avail of ITI training, and, more importantly, children from deprived sections are left behind.

The recent steps taken by the DGE&T, to correct this lacunae, include the introduction of a few trades in the informal sector under the Apprenticeship Training Scheme, the introduction of shorter courses of two to six months duration, and a pilot programme to promote self and wage employment in the informal sector.

There is considerable variation in the quality of ITI training across the country. For example, the training provided in the National and Regional Vocational Training Institutes for Women, run by the Central Government, is found to be far superior to that in ordinary ITIs for women across the country. Inadequacy of resources at the command of the State governments is perhaps the primary cause for such variations. Rapid expansion of the network of training institutions is not always accompanied by adequate resources or the full complement of infrastructure necessary. Obsolescence of trades, equipment and curriculum has long been a problem with the craftsmen training scheme. Though an effort was made during the Eighth Plan to remedy the situation through a World Bank-assisted scheme, it was somewhat of a one-time effort. Industry linkages are sought through national, state, local council and committee levels, but active participation of the industry with a sense of stakeholders is missing. The lack of enthusiasm on the part of the private sector industry to actively participate in skill-building is reflected in the lukewarm compliance with the apprenticeship training programme. Some efforts are now underway to increase the industry's participation in and responsibility to improved training through industrial committees attached to the training institutions at the local level. An attempt was made during the Ninth Plan to increase the institute-industry interaction by setting up Institute Managing Committees under the leadership of local industrialist employers. DGE&T initiated a pilot programme of Formation of Institute Management Committee for ITIs, in collaboration with the Confederation of Indian Industry (CII) to improve cooperation between industry and ITIs. The number of Institute Management Committees organised has increased from about 33 during the Ninth Plan to 292 by March 2004. This also helps in improving the functioning of the institutions, better upkeep of machinery and equipment, development of faculty, placement of trainees for industrial visits, etc., and removing the common perception in industry circles that skills acquired under the scheme are not up to the mark.

Vocational education in schools also suffers from a lack of infrastructure, inadequate equipment, lack of trained vocational teachers working full time, obsolete trades and a lack of weight given to students from this stream in admissions to higher technical education. Though district level vocational surveys determining the trades in demand are supposed to be the basis of introducing vocational courses, a mismatch between demand and supply develops due to inflexibility or delays in altering either the courses, the course content, or the training capacity. Absence of practical training is another drawback. There is now a plan in place to continue the training of those completing the +2 vocational courses through apprenticeship under the Apprentices Act, but coverage is restricted. Full time teachers trained in vocational subjects are also not in place. The States, which implement educational programmes, are rather lukewarm in their approach to the vocational component of education, possibly due to lack of popular demand for it, and unwillingness to make a long term commitment of resources to a centrally sponsored scheme.

There are organisational problems too. Organisational responsibility for skill development in the country is, as has already been seen, scattered over a number of agencies, often without adequate coordination. This leads to avoidable wastage of resources, duplication of effort and lack of uniformity in certification of quality of skills attained. For instance, there is a good deal of overlap between the vocational courses in engineering trades (such as fitter) offered in the schools at the +2 stage and those provided in the Industrial Training Institutes. It is not certain that the levels of skills attained after completion of the courses in the two modes are equivalent. While there is no uniformity in skill certification, even in the formal training systems, there is no skill certification system at all for the skills acquired informally.

During the Tenth Plan period, DGE&T in the Ministry of Labour have taken up a Centrally Sponsored Scheme for testing and certification of skills for workers in the informal sector at a cost of Rs.2 crore. The scheme is expected to become self-financing in the long-run through fee-for-testing and certification.

There is no doubt that a formal employment market information system exists at the national, state and local levels, operated by the Ministry of Labour through State Labour Departments and employment exchanges at the grassroots level. The information system is again geared to the needs of the organised sector and does not offer anything worthwhile for the unorganised labour market. Even in the case of organised sector, the system has gradually been losing its utility over the years due to rigidity, lack of commitment and lack of skills in interpreting labour market signals as well as indifference on the part of training institutions to quickly respond to these signals. The interaction within industrial circles necessary to capture signals for changing patterns of demand for skills is lacking. There is also a practice of conducting vocational surveys in the districts to form a basis for choice of vocational courses for schools. Similarly, the rural development programmes also have a component of assessing the training needs. There are, thus, a variety of bits of exercises undertaken by different agencies to determine the training needs. A more comprehensive all-inclusive effort may be more rewarding.

There is a provision for vocational guidance and counselling in some schools. This enables students to make their career choices. However, only a fraction of schools have these services, which depend on providing a wider knowledge of the world of work rather than on motivating students to take up vocational courses. Quite often, professional counsellors are not available and the work is assigned to a teacher who does this extra assignment on part time basis. Wherever there are trained guidance workers, they are assigned other activities of the school—sometimes they are even supposed to take a regular timetable for teaching. Thus, a professional approach to counselling is usually lacking in schools.

Some Comments on ITI's Efficiency and Organisation

The Industrial Training Institutes form the backbone of the vocational training structure in the States, yet the government institutes generally suffer from sluggishness and inadequacies in management and financial support processes. A recent study by the ILO shows that there are problems of internal as well as external efficiencies with the ITI set up. The study also shows that there are wide variations in the coverage and functioning of the ITI in different States. In Orissa, for example, three districts do not have any ITI under the public sector. Because of the slow growth of the ITI coverage, both in terms of area and the trades, proprietary vocational training institutes have grown. The instructors in these private institutes are often not paid adequately, however, resulting in a poor standard of training offered.

The ILO study has worked out internal efficiency indicators in terms of a percentage of sanctioned training places that eventually produced graduates. The overall internal efficiency of the public sector in Orissa was 73.8 per cent, and in Maharashtra it was 62.6 per cent. In the case of Andhra Pradesh, this factor was as low as 31.8 per cent indicating that there was an over-expansion of training capacity without commensurate market absorption capacity. Trade-wise, analysis shows that minimum efficiencies are in trades like turner, pump operator-mechanic, sheet metal worker, stenographer, draughtsman and mechanic tractor training courses. The low level of efficiency in these trades may also be an indicator of inadequate levels or standards of training in these courses.

One trend that has been noticed is that long-term regular training programmes in basic industrial trades are becoming unpopular with high dropout rates. The percentage of ITI trained persons employed in industry varies widely from trade to trade, from 4.7 per cent in the printing and publishing industry to 90.7 per cent in the synthetic fibre industry.

In the case of women, their low enrolment and graduation rate is due to sociological reasons and also because of the non-availability of hostels, proper transport arrangements and security issues.

The percentage of ITI graduates who are absorbed in wage-employment or self-employment was found to be as low as 16.2 per cent in the case of Orissa, and 35.7 per cent in the case of Maharashtra. For Andhra Pradesh, it was 41 per cent. The activities in which the graduates who were not absorbed in wage-employment or self-employment are engaged, include continuing education, training or apprenticeship, or working as domestic staff, an activity that appears to attract those who do not get adequately and properly employed. The samples indicate that the purpose of using these structures as skill-building agencies for providing gainful employment is not being adequately fulfilled.

It would be interesting to find out whether the skills acquired during training are actually utilised and to what extent. The ILO study found that graduates who utilised the knowledge and skill when they worked in the trade was 48.2 per cent in Andhra Pradesh and 59.9 per cent in Maharashtra. In the case of private Industrial Training Centres (ITCs), these two sample States showed a reverse situation.

The impact of the vocational training system on the unorganised sector is not very significant, since the majority of these institutes are established in urban areas and serve mainly urban needs, while the educated youth in the rural areas are without access to adequate training opportunities. The original purpose of setting up these institutions was to strengthen the urban industrialisation process, not as skill development agencies for the rural poor. In their role of producing skilled manpower for the unorganised sector, since micro enterprises have limited financial strength and are not able to pay reasonable wages to properly trained and certified persons, they are not in a position to employ such formally trained persons.

There is a felt need for changes in the ITI ownership and management structures including the very vital question of operational autonomy and private synergy. The funding levels have to be improved appreciably and the procedural catacomb needs to be demolished and re-done in many states. There is also a need for decentralised decision making at the district levels and for coordination of training needs and ensuring commensurate response from these institutions. A study of different models of revenue generation is also necessary to give them inherent strength and flexibility to meet the changing market demands.

Elements of Skill Development Strategy

It may thus be seen that the training system in the country is generally scattered in nature and suffers from lack of a focused approach, coordination between various departments, convergence of resources and compatibility with changing labour market demands, and a unified certification system. There is also duplication of efforts due to involvement of various Ministries and Departments, not only in imparting skills but also in accreditation of institutions and certification of skills. This also results in indifferent quality of training. For short term training modules and informal training, no uniform or national system is in vogue. If the skill development programmes have to provide necessary impetus to achieve the employment targets set out in the Tenth Plan, the training system needs a thorough overhauling.

Raising the employability of the nation's youth is as important as employment generation to meet their employment needs. Successive Five Year Plans and various committees and commissions mentioned in the previous sections have underscored the prevailing low skill levels among the Indian labour force in comparison to other countries—like the Republic of Korea—and the need to establish comprehensive but flexible systems of skill development to enhance employability and increase productivity and incomes. A number of committees have, in the recent past, looked at the weaknesses of the skill development systems in the country. In particular, the Task Force on Employment Opportunities, The Special Group on Targeting Ten Million Employment Opportunities per Year, the Working Group on Skill Development and Training, and the Second National Labour Commission have each made a number of suggestions. The Task Force referred to features like the low skill endowment of the Indian labour force in comparison to other countries, the strong preference among the young for general education (perceived as a means to landing high-paid government jobs) over vocational training, the inadequacy of the vocational training system in meeting the quantitative as well as qualitative requirements, and the perception among employers that the skills acquired by those coming out of the State-run training institutions are inadequate. It recommended: a major expansion of general education and an increase in vocational content to generate marketable skills; providing additional resources for strengthening Industrial Training Institutes in the public sector to upgrade their facilities; greater industry-institution interaction and joint management of training; expansion of capacity to produce engineering graduates of IIT standards; and, setting up an IIT in each State for this purpose, and encouraging private sector participation in education and training.

The National Commission called for effective coordination between the several official agencies involved in vocational education and training and suggested a labour market information system to ensure better matching of demand for and supply of marketable skills. The system should assess the needs at the district level through the existing official machinery and in consultation with local industry associations, entrepreneurs, NGOs, and professional experts on a continuous basis.

The Industrial Training Institutes should run market-driven courses, reviewing and revising the curriculum every five years and discontinuing obsolete trades. Industry-institute linkages are important, with the industry providing not only advisory but also managerial inputs. The shortcomings in apprenticeship training—namely, lack of flexibility in engagement of apprentices, inadequate coverage of skill requirements, lengthy and clumsy administrative procedures, lack of incentives to encourage modernisation of training facilities, etc.—should be addressed. The Commission recommended a modular approach to a vocational training system, in which training consists of small, result-oriented modules, which help impart skills attuned to the needs of the labour market, introducing timely, need-based changes in curricula and also allowing generation of multiple skills. A system of testing competency and certification should be put in place. Training facilities should be available at the block level for the benefit of rural masses. New computer-based delivery mechanisms as well as distance learning systems should be used to provide training anywhere and any time.

The Special Group pointed out that programmes for development of education and skills should henceforth be geared to the needs of agriculture, small industry, services and self-employment in new areas like information technology, tourism and financial sectors. For vocational training programmes within the Ministry of Labour, the Special Group suggested, a) expansion of facilities through: greater involvement of private sector and NGOs; adequate resources in State Plans; increasing facilities for in-service training; extending apprenticeship programmes to more occupations in high-tech areas, the services sector and informal sector; and adoption of new training delivery methods like distance education and strengthening programmes for training of women and disadvantaged groups; b) improvement in effectiveness, efficiency and relevance through strengthening institute-industry interaction; developing some of the ITIs as centres of excellence; setting up a skill development fund on a partnership basis between government and industry, allowing vertical mobility of skilled persons across levels of proficiency and education; staff development, motivation and strengthening of monitoring mechanism, modularisation and multi-skilling, competency-based certification system, etc; and c) improvement in governance and management of vocational training system through formation of a National Council for Vocational Training by merging the two apex bodies currently dealing with vocational training and apprenticeship training, demarcation of functions of the national and the corresponding state-level bodies with the former setting guidelines, and assigning performance ratings where the latter would be responsible for field level functions like recognition of the institutes, etc.

Role of Government and Private Sector in Skill Development

A common strand running through the strategies recommended by various committees is that the bulk of the skill development effort should be left to the private sector and the community. Experience worldwide shows that institution-based training administered by government has not been very effective in meeting labour market requirements. The cost of training is very high and external efficiency low, therefore a greater role for the users of the outputs of the training systems in planning and implementation of the programmes is critical. The government should concentrate on policy, planning, research coordination, evaluation in collaboration with other partners, etc. and leave the nuts and bolts of skill development to the industry and the community.

It is necessary to classify vocations as those that relate to traditional but stable trades/activities—the demand for which is more ubiquitously distributed—such as carpentry, maintenance of electrical equipment, plumbing, paramedical, etc., those that are emerging, and new ones, such as medical transcription, Information Technology linking, advertising, biotechnology, etc. In the case of the latter, the skill building efforts on a commercial basis are increasingly undertaken by the private sector, and the role of government has been limited to regulatory functions. Successful trainees of these efforts have options in wage-employment and self-employment markets in formal and informal sectors. The large-scale participation of the private sector in ITI training leading to its enormous expansion in the Southern and Western states is an example of what can be achieved through market-demand-oriented private sector initiatives in place of the largely supply-side interventions from the State. Government should gradually divest itself of the responsibility it has assumed in the past to run training institutions in these areas. Capacity building efforts that are socially relevant, such as dry farming techniques, traditional crafts, household industries, etc. could still remain within the ambit of government initiatives and investment. The options for theses trainees are limited largely to the informal sector and self-employment. This would help enhance the base of knowledge-workers at the lower rungs of the employment market. However, the absorption opportunities of formally-trained, skilled workers in the informal sector are somewhat restrictive, partly due to the greater wage expectations of the trained workers and the low profit margin in the informal sector that can ill afford high labour costs.

It is, however, possible that, with an increased private sector role, acquisition of skills could become costlier and render it beyond the reach of the economically and socially weaker sections of the society. Government has a role to play here to assist the deserving aspirants of training. A system of stipends, reservations and other incentives to training providers to extend the benefits of skill development to the poor could go a long way in creating skilled manpower among those without resources and sponsors.

Industry-Institution Linkages

In the past, industry tended to view skill development as a function of the government and more or less remained passive spectators of the process and recipients of the benefits. There is now a greater realisation that the industry is a major stakeholder in skill building. Industry associations like CII are now involved in the dialogue with training institutions. Efforts are also being made by state governments to assess the impact of vocational training on industry and recommend measures for closer interaction. The process of strengthening interaction between industry and institutions has begun and needs to be made more extensive and intensive. Local community and industry should be made to feel responsible to assess local needs, inclusive of those of the informal sector, and to plan and raise resources and develop necessary institutional arrangements. Active involvement of industry/employers should help in establishing a better match of skill levels. A new financially self-sustaining scheme of Training-cum-Production Centre (TCPC) illustrates a demand driven, flexible system of skill development along with the involvement of private sector. This TCPC programme needs to be taken up on a much larger scale.

Apart from assuming responsibilities in the planning and organisation of programmes in collaboration with the local community-at-large, the industry can further the cause of skill development through full-scale participation in the apprenticeship scheme and in training the trainers. Some of the problems of the apprenticeship scheme can be traced to the lukewarm response from the industry, forced by legislation to accept apprentices as cheap labour. These attitudes need to change and the industry should spontaneously find that the apprenticeship programme is in their own best interest.

Box 3.1

Tamil Nadu Scheme for Training-cum-Production Centres

A new scheme has been started recently by the Directorate of Technical Education for running courses with industry tie-ins [vide G.O.Ms.No. 165, Higher Education (B2) Dept. Dt. 7.5.2003]. The features of the scheme are set out below.

A large number of students are discontinuing their education at the VIII, X and +2 level for various reasons. Even those who complete these levels are not in a position to continue some kind of Vocational Education programme, as the present system of Four Year B.E. Degree and Three Year Diploma courses may not be best suited for them, in view of their duration, academic and financial requirements. At present, even the certificate courses of less than one year are more academic and not designed to cater to the specific requirements of today's emerging industries. Many new industries have come up, whereas Educational courses have not been reorganised to keep in tune with new industries. Hardly 10 per cent of the workforce is academically trained and the balance of manpower is recruited locally and trained and made fit for the requirements of the industry by the industries themselves. This includes waste of efforts and resources. Some of the new industries which require large numbers of trained manpower are: Hotel and Tourism, Counter Sales in various Commercial Establishments, Hosiery Industry, Call Centres, Medical Transcription, Direct Sales, Courier Services, Outdoor Catering, etc.

In order to meet the twin objectives—empowerment of youth through purposeful Vocational Education and manpower needs of the merging industries both from the manufacturing and service sectors—'the willing Polytechnics' will be asked to identify potential training fields in their locality. They will further be asked to have a tie up with the neighbouring industry and submit proposals for running short duration Training-cum-Production-Centre (TCPC) Certificate Courses with predominant skill orientation focusing specifically on youth dropouts of formal educational system at various levels. The Syllabi of the Certificate Courses will be prescribed and approved by the Directorate of Technical Education, also charged with administering the examinations and certificates for the said courses. The syllabi and duration of the courses will be finalised in consultation with participating industries, and these courses commenced in the academic year (2003-2004). In the first phase of the programme, five courses of three months duration with 25 students in each course were trained. The scheme is proposed to run on a self-supporting basis.

Another area of industry-institution linkage is the periodic training of vocational instructors by the industry to familiarise them with the latest technological developments. Vocational instructors will have to be trained and retrained to improve the qualifications needed to impart knowledge of emerging skills to the trainees. In the everchanging technology environment, skill acquisition is a continuous process, as skill requirements change with changes in technology. Unless the workers are trained and retrained, their skills become redundant.

Government should consider appropriate tax incentives to encourage the active participation by industry in skill development. Existing benefits to encourage private investment in vocational training include 100 per cent deduction of payments made for the establishment and running of vocational institutions by the private sector in rural areas. Tax benefits also exist on recurring costs in basic training by employers of 500 or more workers. An expanded proposal of fiscal incentives to encourage private sector participation in vocational training has been proposed by the Ministry of Labour.

Training for the Informal Sector

The bulk of production activity takes place in the informal sector. It is this sector that is likely to absorb increasingly large proportions of the labour force to whom the benefits of skill development and the consequent augmentation of productivity should increasingly be extended. The existing training policies and programmes are geared to meet the needs of the organised sector; the labour force in the informal sector does not enjoy the benefits of skills and the resultant gains in productivity. There is enough evidence to show that even a little increase in skills brings in more than proportionate increase in incomes.

An illustrative case is provided by a study of the patch work industry in Uttar Pradesh. The study found that untrained artisans continue to work with traditional designs for which there is not much market, while those with some education and training tend to innovate and augment their earnings substantially. In a globalising economy, the Indian workforce, and particularly those engaged in the informal sector, will have to contend increasingly with internal and external competition from products and services coming from relatively better skilled workers. Survival in the market demands retention of one's competitive edge through acquisition of skills and constantly upgrading the skills acquired. Some of the recent innovative experiments piloted in Andhra Pradesh (Box 3.2) could be replicated by other States.

Box 3.2

Initiatives Taken by the Department of Employment and Training, Government of Andhra Pradesh since August 2003

1. ***Udyogam* (Job):** A Scheme to identify willing and eligible candidates and train them for selection to posts in Para-military forces was launched from 1.9.2003. Recently, against 473 posts of Constables (GD) advertised, 503 candidates were selected under A.P. quota. Usually, only 30 per cent of such posts are reported to have been filled in the past without this kind of pro-activity by the Employment Exchanges.
2. ***Udbhavam* (Emerging):** Under this Scheme, which was experimentally introduced in Vijayawada Region on 5.9.2003, candidates were helped to find private sector jobs through spot submission. In Vijayawada region comprising of five districts, 100 jobs on an average per month/ per district are being provided since September 5, 2003. Over 800 candidates have been placed so far.
3. ***Bhukthi* (Livelihood):** This scheme is aimed at providing domestic help, security guards, cooks etc., to households and institutional employers and big urban centres.
4. **Service Call Centres:** Under the Call Centres Scheme, Service Call Centres have been started in all the ITIs in the State from 18.8.2003 onwards under the 'Earn While You Learn Scheme.' This scheme is helping generate internal resources as well as building self-confidence among the trainees. Revenue generated under the scheme so far is Rs. 7,68,662.
5. ***Ujwal*:** Under this Scheme, skilled candidates registered with the Employment Exchange are helped through Project Report Preparation. Working with an Employment Officer a candidate leases I.T.I. machinery and equipment and secures a loan to the extent of working capital by the Bank. This Scheme was started on a pilot basis in Sadasivpet Mandal in September 2003. One hundred candidates were called, thirty seven candidates attended and nine candidates were selected for sanction of loan. It is hoped that annually over 50,000 candidates can be helped to settle in self-employment. The future prospects of this Scheme are also bright, as it is proposed to combine the technically qualified candidates of ITIs, Polytechnics and Engineering Colleges and provide them assistance under 'Velugu' Project and help them settle in self-employment to the tune of over one lakh candidates per year.
6. ***Keerthi*:** This Scheme is meant to serve the career planning needs of rural students. Under this scheme, one Government High School and one Government Junior College have been adopted by the Employment Exchanges in each district.
7. ***Merupu*:** Under this Scheme, educated, unemployed candidates, mainly graduates and above, from both urban and rural areas, are trained in communication skills and other soft skills required for entry occupations. This makes them marketable with Call Centres, which

Contd ...

... *Contd* ...

are operating throughout India under the out-sourcing programmes of various multinational Companies from India and abroad.

8. ***Asha***: Under this Scheme, on-line service will be provided to job-seekers and employers through Employment Exchanges. This will provide necessary information to employers and candidates and, in due time, it will include Employment Market Information services, Career Guidance Service, etc. The site is presently under preparation.
9. **Short Term Courses:** The training courses conducted by ITIs are one or two years long. Taking the core aspects of short Term courses—some three months long—students are helped to find quick employment or engage themselves in self-employment. The revenue earned so for is of Rs. 9,78,300 as of 31-10-2003. The short-term courses are found to have large demand and have become popular since their inception March 2002.
10. **S2S Scheme:** Raw material given to students of ITIs for doing practicals are being converted into marketable products, thereby adding value of 600 to 900 per cent. Previously, this raw material was sold as scrap, producing insignificant revenue. The products made are: flower vases, field guns, wooden furniture, chemicals, plastic moulded products, etc.
11. **Institute Management Committees:** IMCs were formed in response to the 72 ITIs in the State. The IMCs are comprised of industrialists, representatives of staff, students, unions, etc. The industrialists support the institute by giving jobs, manpower and training advice.
12. **Adoption of ITIs:** Seven ITIs have been adopted by the industrialists. The industries which adopt the ITI provide additional training with sophisticated equipment, facilitate on the job training and sub-contract their orders to the ITIs.

While there is a large institutional network of training and skill development in the formal sector, facilities for the informal and the traditional sector are grossly inadequate. Surveys reveal that only about nine per cent of the workforce in small scale industries are technically trained, most of them only up to the ITI level. Again, an evaluation of the Prime Minister's 'Rozgar Yojana' conducted by The Institute of Applied Manpower Research (IAMR) in 2000 reveals that more than 50 per cent of applications from potential beneficiaries were rejected on grounds of inadequate skills.

The ongoing programmes meant for certain specific areas of the informal sector are too disjointed and routine to have a significant impact. For instance, a study by IAMR in 1997 showed that the courses offered by KVIC were not employment-oriented as about 62 per cent of those trained in 1993-94 had not been employed until 1997 and less than 2 per cent became employers. The existing training capacity is not fully utilised and the infrastructure is inadequate and outdated. Only one-fourth of the teaching staff possessed prescribed qualifications. KVIC had little interaction with other agencies like small-scale industries, community polytechnics, rural development authorities, etc. Subsequently, these issues have been addressed.

Training and development of job-seekers and workers in the informal sector cannot be easily accommodated within the framework of existing strategies for vocational training. The opportunity cost of training for the workers in this sector is high: they cannot afford to forego wages during training. State interventions must address this important area. There is, indeed, as pointed out by the Special Group, a need for a skill development policy in the informal sector. The other suggestions made by the Special Group include: (a) detailed surveys to assess the training needs for the informal sector and the existing arrangements; (b) motivating the associations in the informal sector to help develop skills and entrepreneurship; (c) seeking international assistance in skill development at the grassroots level; (d) opening production-cum-training centres in the informal sector; (e) refinancing facilities for urban micro-credit that creates training facilities; (f) enabling creation of private sector foundations to finance community-based training programmes through tax and credit incentives; and (g) identification of organisations like trade unions, self-help groups, trade guilds, etc. through which skill development can be channeled.

It is also necessary to bring about some amount of uniformity in the skills acquired under various programmes in the same vocation through a system of certification. Promotion of self-employment venture traits, particularly among the vocationally trained, requires a change in the mind-set that is traditionally geared to seeking wage employment.

Accessibility, relevance, flexibility and effectiveness should be the key considerations in establishing any training system. As pointed out earlier, education and training facilities should be equally accessible to all sections of the population, regardless of gender and rural/urban residence. Only one in five of the rural youth—mostly males—has education to the secondary level or beyond. Even in urban areas, this proportion is only two-fifths. It is only this fraction of youth that can hope to go on to higher general or technical education and the recognised forms of vocational education or training, whether in the school system or in the Industrial Training Institutes. The concept of recognised vocational education and training should be more broad-based, covering not only engineering and other skills that are taught at currently recognised institutions at various levels, or in the industrial establishments under the Apprentices Act, but extending to (a) upgrading the traditional skills through the application of technology, (b) imparting of soft and other support skills of various forms needed in entrepreneurship and self-employment, and (c) learning multiple skills required in the present day globalising economy.

Considering that most of the country's population is in rural areas and in small towns, it is essential that the facilities are taken to the block and even village level and should be equally accessible without discrimination against any group. If anything, there should be interventions of positive discrimination in favour of girls and socially and economically backward categories through stipends, scholarships, etc. In undertaking such a massive programme of skill development, there should be contribution from all social partners like government, employers, trade unions, NGOs, employment services providers, and the community at large. Trade unions, for example, could contribute to skill development, as illustrated by the experience of Employment Service Centres in Vietnam, where trade unions organise regular, short-duration, need-based training in skills as demanded by the economy.

Flexibility should be the key word in the training system, without compromising on quality. The present day ills of formal training stem primarily from its inflexibility in the courses, course content, duration of the courses and eligibility conditions for entry. While some basic level of education would no doubt be necessary to absorb training, it is not always necessary for one to pass Class X to be a good welder. Nor is it necessary to have the course for the full two years duration to be eligible for certification. It may be possible to complete the two years course through a system of credits in semesters and be eligible for a partial certification of credits. One could go on to complete the course and acquire the remaining credits immediately or at a later date depending on one's convenience. Such arrangements can possibly net a larger number of persons in the skill development process.

System of Skills Certification

It should be possible for anyone who has undergone any training—formal, informal or self-acquired—to have his/her incremental competence authoritatively tested and certified. There should be easy access at the local level to such testing and certifying facilities too. For those already in employment to augment their skills, the training system should provide for flexible forms, part-time courses, distance learning, computerised learning, etc. The system of information technology training currently in vogue with private centres all over the country and leading to certification by a national body, provides a useful model that can be replicated elsewhere. The Ministry of Labour is implementing a Scheme on Testing and Certification of Skills for workers in the informal sector. The Ministry of Human Resource Development has proposed an elaborate National Competency Testing Agency. The basic tenets of the proposal are summarised in Box 3.3.

Box 3.3

National Competency Testing Agency Proposed by MoHRD

The National Competency Testing Agency will undertake an assignment relating to scientific assessment of individual performance on a specified job/activity. The assessment will be carried out both on process and product, and against pre-identified criteria. In order to make such assessment scientific, reliable and valid, the following testing step procedures and measures are to be adopted: (i) agreed parameters of competency; (ii) identified abilities in terms of knowledge, skills and attitudes; (iii) identified tasks or activities to be performed giving evidence of abilities acquired; (iv) agreed criteria of acceptable performance on Rating Scale; (v) assessment of process through observation by empanelled assessor(s); (vi) assessment of products against predefined measurable and assessable criteria; and (vii) assessment of evidence of prior learning and past performance.

The Agency shall create a database of professionals in different vocations for carrying out testing at various levels i.e., National, State and District. The database of experts shall also be prepared on vocation or occupation basis covering various enterprises, NGOs and Government Institutions.

The Agency shall be initially funded from the scheme and gradually develop internal resource generation so as to sustain its activities upon completion of the scheme.

Labour Market Information

The relevance and effectiveness of vocational education and training imply the existence of close links between the skills being developed and labour market needs, in terms of both quantity and quality. Such relevance and effectiveness can be brought about by putting in place an efficient labour market information system and quickly responding to the signals from that system while considering modifications in the areas of training, training capacity and content.

The IAMR, which maintains an information system for professional and technical manpower, could play a leading role in providing technical support at the local level in coordination with employment exchanges and other concerned organisations, including employers and NGOs. The information system should not only address the needs of the organised sector, but those of the informal sector as well. Skills necessary to identify relevant labour market signals and interpret them meaningfully must be developed at the local level.

Effective Counselling and Motivation

Aspirations for secure jobs in the government and public sector have hitherto been the major cause for the pursuit of general education of higher and higher levels, apart from considerations like status and social stigma. With an increasing squeeze on employment opportunities in the public sector, this is no longer the case. Nonetheless, in view of the difficulties in modifying social attitudes, pursuit of education beyond what is usefully required to meet the demands of production and services will continue for a long time to come. It is here that the counselling services in schools have an important role to play.

The lopsided growth within technical education itself arises out of status and relative expected lifetime earnings, sometimes not linked to what reality presents. The obstacles in correcting the situation are exemplified by the failure date—in spite of policy pronouncements in successive development plans—to expand diploma level and curtail degree level education in engineering with a view to restoring the desirable balance or in expanding the nursing education to lead to an output ratio of 3:1 of medical graduates. Such imbalances, not only in terms of numbers but quality, need to be corrected within the shortest possible time. Another important area where counselling and motivation help is in promoting self-employment.

Coordination between Training Providers

A word on the need for a coordinated governmental effort would be in order. Apart from the Ministries of Human Resource Development and Labour, there are a number of other Ministries and Departments with their own programmes of skill development in specific fields or targeting specific groups. There seems to be a need for complete coordination of all these efforts by a national council for vocational education and training. The need for such coordination is exemplified by the fact that two different agencies provide formal training in the same trade with a different system of certification. For example, engineering trades are taught both in the vocational streams in the schools as well as in ITIs. One could clearly demarcate what areas of skill development fall within the ambit of which agency. The situation at the state level is similar to that at the Centre. An important recommendation made by the Steering Committee on Secondary, Higher and Technical Education set up in connection with the Tenth Plan was to make one department in each state responsible for vocational education at school level, craftsmen training and diploma level education in polytechnics for better coordination, linkages and optimum utilisation of resources.

The need to create a single umbrella organisation in which the entire skill building effort among the workforce—both present and potential—is vested, cannot be overemphasised. Such an organisation could work on a mission mode cutting across various departments and ministries, since the arena is too important to be mired by inter-ministerial turf tussle.

Summary and Recommendations

The essential problems in the area of vocation training can be subsumed under four main issues:

(1) Absence of a co-ordinating and regulating institution to ensure standards, relevance and costs of vocational training.

(2) Grossly inadequate intake capacity in the formal system with limited reach and absence of a credible testing and certification system for those trained in the informal system.

(3) Vocations offered by the formal system are not informed by the labour market demands.

(4) Rigidity of the formal system of vocational training.

The challenges of globalisation are better addressed by providing required institutional systems and incentives in order that a mismatch in skills does not restrict economic expansion. Such systems should include: efficient labour market information, an institutional mechanism for planning and implementing skill development programmes at the local level through collaborative effort between the community, industry and business, local administration and NGOs, with the government playing mainly a regulatory role; a mechanism for national and regional level coordination to ensure optimum utilisation of resources; and, a national system for certification of skill levels. Preparation of a Human Resource Map of the country with a 10 to 20 year perspective also needs to be initiated. The critical action points arising out of the preceding sections are as follows.

Developing an umbrella organisation/mission to coordinate all efforts to increase the skill levels of the present and potential labour force is critical. In the interim, defining skill arenas for major training providers—trades relating to manufacturing/secondary sector through the ITI system; white-collar-related vocations through vocational stream of 10+2 school system; primary-sector related skills through institutions under Ministry of Agriculture; and short duration courses of three months or less in household industrial sector through KVIC; expansion and strengthening of Community Polytechnics to cater to children dropping out before completing eight years of schooling—all represent a start.

Creating a space for NGOs at the grassroots level to enhance the skill level of the workforce and to link it with the informal sector in secondary and tertiary sectors of the economy is important. Making an inventory of non-governmental skill training providers, particularly in rural areas and drawing on the capacities of NGOs in clearly identified vocations for short-term courses on a large scale would enhance their role.

Utilising the technical and financial cooperation of bilateral and multilateral agencies to enhance skill development among the labour force, particularly in the informal sector is an important step. States may be encouraged to seek cooperation from such agencies as per their needs.

Increasing intake capacities by intensive utilisation of existing institutions rather than creating new facilities is most prudent. Removing regional imbalance in the distribution of training facilities and promoting private-public partnership for creating additional facilities in regions that are poorly served will make a difference.

Finally, disinvesting publicly managed vocational training institutions to purposefully follow public-private partnership in management of such institutions is critical. Substantially augmenting training infrastructure in select centres to serve as centres of excellence for a cluster of districts is an important step in that direction.

Actions required to revamp the skill building system cannot be perfunctory and in small steps but needs a paradigm change, although one could identify some small immediate steps to address specific problems till such time the paradigm shift takes place. The framework of the new paradigm could be summarised as follows:

(1) Creating an entity (Ministry or a Mission) responsible for employment promotion and skill building, cutting across all sectors. The functions of the entity should include:

   (a) facilitating and creating a robust system of testing and certification of citizens trained in the informal and formal streams of skill formation;

   (b) establishing training standards and competency levels needed for certification;

   (c) put into place a decentralised (district) labour market information system and facilitate preparation of district business opportunity maps at regular intervals;

   (d) create vocational trainers' resource groups that include retired vocational instructors, NGOs that offer vocational training, private training providers, and local entrepreneurs at the district level;

   (e) prepare and update periodically a large shelf of vocational training modules that are additive to facilitate higher levels of training and vertical mobility in skill acquisition;

(f) create a system of outsourcing for the preparation of training and learning material from diverse sources;

(g) collate and disseminate information on publicly funded employment schemes;

(h) provide a decentralised, mutually beneficial forum to bring about convergence between training, labour and product market information, credit facilities, small entrepreneurs, small scale industry;

(i) create and operate a corpus for skill building and self-employment;

(j) promote small entrepreneurial initiatives; and

(k) create a state level, nodal organisation to support the entity thus created by reallocating surplus staff in the government departments.

(2) Restructure and redefine the functions of the Employment Exchange to make the employment promotion and information hub at the district level. The restructured Employment Exchange could perform the following functions at the district level:

(a) identify trades that are locally in demand both in the formal and informal sector, through quick, district-level market surveys;

(b) establish a computerised, Labour Market Information System to cover the informal sector at the district level;

(c) identify business opportunities for self-employment;

(d) provide electronically accessible classified information on job-seekers;

(e) undertake periodic labour market demand surveys to inform the training providers;

(f) provide guidance and counselling services for job-seekers and students to help choose career paths[6]; and

---

6. The Small Industries Services Institute, Chennai attempted this approach (Personality Profile Mapping).

(g) bring about a synergy between self-employment programmes, vocational training institutions, and Employment Exchange.

In the interim, the short term measures that could be taken are:

(a) increase in-take capacity by introducing double shifts in the institutions currently offering vocational training;[7]

(b) introduce, in the second shift, short term modular courses of three to six month duration and relax entry level qualifications, where feasible;

(c) identify a set of vocational courses that are market driven without necessarily waiting for elaborate market surveys (a list of such vocations associated with the sectors identified by the Special Group for creating 10 million employment opportunities is given in Annexure XII); and

(d) earmark ongoing development schemes and tap bilateral and multilateral technical and financial assistance available, particularly to promote informal stream of training provided in the Order of Constitution of Working Group on Vocational Training Programme (No. P-12049/30/03-LEM/ERS dated August 28, 2003).

---

7. Second Shifts have been introduced in about 1000 existing ITIs.

4

Cluster Development

Introduction

The earlier chapter emphasised the need for vocational training and skill development for all unemployed and under-employed workers in low productivity jobs to enable them to qualify for high priority jobs and enjoy gainful employment. This is an ambitious task, when the total under-employed and unemployed labour force adds up to 60 million in a total labour force of near 300 million, with hardly 10 per cent skilled.

Arranging finance and developing a proper delivery system, training and arranging mentors in response to such a gigantic scale seems rather impossible even over the medium term, given India's financial constraints, institutional rigidities and shortage of infrastructure both physical and human. The book, therefore, recommends that we should try to approach this problem by identifying suitable natural clusters of high priorities where the holistic approach of both infrastructure and skill development can be attempted. It has been the experience in many other countries that this cluster approach can combine the benefit of small and medium production units with their labour intensity and at the same time draw upon the advantage of a large scale operation in technology, finance, marketing, entrepreneurship development and related issues. The subsequent section explains some of the programmes in Cluster Development in the pipeline.

Targeting of Small Scale Industries (SSIs) through cluster based programmes started with the State Bank of India initiatives in 1989 followed by Small Industries Bank of India (SIDBI) in 1991. UNIDO started the Cluster Development Programmes in four Indian Clusters in 1997. The Ministry of SSI, through its office of the Development Commissioner (Small Scale Industries) launched the cluster based

UPTECH scheme in 1998. This was followed by the National Programme for Rural Industrialisation (NPRI) started in the next year. Various State governments, institutions and some NGOs also picked up a cluster- based growth approach for SSIs. Prominent among these are the State governments of Andhra Pradesh, Gujarat, Kerala, Madhya Pradesh and Ministries/Institutions like Department of Science and Technology, Government of India, Development Commission (Handicrafts), KVIC, NSIC, Textile Committee and NGOs like Rajasthan Chamber of Commerce and Industries, Grameen Development Services. To start with, these initiatives were theme-based, with technology upgradation and infrastructure development being the most popular themes.

According to the quick estimates derived from the Third All India Census of Small Scale Industries (SSIs) conducted by the Ministry of SSI in 2003, there are 1200 SSI clusters consisting of 280,500 registered SSI units, employing 13.75 lakh persons with an estimated output of Rs. 32,300 crore per annum. The UNIDO has separately published a list of 388 Small and Medium Enterprise (SME) clusters covering 490,000 SMEs, with an estimated annual output equivalent to Rs. 157,000 crore and employment to the tune of 75,00,000. The variation between the data bases are explained by the fact that, unlike the Ministry of SSI estimates, the UNIDO data covers Small and Medium Enterprises SMEs, and not merely SSIs. In the clusters, unregistered units provide complementary goods and services, showing the existence of some parallel economy.

The UNIDO initiative introduced a holistic and demand-led approach for identification of the problems in a cluster and designing suitable interventions for their solution. The initiatives thus identified are being implemented under this approach through local intermediaries like associations/networks of SSIs and technical agencies/service providers.

It is estimated that the cumulative expenditure incurred so far by different institutions on cluster development as on January 1, 2004 amounts to Rs. 45 crore. The major share of this amount has been spent by DC (SSI) and UNIDO (Rs. 15 crore each) followed by SBI (Rs. 4 crore), SIDBI and Government of Gujarat (3 crore each) and NABARD (1.5 crore).

In view of the diversity of products being produced in the clusters and multiplicity of development institutions launching new cluster development programmes with increasing frequency, the Indian clusters need to be developed under a 'Multi-Agency Development Initiative,' with a suitable coordination mechanism at the national level.

In view of the increasing importance and contribution of the services sector to the national economy, services clusters cannot be kept out of any comprehensive programme of cluster development. Therefore, relevant types of service clusters must be covered intensively by various implementing agencies of cluster development programmes.

The number of State governments who have initiated cluster development programmes are barely half a dozen, although the enthusiasm and initiative shown by them is encouraging. Therefore, there is a need to further sensitise state government officials towards the cluster approach. The next logical step would be to motivate state governments to recognise cluster development programmes as their main strategy for revitalising the SSI sector and to make adequate budgetary provisions for the same. Local resource centres need to be established in each State as a nodal point for building databases on clusters, training of cluster development personnel, documentation and dissemination of best practices and networking with similar institutions elsewhere.

Status of Clusters and their Problems

Clusters, whether industrial or artisanal, have existed in the country for a long time. Often, the locations of these clusters have been synonymous with the products, thanks to the historical patronage of satisfied consumers through the generations. There is no reliable database on cluster. The recognition of such clusters for policy support is rather recent, and this explains the absence of a national and regional database on clusters in India in the earlier years.

Involving Large Industries in Cluster Development Programmes

Cluster Development initiatives have a long gestation period and the fact that financial gains accruing from such initiatives are shared by a large number of industrial units makes it difficult to perceive a model wherein the large scale sector would initiate and finance cluster development programmes. However, large industries can be motivated to join as catalysts or active participants in the development of networks, consortia and other cluster development initiatives.

In view of the fact that the SSIs, playing the role of ancillaries, need to have better quality machinery, testing equipment, and technology so as to measure up to the reputation of the large purchasing industry, there is a need to re-examine the re-introduction of ancillary industries with a higher limit of investment in plant and machinery.

As per the Industries Development and Regulation Act 1951, the Government of India, through its Administrative Ministry (Industry), was empowered to specify the parameters for defining small-scale industries as well as ancillary industries. Since then, besides other parameters, the Government of India defined small-scale industries based on original investment in plant and machinery. The GoI, for definite reasons, defined ancillary industries based on investment in plant and machinery, which was always kept distinctly higher than the investment for small-scale industries.

Every time the limit for small-scale industries was enhanced, the limit for ancillary industry was also enhanced and always ensured, until 1997, when the investment limit for ancillary industries was kept distinctly higher than the investment limit (plant and machinery) fixed for small-scale industries. However, in the year 1997 the investment limits for both small-scale and ancillary industries were kept at Rs. 3 crore, subsequently reduced to Rs. 1 crore each in December 1999. The other distinct parameters applicable to ancillary industries were so modified that, since 1997, there remained no differences between a small-scale industry and an ancillary industry.

Further, the Government of India, through the Bureau of Public Enterprises, came out in May 1978 with specific guidelines to promote ancillarisation/outsourcing with a view to encourage partnerships and long term business linkages between large and small-scale industries. To begin with, these specific guidelines were directed towards the central public sector undertakings with an idea that such a move would not only help in generating additional employment opportunities but would also add to the quality of the produce while cutting down the cost at PSU level.

However, the dilution of government support to the development of ancillary industries, in part due to the latest definition in vogue—BPE Guidelines—were also withdrawn and the concept of 'Vendor Development' adopted for outsourcing. Such vendors are to arrange everything by themselves, such as techno-managerial consultancy, testing equipment, laboratory, raw material including scarce raw materials at prevailing market prices, besides other paraphernalia. This requires much higher investment in plant and machinery units.

Governments (Central/State) are the biggest buyers of produce from SSI and Ancillary units. However, its support through the government's purchase programme leaves a lot of gaps in what exists *vis-à-vis* what should be optimally available to industries. Therefore, appropriate measures need to be taken to ensure that Central/State government's procuring organisations, departments/undertakings, patronise supplies from the small-scale sector.

At the present juncture, the Ministry of Small-Scale Industries has issued guidelines to Central/State public sector undertakings that they should provide price preference up to 15 per cent to small-scale units *vis-à-vis* the offer of the large scale units. However, these guidelines are not followed in letter and spirit and such price preferences often are not made available. Price preference should be made mandatory to small-scale/ancillary units by all government/semi-govt. procurement organisations without compromising on the quality.

Besides providing several benefits to the parent unit(s), the concept of outsourcing also provides major gains to society as a whole, by creating additional employment opportunities through the horizontal spread of wealth and economic benefits to consumers.

In order to encourage ancillarisation, the following additional measures are warranted:

(a) Recognising the need for a higher limit of investment in plant and machinery for SSI ancillaries leads us to define another category of medium industries, with an investment limit of, say, Rs. 10 crore, to which the ancillaries and other SSIs may graduate.

(b) Ensuring adequate flow of credit to ancillary units.

(c) Increasing the limit for coverage under credit guarantee from the present level of Rs. 25 lakh.

(d) Making mandatory provisions to ensure that departments, undertakings, and procurement organisations under Central/ State governments make procurements from the SSI Sector.

(e) Encouraging ancillary units to enter the export market.

(f) Tax holidays to parent units who source a minimum specified level of their requirements from ancillaries on a graded scale.

Employment Generation

The key role of the SSI sector in the creation and sustenance of large-scale employment in India has already been recognised. Development of SSI clusters has been identified as one of the important elements of the strategy for revitalising the SSI sector, resulting in additional creation of employment besides other benefits to the industrial economy.

In order to ensure accelerated employment generation, the following thrust areas are important:

- Fuelling growth in existing clusters through creation of new enterprises and revitalising existing ones.
- Classifying clusters into technology-intensive, labour-intensive, export-oriented and skill generation categories. Bulk of the additional employment will be generated through focusing on those clusters which are labour intensive, or have a higher capacity for generating employment with each unit of additional investment in capital.
- Identifying and focusing on 'potentially feasible clusters,' presently small conglomerations of industrial units which may not be defined as full-fledged clusters as yet, but which may be developed into full clusters with a very high potential for the creation of additional employment.

Themes like 'business expansion', 'induction of new technologies,' 'innovation,' 'brand building,' and 'infrastructure development,' have frequently been selected as the goals of cluster development programmes at the initial stages, later fanning out to other needs. However, generation of additional employment has not been set as the main objective in any of the cluster development programmes taken up so far in India, and in more than 500 listed cluster development initiatives around the world.

Increasing the overall competitive strength of the cluster under a holistic framework is the most favoured approach for cluster development in our country. Since this is also bound to generate additional employment at a substantially higher level, this approach is sufficient to meet the targets for employment creation at the same time. However, it does not appear to be feasible (due to practical reasons) to estimate the likely generation of employment through SSI clusters and to monitor the status of employment creation through cluster development separately. Rather, the target of creation of 0.55 million employment through development of SSI clusters may be considered together with the target for creation of 3.86 million employment through growth-based schemes for SSIs to achieve the overall target of 4.41 million employment opportunities.

Emergent Sub-sectors

There are sub-sectors which, at present, support relatively little employment but which have potential for growth in the near future because of unmet demand. These sub-sectors usually emerge in response to rapidly growing niche markets, often export demand, and are based on hitherto under-utilised raw materials and skills. Examples of such emergent sub-sectors are fruit processing and granite processing in Andhra Pradesh; agro-services and rural transport in Assam; readymade garments, cement-ware and small engineering in Gujarat; tussar silk, fish processing and rural tourism in Orissa; food processing and rural business in Punjab; minor minerals, leather and rural tourism in Rajasthan; sericulture and rural tourism in Tamil Nadu; and fruit and herbal processing and rural transport in Uttar Pradesh.

High Growth Sub-sectors

These are sub-sectors which register high employment growth rates due to demand in the domestic and/or export market. Examples of these types of sub-sectors are silk textiles and repairs in Andhra Pradesh, fibre products and construction in Assam, textile products and cement products in Gujarat, spice processing and rural tourism in Orissa, freight transport and metalware in Punjab, oil seeds processing and handicrafts in Rajasthan, power looms and hosiery in Tamil Nadu, and leather products and pottery in Uttar Pradesh.

High Share Sub-sectors

These are sub-sectors which at present account for a high share of employment in the SME sector, even though the demand prospects for some of them are uncertain. Examples of these types of sub-sectors are paddy processing and manufacture of *bidis* in Andhra Pradesh, cane and wood products and handlooms in Assam, food products and pottery in Gujarat, fish processing in Orissa, grain milling and brick manufacture in Punjab, gem processing in Rajasthan, matches manufacturing in Tamil Nadu, and carpet weaving in Uttar Pradesh.

Self-Employment Exchange

Identification and selection of trainees is most crucial in the successful implementation of the programme. Since the programme has to be on a massive scale, a mechanism for identifying the most qualified workers must be carried out. This could be done by decentralising such programmes at the district level and by constituting a committee at the district level with District Collector as its Chairman and NABARD, Lead Bank, District Industries Centre (DIC), District Rural Development Authority (DRDA) and major banks as its members.

Each district should consider opening a self-employment exchange (SEE). These SEEs will work under a committee headed by the District Collector. This way, there can be a mechanism for registering the names of persons interested in taking up self-employment activities. A massive campaign may be implemented through the machinery of DRDA and DIC, and public awareness could be generated to register jobseekers' names with basic details as per a proforma, in a nearby bank branch or village office or block office.

These applications could be scrutinised at the district level and based on the interest and details furnished, a series of training programmes could be organised for entrepreneurship and skill development. These trained persons could be assisted to establish their units with bank credit, or could also be absorbed in some of the existing schemes of the government/*panchayat* etc.

Self-Help Groups

Self-Help Groups (SHGs) are potential clients for such employment generation programmes. There are already more than seven lakh

SHGs credit linked in our country, and is likely to soon cross one million. The present SHGs already linked to banks cover more than 10 million families. Many of them could be suitably assisted in taking-up smaller enterprises. The advantage of SHG members are:

- they are self disciplined due to their association with SHGs;
- they are a motivated group;
- they are aware and knowledgeable of account keeping and financial matters;
- credit is made available easily through the linkage of banking mechanism;
- group ventures are encouraged;
- cluster approach could be adopted for procuring the raw material and marketing; and
- peer pressure would ensure proper implementation of the programme, repayment of loans, and other activities.

These SHG members with limited training could be supported in micro enterprises, mostly in the nature of traditional activities and agro-based activities, and their choice of markets, customers, etc.

Strategy for Employment Generation in Rural Clusters

Obstacles to rural clusters may include: the social preference for employment in organised sectors; lack of awareness about the employment opportunities in rural clusters; lack of technical skills or entrepreneurship abilities; non-availability of credit; difficulties in marketing, and other challenges.

In identifying the high potential rural cluster the following has to be kept in mind:

- traditional labour-intensive clusters like handloom and handicrafts;
- clusters based on local resources;
- clusters with a high potential to employ persons with easy-to-acquire skills; and
- clusters producing goods which can cater to local markets or supply to outside markets through common marketing outlets.

Rural clusters that fall under any of the following three categories should form high priority areas for employment creation:

i) Emergent sub-sectors which have a high potential for growth, or rapidly growing niche markets, or may be based on hitherto under-utilised raw materials and skills;

ii) High growth sub-sectors; and

iii) High share sub-sectors (having a high share of employment).

Also, in order to maximise employment of fresh talents into rural clusters, entrepreneurship development programmes will have to be intensive. It would require a survey of the area to identify suitable, demand-oriented activities followed by carrying out of a systematic selection process to identify the most suitable candidates to undergo training programmes on entrepreneurship, management and technical skills. Subsequently, follow-up and escort services/hand-holding should be provided to the trainees. SHGs may also be promoted as a major tool for providing employment in the main or supporting activities in a cluster. Availability of micro credit through SHGs and other channels will also be necessary for development of rural clusters.

In so far as the artisan clusters are concerned, very limited information is available pertaining to the handicraft and handloom clusters in terms of their number. As per a compilation undertaken by UNIDO in the year 2000, based on a variety of available secondary sources over the last few years, an initial list of 1657 clusters has been prepared for handicraft and handloom clusters.

The office of the Development Commissioner, Handicrafts has compiled a list of handicraft clusters in the country (that is a far more authentic database in terms of the number of clusters). According to this data, there are more than 3000 such clusters in the country. However, their gross contribution in the handicraft sector as a whole is not available. Similarly, in the area of handlooms, the office of the Development Commissioner (Handlooms), has compiled a list of handloom clusters in the country. The list provides names of 415 such clusters, although their contribution to the handloom sector as a whole is not available. In case of tiny SSI clusters, comprised mainly of unregistered SSI units, the listing along with gross estimates of contributions needs to be worked with the available census data.

Services Clusters

In the third category of services, which is a fast growing and potentially highly contributing part of the Indian economy, several clusters have emerged in the recent past. Services clusters by their very nature contribute significantly to employment generation while also contributing to exports. Identification of such clusters, and their potential role in tourism, health, food processing and information technology, could be very useful in creating employment opportunities. No database is presently available on this segment.

Credit Availability

The clusters are served in their credit needs by both formal and informal means. It is estimated that the quantum of credit available through informal channels far outweighs the institutional credit, due to the informal and parallel economy as well as the well known constraints pertaining to credit delivery through institutional means. The cluster-specific knowledge from institutional channels that offer efficient and effective credit to clusters is low.

District Credit Plans (DCPs) do not take into account cluster related information in the districts nor focus on the common credit requirements of the firms. Clusters with their specific requirements, due to the nature of products that they make and the kind of markets they serve, are not effectively taken into account while preparing DCPs. The mutual knowledge and trust among the borrowing firms in the clusters, due to their proximity, provides a basis for collective delivery systems that has been tried, tested and exploited in the artisan sector and rural economies.

Such a principle duly supported by mutual guarantees, however, has not been exploited in industrial clusters in order to provide greater credit through institutional means and ensure lower NPAs for lender institutions. The system of coaxing banks to lend without collateral, requires appealing to a broad-minded approach among bankers, and has not served the objective of increased credit delivery, nor it is likely to, because of the commercial means of assessing the loan portfolio and bankers' performance in the banks.

Instead, credit guarantees that rely on innovative means—assessing creditworthiness of firms and seeking collective comfort levels—will certainly serve the need. The Mutual Credit Guarantee System (MCGS) for industrial clusters, successfully used in several industrially developed parts of the world, has not yet been tried and tested for wider replication. The instrument has the potential to serve both the short- and long-term credit requirements of the industrial clusters.

Technology

Most industrial clusters reflect wide cross section of technology levels, ranging from the labour intensive to highly automated levels. The coexistence of such a diverse range of technology levels is best explained in terms of the range of the quality of products and the type of markets served. However, only a few use the advanced technology, while a large number of them use manual systems. Within a firm, a diverse range of technologies can co-exist, justifying the economics of using the different levels and taking into account the cost of labour and cost of capital.

The technology usage pattern of industrial clusters generally reflects extremely low levels of innovation. Linkages between industry and technical institutions, including universities, defence laboratories and research organisations, are negligible. The mutual role of private consultants, machinery makers, and machinery has led to significant technology improvements in several countries, but is also limited in quantum and significance. In such a scenario, while the copying of tried and tested technologies is widespread, adaptations of technological improvements is moderately low and innovations virtually absent in most industrial clusters.

Marketing and Export Promotion

Character marketing and export has always been a private sector domain. In order to assist small firms to overcome their initial disadvantages *vis-à-vis* large firms, however, small industry promotion for price preference and purchasing goods by the government and public institutions must be provided. While artisan clusters in State marketing organisations were set up to actually procure goods and sell on a detail basis to consumers, such an arrangement was never felt necessary for industry clusters.

Infrastructure

The creation of infrastructure for small industry clusters can itself be an employment generating activity. Besides general infrastructure, which includes roads, rail networks, ports, electricity, etc., cluster specific infrastructure also includes common facilities for designing, effluent treatment, testing, training, display, marketing and research, development and human resources.

Over the last two decades, the number of new centres providing the required services are very few. Almost all these centres have been set-up and managed by public organisations with little support drawn from the private sector. The status of public-private partnerships in most of these clusters can be stated as poor. Upgradation of facilities in these centres, training of technical staff and level of motivation require boosting. At the same time, the requirements of the industry have undergone rapid change in the last two decades that call for provision of upgraded and new services that may require several new facilities to be created. The diagnosis of such needs and the availability of these services indicate extensive gaps at the cluster level and sectoral level.

An analysis of the different cluster initiatives in terms of parameters—implementation channel, major areas of interventions and whether social capital building is a thrust area—is indicated in tabular form (Box 4.1) below:

Box 4.1

An Analysis of Cluster Development Initiatives

	Implementation Done by		*Major Areas of Interventions*				*Is Social Capital*
	Own	*Institutional*	*Credit*	*Techno-logy*	*Employ-ment*	*Infra-structure*	*Building a Thrust Area?*
Andhra Pradesh		✔					✔
DC (HC)		✔		✔		✔	✔
Gujarat		✔		✔			
KVIC		✔	✔			✔	✔
Madhya Pradesh	✔						✔
NABARD		✔	✔		✔		
NSIC	✔		✔				
SBI	✔		✔	✔			
SIDBI		✔	✔	✔			
SIDO	✔			✔	✔		✔
Textiles Committee	✔			✔			✔
UNIDO	✔						✔

Notes: 1. There may be other thrust areas too and absence of a primary thrust area does not mean that it is not a thrust area at all for that organisation.

2. Absence of any upfront thrust area implies that the organisation necessarily has an open mandate.

The major problems that are encountered in the process of cluster development are as follows:

(a) Absence of intermediaries: It is difficult to locate proactive and functioning associations in clusters. Again, in most occasions the associations at present do not have the necessary functioning infrastructure and necessary secretarial support to initiate activities.

(b) Involvement of limited support agencies: The agencies involved in development often lead the programme and are not adept in involving other available support institutions in the programme. This reduces the leverage capacity of the programme by the implementing institution.

(c) Lack of flexible support mechanism: The support mechanisms of the agencies are pre-defined and often do not suit the ground realities of the cluster. The mandate for creating new support tools often does not exist.

(d) Lack of service providers: Technical service providers who understand the operational problems of an SSI and are willing to work under those constraints are also not found easily in a cluster.

It has been observed that firms in the cluster usually operate in isolation. There is a feeling of distrust and general lack of cooperation among them. Usually, as a result of mutual competition over a large number of years, the feeling has further been intensified by real and imaginary threats of liberalisation and globalisation. Moreover, linkages with raw material providers, machinery suppliers, channel members (for domestic marketing as well as exports), local training institutes and R&D institutions also are either non-existent or very weak. As a result, hidden potentials remain unutilised. Possible savings through formation of networks and consortia for procurement of cheaper raw material exploration of new market and better affordability of Business Development Services (BDS) providers remain untapped.

These problems become even more significant, especially in the artisanal and rural handicraft clusters, where the level of education is low and the question of survival is even more pronounced.

Developing a Feasible Model for Cluster Development

Out of the large number of various types of existing clusters in India, the following broad types can be identified easily:

Sl. No.	*Type of Clusters*	*Production Relations*	*Market Relations*
1.	Artisan Clusters	Local	Local
2.	Cottage Industry Clusters	Local	Local/National
3.	Ancillary Clusters	Local	National
4.	SSI (Other than Ancillary) Clusters	Local/ National	Local/ National
5.	Export-oriented	Local/ National	National/ International

The process of cluster development in the above context is aimed at converting each of the above five types into 'Globally Competitive Clusters,' with international production relations and national/international market relations.

Criteria for Selection of Clusters

Utmost care and application of mind through detailed study of the ground conditions in the clusters and their logical analysis is a must for selection of the right type of cluster before development interventions are planned. The criteria may, to some extent, vary depending on the type of clusters, nature of operations of the agency preparing to take up the clusters for development and the goals sought to be achieved through the Cluster Development Projects. However, broadly it can be said that the importance of the clusters, existence of critical gaps, their viability, promotability, out-reach and subsidiarity may form the main cornerstone for making the selection. Existence of a suitable policy/institutional framework at the national level and its continuous improvement by making suitable adjustments is a necessary pre-condition for the success of the endeavour.

Measures for Involving State Governments in the Programme of Cluster Development

About half a dozen state governments have initiated cluster development programmes in the past, and some of them have further broadened the base and intensified initiatives in the current year. However, there is a need to involve the remaining States, for which the following steps are advised:

- Sensitising policymakers and officials towards the cluster approach (Ministry of SSI may organise orientation programmes).
- Motivating State governments to:
  a) recognise and declare cluster development an important strategy to revitalise the SSI sector;
  b) create specialised divisions/cells in the secretariats and field offices to design and implement cluster initiatives; and
  c) make adequate budgetary provisions for cluster development.
- Creating one-stop facilities in States for:
  a) building databases for clusters and their mapping;
  b) training of cluster development personnel;
  c) documentation and dissemination of best practices; and
  d) networking with similar resource centres in other States and at national level.
- Tracking employment generation in old and new clusters.

Measures for Involving Large Industries in the Programme of Cluster Development

Coopting large industries to act as catalysts in the cluster development process. In particular, large industries can be motivated to play the following roles:

- Sharing and dissemination of best manufacturing processes to small-scale units.
- Acting as 'pioneer units' for adoption of new technologies, so as to build confidence among the small units to adopt the same.
- Increasing the awareness about and adoption of ISO-Certification, CE Certification, etc.

- Taking the lead to conceptualise infrastructure development initiatives and networking of potential partners in the execution of infrastructure development initiatives.
- Partnering with SSI units in activities like common procurement of raw material which may bring much larger economies to participate through large firms.
- Building the 'brand' image of the cluster which is going to benefit small units.
- Building up a vertical network (or sub-contracting relations) between the large and small units in the cluster.

Skill Upgradation in Clusters

In the face of emerging pressures on competitiveness of the SMEs in general and clusters in particular, the need for skill upgradation will only grow at all levels. The present level of skill related institutions in the country are not only ill equipped but also severely inadequate to meet the requirements. A detailed analysis of the training requirements in this connection has been made in the previous chapter.

In general terms, there is an urgent need to upgrade the available facilities, revamp available courses, and cut them into acceptable short-term modular courses so that the industry can sponsor their candidates on a part time basis. Besides formal institutional training, innovative means to deploy supervisors, private BDS providers, machinery suppliers and creation of cadre of trainers in the clusters is warranted. This can only be meaningfully undertaken after a clear mapping of skill requirements by competencies at every segment of the productive value chain of the cluster. The strategy, resources and means will therefore have to be cluster specific, at best integrated across clusters of similar types within a sector.

It is of utmost importance to involve the private sector in designing the required new training modules, upgrading available facilities, and sponsoring of candidates for training in order to utilise the upgraded skills effectively on a sustainable basis.

5

Business Process Outsourcing: Potentialities for Employment Generation

The growing prominence of India's Business Process Outsourcing (BPO) industry, an offshoot of the Information Technology sector has brought the nation to the cover pages of some of the leading international magazines. The BPO industry, the emergence of which could not have been imagined some 10 years back is, today, thriving in India and in a number of other emerging market economies.

The potential of this sector is highlighted by the fact that, while today it employs close to 250,000 individuals, by the end of the fiscal year 2005 this figure is likely to touch the 400,000 mark. Equally important is this sector's contribution to India's exports, which are presently US $2.4 billion and are expected to climb to US $5.5 billion by the end of the fiscal year 2005.[1]

On first look, the employment potential of this sector may not appear significant, as it covers only .05 per cent of the present workforce. But in incremental terms, for the next five years it comes to 30,000 per annum, which is nearly 0.3 per cent of the additional employment generation in a country (targeting 10 million additional jobs a year). In addition, this field mostly attracts educated youths. There, it covers nearly 2.5 to 3 per cent of incremental employment among educated youths per annum, averaged over the next five years. While compared to the number of jobs needed in India this sector may seem insignificant, for the educated youths who come mostly from middle or upper income classes, it is comparatively large.

While the forecasts for the BPO industry are likely to improve, certain adverse developments of the recent past—the backlash in the

1. All India Management Association (2003). *India's New Opportunities-2020, Report of the Strategic Group,* The Boston Consulting Group (Consulting Partner), Confederation of Indian Industry (Implementing Partner).

Western economies—could play spoilsport and therefore need to be dealt with in a structured manner. Why such developments cannot and should not be taken lightly is due to the considerable employment potential that this industry presents, especially to the urban middle class population in India.

While the software and IT industry employ highly trained professionals, the BPO industry gives employment to ordinary, mainstream graduates. This industry, therefore, has a major role in providing jobs to educated youths. Its contribution does not end here and goes far beyond direct employment generation.

Business process outsourcing can broadly be defined as management of one or more specific business processes or functions, essentially the ones which are non-core in nature and do not add to the competitive advantage of the business by a qualified third party. However, for the third party entrusted with the task of managing the non-core functions, the same processes are in the nature of their core functions and it is, therefore, able to add greater value to them.

Such a transfer benefits the organisation by freeing up resources, both human and physical, which it can now focus on its core operations. It also generates benefits in terms of lower costs of the processes outsourced, as the service provider can undertake to do the same at a fraction of what it cost the company. BPO is, in this sense, both liberating and strategically valuable.

An important point in the context of business process outsourcing is that it is different from the normal purchase of services as well as contracting of services. While in the case of purchase an organisation buys a product or a service, in the case of outsourcing, an organisation is essentially buying the results of a process. Further, while in the case of contracting a process the organisation retains control over the process, in the case of outsourcing, the organisation allows the supplier or the vendor to exercise control over the process.

Difference between Business Process Outsourcing and IT Outsourcing

Although the concept of business process outsourcing is not a new one, what has contributed to its sudden rise to prominence is the scope and the number/types of processes that one finds being outsourced. Talking about the types of processes being outsourced, one must be clear on the distinctions between IT outsourcing and business process outsourcing. A typical IT outsourcing deal would involve handling the IT component of a single or number of, and often unrelated, business functions of an organisation. BPO, on the other hand, refers to the outsourcing of one or more business processes along with the technology structure supporting it. Further, the process being outsourced may or may not be IT intensive.

Forms of Business Process Outsourcing

While the most common form of outsourcing is to enter into a contract with a third party or a vendor, it is not the only form in which a company can go for outsourcing. There are instances where a joint venture has been formed between the service provider and it's client.

Another route which can be followed by companies is through the set up of it's own subsidiaries. Through such captive subsidiaries the company can not only outsource it's own business, but it can also cater to the demand of other organisations.

The Probable Range of Processes Outsourced

The handling of calls from existing organisations and/or prospective customers is the first example that one comes across when studying about business process outsourcing. However, there is much more to BPO than just call centres or medical transcription. In fact these services are placed at the lowest rung of the BPO ladder and as one moves up the ladder, one comes across complex and technical processes like insurance underwriting, payroll processing and management—functions which require specialised skills and training. A large number of companies have either set up their own BPO centres or are outsourcing to Indian companies/MNC's various internal processes. An indicative list of internal processes, which are increasingly being outsourced, is provided in the Box 5.1.

In fact, the spectrum of business processes as the subject of outsourcing is likely to grow further as companies identify non-core areas that may be effectively managed by a third party or, if outsourced, will lead to a reduction in costs.

Box 5.1

Indicative List of Internal Processes Outsourced

- Internal Audit
- Customer Relations
- Insurance Administration
- Employee Benefits
- Travel Services
- Logistics and Sales Management
- Content Development
- Market Research and Surveys
- Order Entry and Data Mining
- Billing and Collection
- Benefit Administration
- Records Management
- Finance and Accounting
- Tax Compliance and Management
- Cash and Investment Management
- Financial Analysis Risk Management

The Reasons for Outsourcing

Over time, a major change has taken place in the perception of decision-makers regarding outsourcing. Earlier, outsourcing was viewed as an activity to be undertaken during troubled times, to hide inefficiencies, or, for mere convenience. Today, however, it is viewed as a legitimate competitive tool. Corporations have come to realise that it is essential for them to focus their resources—management time and talent—only on those functions that would differentiate their product offering in the market and give them a competitive edge. To spend time on anything that does not contribute to customer and shareholder value is just not acceptable. Processes that are too expensive in terms of money, time, people or technology and do not bring commensurate returns are taken to be better outsourced. Some of the compelling factors that favour outsourcing are as follows:

- Strategic outsourcing enables an organisation to focus on its core competencies. The management can focus on increasing sales and market shares, developing new and improved products, expanding into new markets, and enhancing customer service and satisfaction.
- Outsourcing gives an organisation the opportunity to benefit from industry knowledge and experience as well as share in the industry resources and technologies.
- The company can focus more on strategic growth.
- The service provider can develop as a consultant and suggest better ways to manage processes. Outsourcing enables the

companies to obtain outside expertise, which they may not have in-house.

- It can help keep a check on the employee headcount.
- It requires less upfront investments and at the same time the benefits are more easily and readily quantifiable.
- The company can more easily comply with the regulatory changes as and when they take place.
- The service providers also provide strategic benefits like cost reductions through re-engineering, process improvements, and use of advanced technologies. This on one hand eliminates unnecessary operating costs and, on the other, reduces and brings other administrative costs under better control.

Current Backlash

The backlash against outsourcing, which we are witnessing along with protests over the use of L1 visas by companies to shift personnel from home country to the client's premises abroad, are part of a larger campaign whose intensity is likely to increase in the coming months. While restrictions on the number of L1 and H-1B visas issued is going to affect the software companies doing onsite work, any restrictions imposed on outsourcing of work would be detrimental to the interests of Indian BPO service providers.

These protests have two dimensions, political and economic. We have to realise that, as in the US, with the unemployment rates as high as 6 per cent in some of the States, job loss is bound to be on the political agenda of some leaders. It is expected that if the US economy shows signs of a pick-up in future, these protests would mellow out.

The point to be noted is that the outsourcing model is commercially attractive and makes companies more competitive. The commercial benefits associated with outsourcing are immense and it is fast becoming a compulsion rather than a choice. Any move to place restrictions in developed economies on free movement of people and work would prove detrimental for them, as their resources would be sub-optimised. Though sections of US population are bound to be affected by the current trend of outsourcing, this micro-level upset would not over-shadow the macro level benefits.

The skill sets offered by India for performing such functions are much superior to what is available in the US. While college graduates in India are employed to perform functions such as receivables management, in the US this task is performed by high school graduates. Consequently, the quality of output and productivity are higher in India. What makes the India proposition all the more attractive is the much lower attrition rates. In collections, for example, attrition rate in US is 150 per cent as compared to 30 per cent to 40 per cent in India.

It is a reality that jobs in the services sector are being taken away, and this situation finds a parallel in a similar yet different form of outsourcing that took place in the US manufacturing sector in the 1970s and 80s. During that time, while mass-scale manufacturing moved to the developing countries, high-end manufacturing in the fields of aeronautics and defence, for example, grew in importance in the developed world. A similar movement is expected in the services sector, with the developed countries continuing their upward movement in the value chain and with the low end services being filtered to the developing nations.

The present wave of protectionism, however, differs from the one witnessed in the 1970s, and for today there exist genuine fears in the US regarding the outside world. American companies are more concerned than ever before about business continuity planning and disaster recovery practices. Companies in India will have to allay the fears of their clients on these accounts, assuring them security of their investments and an uninterrupted provision of services.

The fundamental challenge of resistance to outsourcing remains the same for both captive players and third party service providers. The resistance, however, is much lower in the case of captive players.

Greater resistance will also have to be faced by companies that are outsourcing for the first time directly to other countries, as compared to companies that are moving from outsourcing to off-shoring. We should not be discouraged by such developments and instead focus our efforts on promoting India as USA's services partner, just as China is now seen as their manufacturing partner. The benefits that would accrue from such a win-win situation need to be driven home.

The partnership between the US and India is leading to increased competitiveness of the US companies. The savings generated from outsourcing, primarily aimed at engendering a 24/7 work-cycle, help create additional jobs and prevents layoffs which otherwise would be necessitated. Further, if the costs of US corporations went up, US taxpayers would, ultimately, have to bear the burden. The choice, therefore, for US firms is simple: either cut costs by moving services offshore, or lose market share to firms from other countries.

This shows that there exists a clear gap in perception, and that it needs to be bridged. Indian BPO players who are currently being branded as 'villains' are actually helping Western companies to become more efficient, and are providing greater value to their stakeholders, shareholders, debt holders, suppliers and customers.

How to Deal with the Emerging Scenario

The situation as it is unfolding is essentially transitory in nature and does not present an alarming scenario. However, certain corrective measures are called for to dispel the notion that the outsourcing of work to low cost destinations abroad is a zero-sum game.

The backlash is largely on account of the high visibility this sector has attracted in media circles. The players should understand that such hype harms them and the industry. We need to learn from countries like China, Taiwan and Korea—big players in both manufacturing and services outsourcing—how to continue to reap the benefits by maintaining a low profile. 'Doing business in the silent mode is therefore the recommended strategy.'

The fundamental principle in a free market economy is that production moves to the lowest cost destination. This dynamic, which played itself out in the manufacturing sector, is now being replicated in the services sector. Any move to stop or reverse the global redistribution of labour would prove futile and counterproductive. This needs to be communicated to the concerned parties in a subtle yet strong manner. Business cases that bring out the advantages of outsourcing should be developed and disseminated.

The use of inaccurate images to stir up consumer opposition—with allegations like working conditions being similar to 'sweatshops'—needs to be countered. Working conditions made available by Indian companies to their employees are comparable to the best in the world, and a combination of HR practices is applied to retain employees for a long period of time.

The Indian BPO industry must further benchmark with global standards in workplaces. Here employee welfare becomes a priority. Further, it should maintain a low-key stance, employ more locals while setting up onshore development centres, engage with trade bodies and customers in other outsourcing distribution, provide credible research and facts, sensitise the Indian government on issues, and drive strategy and actions to open up Indian markets.

The government, on the other hand, needs to play a very active and strategic role. It must bring the negotiations on the services sector higher on the agenda.

Developed Countries–The Demographic Shift

While outsourcing has strong economic justification, another aspect that increases its importance is the changing demographic profile in the developed nations. Two distinct trends have emerged over the decades and would continue into the future. These are a reduction in the successive additions to working age population, and secondly, a concomitant and substantial increase in the numbers added to the elderly population each decade. The fallout of these two developments is the rapid rise in the elderly dependency ratio in developed nations.

The question that merits attention in such a scenario, therefore, is how developed nations will provide for their ageing population when the likely availability of an economically active population is on the wane? How are they going to maintain a minimum level of economic growth, which is already gasping for a new lease of life?

There are different estimates available from several non-governmental institutions in India. One possible solution is to cope with the changes in demographic character by drawing on the workforce in India and other developing countries in the form of IT enabling services, health related services, tourism etc. and their dimensions. Estimates of labour demand from India, received from different sources, vary widely. One of the major sources is the report of the All India Management Association.[2] This report gives the most

2. *ibid.*

optimistic picture, generating 20 million jobs in these sectors in India by the year 2020.

No detailed sources are mentioned in the report and, therefore, it has not been possible to make an assessment on the predictability of this report. The report assumes a net workforce shortfall of around 32 to 39 million by the year 2020, taking all developed countries together. The benefit of this shortfall to India has been estimated to be 20 million new jobs. This seems to be too optimistic, and there are other competitive sources among other emerging developing countries which may also share in this gap.

Considering that high levels of unemployment in many developed countries range from 5 to 8 per cent of the labour force, it will take a minimum of 5 to 7 years before those jobs start trickling over to India.

Lastly, the technology trend in the developed world is moving fast to automation, even in many of the employment intensive labour services sectors. Given this scenario, the report assumes that by the end of the Tenth Plan, a maximum of 10 to 15 lakh job opportunities may arise from those sources. Because of the low growth and high unemployment, there is already significant social and political pressure in many of these developed countries against outsourcing and against workforce migration from the developing countries.

An independent estimate made in the study shows that assuming the growth rate of the high income countries for the next decade (from 2005) at 4 per cent per annum (seems to be optimistic), and assuming an employment elasticity of 0.15 (taking into consideration the trend towards automation) and the base period unemployment rate at 5 per cent, the demand for workforce will be maximum 414.2 million.

Given the base period total labour force in the high income countries, the total supply of labour force 10 years hence will be hardly 393.8 million; this gives a gap of 20.9 million as shortage (World Bank, 2004). Grouping the developing countries like East Asia Pacific, South Asia, Latin American countries and Central Asia, and assuming a growth rate of 6 per cent per annum over the next decade and a comparatively high employment elasticity of 0.25, the demand for labour force will be around 2059 million. Similarly, assuming a 2 per cent growth in labour force for the next 10 years and a base unemployment of 4 per cent, the unused labour will be around 342.6 million. Therefore, to compete for the share of the shortage in the labour force in developed countries, the competition is in the order of 16 to 1. All this show that in the near future the opportunities that we are looking for, based on demographics, may not be as rosy, given the number of global competitors and the way many of the reports are presenting.

Prudence demands that they look beyond their national frontiers and engage human resources elsewhere, to give a thrust to their sagging economies. Capping the level of migrant workers is equivalent to imposing quantitative restrictions on the free flow of human capital. Similarly posing restrictions on the outsourcing of work to low cost destinations abroad is tantamount to non-tariff barriers on service exports. Both these measures are not only WTO incompatible, but are also detrimental to their economic and business interests.

6

Status of Employment Exchanges

Historical Background

The National Employment Service (NES) emerged in July 1945 for the purpose of resettling demobilised Defence service personnel and discharged War Workers through a network of employment exchanges controlled by the then Directorate General of Resettlement and Employment (DGR&E), now known as DGE&T. After Independence, the Directorate was called on to handle work relating to displaced persons from Pakistan. Subsequently, the scope of the Directorate was extended to cover employment service to all categories of job-seekers in early 1948. In pursuit of the recommendations of the Training and Employment Service Committee (Shiv Rao Committee set up in 1952), the day-to-day administrative control of the Employment Exchanges was transferred to the State governments/Union Territory Administrations with effect from November 1, 1956.

The present National Employment Service functions within the conceptual framework of the ILO Convention No. 88 on Organisation of Employment Services—'services are free'. The primary objective is settlement of job-seekers either through regular jobs or through self-employment. To enhance the employability of job-seekers, NES collects employment market information, and career counselling and vocational guidance are inbuilt in the system.

The employment service consists of about 940 employment exchanges run by State governments. Private placement agencies also operate on a limited scale, primarily in urban areas to cater to the requirements of specialised fields in the organised sector. Such agencies generally charge fees of varying amounts, both from the job-seekers and employers.

Functions of the National Employment Service (NES)

(1) The National Employment Service, and, for that matter, Employment Exchanges, function within the ambit of the Employment Exchanges (Compulsory Notification of Vacancies) Act 1959, enacted within the framework of ILO Convention No. 88. According to the Act, notification of vacancies arising in all public sector establishments, and all non-agricultural establishments in the private sector employing 25 or more workers, is compulsory. The Act also makes it obligatory on the part of such employers to furnish employment returns (called ER-I and ER-II), which give the government information on employment, vacancies occurred, mode of recruitment, occupational distribution of employees, and educational requirements for those occupations. Therefore, noting that NES is not responsible for employment generation nor do they implement any employment generation scheme, the objectives of the National Employment Service are as follows:

(a) Collect, compile and disseminate information on vacancies notified, employment in various industries, types of occupations in existence, qualifications required for various occupations, emerging trend of employment in various industries, etc.

(b) To have an assessment of demand (from notification of vacancies) and supply of labour (from registration of job-seekers) in the labour market and adjust them.

(c) Create requisite database for manpower planning and management, career counselling, and vocational guidance, with a view to effectively guide job-seekers.

In order to achieve the above objectives, the NES which operates through the network of Employment Exchanges carries out the following functions:

1. Registration and placement of job-seekers, so as to ensure a proper balance between demand and supply.
2. Collection of comprehensive Employment Market Information on a quarterly basis for creation of a database for use in

effective management of the demand and supply of labour, preparing career literature for counselling and vocational guidance.

3. Career Counselling and Vocational Guidance.
4. Conducting area specific, specialised studies/surveys to assess skills available and the marketable skills required for encouraging job-seekers to pursue self-employment, particularly in the rural informal sector.
5. Some of the state governments arrange disbursement of unemployment allowance to certain, specific categories of job-seekers out of their own resources, through the employment exchanges as registered with them.

NES, from its very inception, restricted its activity to those sectors of the economy which are covered under the employment exchanges (Compulsory Notifications of Vacancies) Act, 1959, in view of statutory backing for notification of vacancies and submission of employment market information. At the initial stage, job-seekers registered with the employment exchanges and the placement made through employment exchanges compared well, due to the emergence of a large number of public sector undertakings and the existence of employment exchanges to meet the manpower requirements. Attention was given mainly on registration, placement, and other legitimate functions, namely creation of a database, while career counselling and vocational guidance were relegated to the secondary tier.

Subsequently, a large number of recruiting agencies like the Staff Selection Commission, Railway Recruitment Boards, Banking Service Commissions, etc., came up and restricted the area of operations of the Employment Exchanges. In fact, today almost all the major establishments, both in government and outside, have their own recruitment agencies. Therefore, Employment Exchanges are left with only stray cases at the lower levels of appointment.

Recent judgments of the Supreme Court, which make it obligatory that employers advertise vacancies in other media and consider candidates not only submitted by employment exchanges but also by those responding to open advertisements for the selection of candidates, made the matter worse. Therefore, on the placement side (regular wage employment), the role of employment exchanges is definitely not very significant. This does not mean, however, that the work in the employment exchanges has been reduced.

Though placement (around 0.2 million a year) has reduced substantially, the pressure on registration (around six million a year and around 42 million live register) and maintenance of live register went on increasing. The heavy incidence of registration and renewal continue to consume employment exchanges, giving them very little time to devote to other activities. Therefore, the workload as a whole in employment exchanges has increased, primarily due to the large number of job-seekers approaching employment exchanges even today, knowing fully well that chances of getting placement through employment exchanges are bleak.

Public Perception of the Employment Service

Why, then, in spite of the fact that employment exchanges are not providing substantial placement, do job-seekers continue to register and periodically renew their names, and what is the public perception of these employment exchanges?

Broadly, the public in general has the perception that Employment Exchanges are only to provide jobs. They are seen only as placement agencies and as a source for securing wage employment. The job-seekers approach employment exchanges with high hopes and expectations. But then, after a long wait to secure sponsorship—which is quite frustrating and often leads to the feeling that employment exchanges are not impartially serving the job-seekers—hopes and expectations are dashed. Questions are raised as to why the NES should exist in terms of expenditure, expectations, and limited role left in the present scenario of the labour market.

Present Employment Scenario *vis-à-vis* Employment Exchange Operations

Currently, employment in the organised sector is shrinking. The employment exchange strategy so far has been primarily identifying those jobs which were generated in the public sector. Emphasis on private sector jobs was not there. Therefore, placement through employment exchanges was primarily in the public sector. But now, employment generated in the organised sector (both Public and

Private) is not appreciable enough to absorb the job-seekers registered with the employment exchanges. In the present scenario, a job-seeker is expected to wait for a long time before becoming sponsored. By the time his seniority comes up for sponsorship, he has sufficiently aged and the employer naturally feels reluctant to appoint him.

During the last three national plans, the emphasis was on promotion of self-employment, development of small-scale industries through provision of assets, skill development and expansion of other support facilities to the unemployed and poor. These self-employment ventures are primarily in the unorganised sector. The results of the survey carried out by National Sample Survey Organisation (NSSO) during 1987-88 and 1993-94 indicate a decline in regular, salaried employment and in self-employment, and an increase in casual wage employment.

NES should have played a proactive role within the overall perspective of the national plan. It was therefore necessary to tap the unorganised sector and create a database for informal activities, so as to guide the job-seekers for suitable self-employment ventures with proper coordination and banks giving credit for such purposes. Though, the poverty alleviation programme implemented through different agencies actually created casual employment, it was not sufficient for the permanent settlement of the job-seekers.

Private Placement Agencies

Private placement agencies, which normally consider placement in relatively large industrial establishments, utilise data collected through the NES, collected by their personal contact, through public notifications in newspaper and periodicals, the Internet, etc. These agencies generally charge fees from both the job-seekers as well as from the employers. These agencies function primarily in metropolitan cities, and a very rough estimate places its number at around 800. These agencies again are very small (one or two men show) and concentrate on placement only.

Fake placement agencies also exist. These fake agencies collect money from the job-seekers and arrange fake interviews in connivance with some of the industries or agents. Such agencies serve a limited purpose to a selected section employers and cannot have an overall perspective on the country as a whole. Therefore,

Governmental efforts cannot be diluted and at the same time the private placement agencies should be subjected to some regulatory guidelines to prevent their exploitation.

Are the Employment Exchanges Relevant Today?

As has already been indicated, the employment exchange has primarily three major objectives and to achieve these objectives four major activities are being earned out. Let us now examine whether such functions are required to be performed.

1) The points in favour of Employment Exchanges are:

- Performance of employment exchanges are to be seen as a whole and not only on the basis of placements. It should also be recognised that this is the only government organisation where the poor job-seekers can have access to jobs and other information to shape their careers.
- Employment exchanges are the only organisation of its kind which provide a meeting point for large numbers of employers and job-seekers, free of cost.
- In the present day scenario, career counselling and vocational guidance are important and employment exchanges represent the only agency where a large number of the unemployed are available for career counselling and vocational guidance. Private organisations, if they exist, are in urban areas and their services are limited and not always free of cost.
- Career literature and vocational guidance materials are available. Career talks at school and college levels are useful for the students in considering a career. No other organisation has such network.
- Registration with the employment exchanges gives an idea as to the prevailing unemployment situation. Of course, some adjustments are necessary in view of the limitations of the employment exchanges such as (i) all unemployed need not register, and (ii) all registered need not necessarily be unemployed. This also gives an idea about the availability of labour in the labour market.

- Data collected by the employment exchanges—on industry-wide employment, occupational and educational pattern of employees—are unique and unparalleled. This actually throws light on the demand of labour in the labour market and the educational and skill requirements of the industry. It is only through this source that employment in the organised industry is assessed. This also is used to make an assessment of employment in the unorganised sector by utilising the results of the National labour force survey conducted by NSSO. Data are comprehensive and minute; industry-wide data are available.
- Employment exchange networks are also used for collection of data on various issues, such as (i) Census of central government employees, (ii) revision of national classification of occupations, and (iii) bulletin on job opportunities. These are important activities.
- Data are used for national Five Year Plans, manpower development and various other manpower planning initiatives both by Centre and state Governments.
- Employment Exchanges act as a pivot for selection of persons for various employment generation programmes run by various organisations.

2) Disadvantages to the operations of the Employment Exchange include:

- Placements through the employment exchange are declining day by day, whereas the expenditures are increasing.
- Job-seekers are frustrated since, due to various reasons, they do not get nominations within a reasonable time, and by the time they are nominated they become overage and must engage in less desirable work.
- The Act is not enforced in letter and spirit, particularly for the private sector. As a result, many private sector vacancies do not get reported in the employment exchanges.
- Employment exchanges have not been able to adjust, as per the requirements of the market and have concentrated on the public sector only. When employment generation in the public sector was not significant, it should have enhanced operations

in the private sector, unorganised sector, self-employment sector or any other area in need of jobs.

- Career counselling and vocational guidance were never taken seriously. Employment market information was not used effectively for the preparation of career literature and vocational guidance materials. In the absence of such materials, the career talk given—or supposed to be given—was not very effective. Gradually, this talk was almost stopped.
- Collection, compilation and analysis of employment market information were relegated to secondary, functional areas, the result of which was a long lag time. Periodic updating of the employer's register is not taking place, which leads to non-coverage of a large number of new establishments. This leads to under-estimation of the data.
- Employment exchanges are still working manually in the traditional way. Some of the employment exchanges are computerised, but such isolated computerisation does not make the network of employment exchanges modern. The result is a delay in all the operations of the employment exchanges, providing scope for malpractices.

Whether the Employment Exchange is Necessary Today

In continuation to the merits and demerits of the Employment Exchange discussed above, we now examine in detail the four major functions performed by the employment exchange to achieve its objectives:

Registration and placement of job-seekers so as to ensure a proper balance between demand and supply

Let us assume that in view of the fact that placement through the employment exchanges is not much, there is no need of registration and placement through any government agency and this should be left to the market forces. This may lead to the following:

- Emergence of a large number of placement agencies and exploitation of job-seekers by these agencies. Whatever placement is being made now by the employment exchanges will be handled by private placement agencies. Both the employer and the job-seeker will have to pay a price for advertisements, selection, and for utilising the services.

- Country may not have any idea about the persons looking for the jobs. What type of manpower available and what is required to make them employable may not be known. Getting such data from private placement agencies is difficult, if not impossible.
- Private placement agencies will have only the profit motive without any social cause, and therefore these will function only in selected places, primarily in the metropolitan cities.
- We will have no idea of the social dimension of the problem. The data available, if any, will not give a picture for the country as a whole.
- We will not have any storehouse of manpower to nominate for various purposes such as self-employment, wage-employment, and other programmes being operated by various departments.
- Without a list of unemployed or job-seekers, it would not be possible to extend any type of welfare, social security, etc., to those belonging to the specified group and the unemployed.

One can go on enlarging the list, but one message is clear: such a government system should exist.

Collection of comprehensive Employment Market Information on a quarterly basis for creation of a database for use in effective management of the demand and supply of labour, preparing career literature for counselling and vocational guidance

Primarily there are three sources of statistics relating to employment, unemployment and related aspects. These are: (i) Population Census, (ii) Labour Force Surveys conducted by NSSO, and (iii) Employment Exchanges' Statistics and Employment Market Information Programme of DGE&T.

The first two sources—Population Census and Labour Force Surveys of NSSO—give an aggregate picture of the various levels of the economy as a whole, and considering both the organised and the unorganised sector. The persons are not identifiable. The definitions are from an economic point of view and therefore consider the work available and a person's time utilisations, without taking any cognizance of the income or quality of work. The employment exchanges' statistics and the employment Market Information Programme, implemented through the network of employment exchanges, identify the following:

- Persons who are unemployed and better job-seekers. The live register gives the details.
- The occupation(s) in demand and which are obsolete in the labour market.
- The type of manpower available and required in the market.
- The organised sector plays an important role in the economy. Employment Market Information Programme is the only source of employment data for the organised sector and covers all the sectors of the economy. This data alongwith the data thrown by Census or NSSO surveys are used to estimate employment in the unorganised sector which is vital in the present economic scenario.
- The data collected give industry-wise occupational and educational distribution of employment in the organised sector. These are vital inputs for vocational guidance and career counselling to those who are future or recent entrants to the labour force.

Data generated through the employment exchanges are supplementary to the data generated through other sources. The aggregated data of census or the data of NSSO can only be useful for macro level planning, whereas the data coming out of the network of employment exchanges is helpful for micro level planning and in actual adjustment of demand and supply of labour, and to address employment and unemployment issues.

Career Counselling and Vocational Guidance

In the present employment market, with around nine million open unemployment and around 122 million working poor, career counselling and vocational guidance assumes utmost importance. Its basic objective is how to guide the prospective workforce so that they can select their career and pursue vocational studies in such a way that they are useful (i.e., they find gainful employment in the labour market). In order to do this job effectively, career literature, vocational guidance materials, consideration of the job opportunities (both wage and self-employment) prevalent in the area and outside the area, are critically important. It is also necessary that such materials are disseminated to as many persons as possible either through the print media or through personal interactions.

Outside the employment exchanges, career counsellors in various organisations—like National Council for Educational Research and Training (NCERT)—are functioning. Some schools, colleges and universities also have career counsellors to guide their students. Some of the non-governmental organisations do provide career counselling, either free or on payment basis. There are private individuals who run career counselling as an enterprise. All these mostly concentrate on high profile, wage-paid jobs and therefore serve only a fraction of the totality.

It must be made clear that those who are of high calibre do not have much problem and they find career information of their own through various sources and shape their career themselves. It is the average and below average calibre job-seekers who are actually required to be guided in details. This section constitutes the majority, and for them wage employment and self-employment must be considered. A large percentage of these job-seekers are lower middle class or poor and may not have means to approach the above mentioned other agencies for their career counselling.

Considering all these aspects and the availability of the job-seekers in employment exchanges, career counselling and vocational guidance can only effectively be done in the employment exchanges as they currently exist today. All the job-seekers do visit the employment exchanges periodically and know that services are free. Therefore, they can approach the officials of the employment exchanges and seek guidance.

The data collected by the employment exchanges equip these officials with information as to the types of jobs, including the new emerging jobs, possible self-employment ventures and the requirement for various jobs that their clients seek. The officials of the employment exchanges can even visit various schools, colleges and universities and deliver career talks and guide the students. This, however, does not mean that other sources should not exist. This work is gigantic, and various organisations are to play a role in guiding the students toward a career.

Conducting area-specific, specialised studies/surveys to assess skills available and the marketable skills required for encouraging job-seekers for self-employment, particularly in the rural informal sector

Necessity of such study needs no emphasis. Various agencies may be carrying out such studies, but most of these are in select areas and do not have totality perspective. To have separate organisations and financial constraints restrict such study. District or *Tehsil* level organisations may be suitable for such studies on a regular basis. But these organisations are entrusted with various works by various authorities because it is only through such organisations that local level information can be collected. Therefore, to what extent these organisations can be burdened is a question.

All the districts in the country do have employment exchanges. In a large number of cases, these are located even at a lower level. The employment exchanges concerns, regarding manpower requirements and developments, are perhaps more suitable for such studies and its dissemination to prospective workers. In fact, if the employment exchanges are to do the jobs expected, they will have to get this information formally or informally, and use it for career counselling and vocational guidance.

Cost Effectiveness of the Employment Exchanges

Expenditures incurred by employment service operations consists of five different activities, namely: (i) registration and placements; (ii) collection of employment market information; (iii) vocational guidance and career counselling; (iv) area specific study; and, (v) providing unemployment allowance (in the States where it is provided). These operations are so intermixed that it is difficult to segregate the expenditure for individual items.

A rough estimate suggests that maximum expenditure would be on providing unemployment allowance, followed by collection and compilation of information, registration, and placements, vocational guidance and career counselling and area specific study. These rough estimates reflect the importance the employment exchanges give in the present situation, and this may not be uniformly true for all the employment exchanges throughout the year. For example, during the months, when the result of the examinations are out, there will be a rush for registrations and at that time almost all the officials will be deployed for registration.

Similarly, there are periods (sometimes between December to March) when notification of vacancies are greater and therefore extra efforts are necessary for nomination. As per the present information, unemployment allowance is paid to some section of the job-seekers in the states of Andhra Pradesh, Haryana, Madhya Pradesh, Maharashtra, Punjab, Tamil Nadu, and West Bengal.

The government tries to separate the unemployment allowance from the total expenditure of these states to determine the amount of expenditure for the remaining activities. Collection, compilation of employment market information in the ER-I return (from around two lakh establishments every quarter), compilation of educational and occupational information in ER-II return (from around two lakh establishments every year), compilation of administrative data on employment exchange statistics i.e. registration, placement, updation of the employer's register, etc. involve substantial work which normally goes unnoticed by the public. This accounts for at least half the expenditure, if not more. Remaining half, for simplicity is apportioned between (i) registration and placement, and (ii) vocational guidance, career counselling and area specific study. Therefore, about 1/4th of the expenditure can be attributed to registration and placement.

Attempts have been made to collect expenditure incurred by the state governments on the employment service operations, i.e., expenditure on employment exchanges and expenditure on the directorate of employment, the headquarters of the employment services in the State.

Twenty-five states have responded to our request and furnished the expenditure accounting. On the basis of the expenditure pattern observed in these states, it is estimated that the total expenditure for running an employment exchange has shown an increasing trend and in the year 2000-2001, when it was of the order of 14.3 lakh per employment exchange. Considering this average expenditure, the estimated total expenditure for running 939 (as on November 2002) employment exchanges comes out to be of the order of Rs. 134 crore.

If we consider that 1/4th of the expenditure is on registration and placement, which involves registration of around 60 lakh job-seekers in a year, renewal of registration of around 60 lakh job-seekers already registered, maintenance of live register of around 410 lakh job-seekers, and nomination of around 20 lakh job-seekers (out of which around 1.70 lakh job-seekers are placed), the total estimated expenditure would be of the order of around Rs. 33.5 crore on this account.

If we attribute this expenditure on placement, then the average expenditure per placement comes out to be around Rs. 2000. Large interstate variation has been observed. Since this is directly related to placements, states like Jammu and Kashmir, North Eastern States, Bihar, etc., where placement was not significant, expenditure per placement was found to be very high.

On the other hand, states like Gujarat, Maharashtra, and Tamil Nadu, found that expenditure per placement was comparatively low. Argument on cost can be on both sides. Some may try to compare expenditure of the earlier days and find this quite exorbitant. Some may like to compare with the money involved in placement by any private placement agencies and argue that the cost per placement is not much considering the charges the private placement agencies take from job-seekers as well as from the employers. (There is no uniformity in the charges by the private placement agencies. Normally, they charge Rs. 100-200 for registration of the job-seeker and one month or 15 days salary both from jobseekers and employers, or, one month or 15 day's salary from the employer.)

As regards collection, compilation and publication of quarterly data from two lakh establishments, even if we take a meagre amount of Rs. 100 per quarter per establishment, the amount involved would be approximately Rs. 8 crore. For collection, compilation and publication of educational and occupational employment from around one lakh establishments, the amount involved would be of the order of Rs. 5 crore (considering the information collected and the volume of data to be processed, expenditure would be quite high and cannot be less than Rs. 500 per establishment). Processing of these data and publication of the (i) quick estimate of employment, (ii) quarterly employment review, and (iii) annual employment review, and (iv) educational and occupational pattern of employment are very costly.

Beside this, the collection, compilation of statistics which follow day to day operations of the employment exchanges and publication of employment exchange statistics, involve a substantial expenditure. All these taken together equal an expenditure to the tune of around Rs. 67 crore by all the 35 State/UT Governments.

Vocational guidance and career counselling and area specific study to make an assessment of the demands in the local labour market assumes importance in view of a near stagnant situation of employment in the organised sector. Labour market demands, particularly for the unorganised sector, play a vital role to encourage the youth to go in for entrepreneurial activities and activities which are area specific. Literature for vocational guidance and career counselling is required to be prepared and periodically updated.

A large scale investment in modernising, networking the employment exchanges and electronic data communications, must be done, lest the purpose of the employment exchange may not be served. Development of a kiosk system, so that the job-seekers may access all relevant information without any contact with officials and decide the career to be pursued. Once the career is decided, the vocational education required can also be had in the kiosk itself.

Are Employment Exchanges Doing the Jobs as Effectively as Expected?

One would tend to believe that employment exchanges are not doing their jobs effectively. To some extent it is correct in view of the following:

- Placement through the employment exchange is insignificant.
- Career counselling and vocational guidance are not taken seriously, therefore, the officials of the employment exchanges do not know what type of counselling or guidance is to be given, nor do they actually try to do so. In fact, in most of the employment exchanges, career literature and vocational guidance materials are not prepared.

- Employment Market Information to be collected by the employment exchanges are never up to date, therefore the publications are always delayed, resulting in obsolescence of information for use.
- The studies to have an assessment of skills available and the marketable skills required for encouraging job-seekers for self-employment, particularly in the rural, informal sector, are not effectively carried out. Therefore, they do not have any employment perspective in their approach.
- Enforcement of the Act is not taken seriously. The data collected, therefore, suffers from serious underestimation. In fact, a large number of public establishments and a majority of private establishments do not report vacancies arising in their establishments and do not submit the returns prescribed under the Act.
- Lack of coordination among employment generation schemes being implemented by various organisations. The role it has for economic rehabilitation of the job-seekers is not being played. In fact, they are behaving like post offices.
- Data to update employer registers and many other work-like interactions with the industry, schools, colleges and universities are missing.

The problem, therefore, is the work culture and sincerity of the persons working in the employment exchanges. In fact, the mental set up which was developed from the beginning—when placement was quite large—did not change with time. The social importance the officers get on placement resulted in employment exchanges giving more emphasis to registration and placement and neglecting other legitimate functions, which, though important, do not have much public interaction and which do not have any immediate effects.

All these have resulted in the perception that employment exchanges are the only placement agencies. This is not only true in the minds of the general public, but also with the various officials of both the Central Government as well as of the State Governments. The officials who matter, therefore, do not lend any weight to employment exchanges, since the placement is less and accordingly feel any investment in the employment exchanges is a waste. As a result, employment exchanges do not get modernised and work in the primitive way. It has also been observed that the head of the employment service (who is generally Director of employment) in the State is changed very frequently. As a result, even they do not get sufficient time to understand the operations and change their perceptions.

Under such a situation, unless the employment exchanges change their attitude, this network will soon be considered outmoded, not useful and closed, and a new set-up will be developed for the various activities which are unique to the employment service.

What Employment Exchanges Should Do in the Present Scenario?

i) Change the mindset of the officers and staff working in the employment service, as the work expected of employment exchanges includes registration and placement of job-seekers.

ii) Collect, compile and disseminate comprehensive labour market information, not only for the organised sector but also for the unorganised sector to use in developing a database for use in effective management of demand and supply of labour, preparing literature for career counselling, and vocational guidance.

iii) Coordinate with the various training providers to equip job-seekers registered with the employment exchanges, with the requisite skill for which either wage-employment or self-employment can be pursued.

iv) Provide effective career counselling and vocational guidance to the job-seekers.

v) Coordinate and monitor employment generation in the area under the jurisdiction of the employment exchanges, both through the normal growth process and through special employment exchanges, implemented by various departments of the State.

vi) Conduct an area specific study/survey to have an assessment of the skills available and the marketable skills required for encouraging job-seekers to pursue self-employment, particularly in the rural informal sector.

Though, the activities indicated above are not new to the employment exchanges and these are part of their activities, what is needed is that:

- State government, as well as the officers engaged in the NES, must abandon the impression that the employment exchanges are only to provide jobs, and should concentrate on all the activities indicated above.
- Planning Commission may like to impress upon the state governments to change their attitudes and take effective measures to help the State government in modernising and networking the employment exchanges on a uniform line.
- Employment exchanges are to be strengthened both in terms of manpower and finance, in view of the fact that during last few years state governments have diverted the manpower and money to other areas. What is needed is to restore the manpower and the financing required.

7

Labour Welfare and Social Security

SECTION I

SOCIAL SECURITY FOR THE ORGANISED SECTOR

Introduction

Social Security caters to the universal need for reassurance and support in times of unemployment, illness, disability, death and old age. The State bears the primary responsibility for developing appropriate systems for providing protection and assistance to its workforce and their families. Public support systems for social security in India have gained prominence over traditional family support in tune with the trends of urbanisation and work place migrations. The dependence on social security varies as per the need and income status.

Social Security Laws

The principal social security laws enacted in India are the following:

- The Employees' State Insurance Act, 1948 (ESI Act).
- The Employees' Provident Funds & Miscellaneous Provisions Act, 1952 (EPF & MP Act). (Separate provident fund legislations exist for workers employed in coal mines and tea plantations in the State of Assam and for seamen).
- The Workmen's Compensation Act, 1923 (WC Act).
- The Maternity Benefit Act, 1961 (M.B. Act).
- The Payment of Gratuity Act, 1972 (P.G. Act).

Administration of Social Security Acts

The EPF & MP Act is administered by the Government of India through the Employees' Provident Fund Organisation (EPFO). Cash benefits under the ESI Act are administered by the Central Government through the Employees State Insurance Corporation (ESIC), whereas the State governments and Union Territory administrations administer medical care under the ESI Act. The Payment of Gratuity Act is administered by the Central Government, and establishments under its control and having branches in more than one state—major ports, mines, oil fields and the railways are also adminstered centrally, while state governments and Union Territory administrations manage all the other cases.

This Act applies to factories and other establishments. In mines and the circus industry, the provisions of the Maternity Benefit Act are being administered by the Central Government through the Chief Labour Commissioner (Central) and by the State governments in factories, plantations and other establishments. The provisions of the Workmen's Compensation Act are being administered exclusively by State governments.

Employees' Provident Funds and Miscellaneous Provisions Act, 1952

The object of the Act is the institution of compulsory contributory provident funds, pension and insurance for employees. Presently the following three schemes are in operation under the Act through the Employees' Provident Fund Organisation:

- Employees' Provident Funds Scheme, 1952.
- Employees' Deposit Linked Insurance Scheme, 1976.
- Employees' Pension Scheme, 1995.

Coverage of Establishments and Members

Presently, the Act is applicable to 180 specified industries/classes of establishments as is specified in Schedule I of the Act or any activity notified by the Central Government in the official Gazette and employing 20 or more persons. As of 31st March, 2003, there were 3,44,508 establishments and factories covered under the Act with a membership of 394.98 lakh under EPF Scheme, both in the exempted and unexempted sectors. With effect from 01.06.2001, an employee, on joining the employment in a covered establishment and getting wages upto Rs. 6500 is required to become a member.

Benefits under the Scheme

Partial withdrawals by way of advances are allowed to members for specified purposes. During the year 2002-2003, financial assistance was provided to the members through partial withdrawals, settling 4.62 lakh such cases and disbursing an amount of Rs. 1,373.73 crore. Further 18.31 lakh claims under the Act were settled and an amount of Rs. 6621.34 crore was disbursed.

Employees Provident Fund Arrears

The Provident Fund arrears as on 31.03.2003 were of the order of Rs. 1511.79 crore. The EPF Organisation launches prosecution against the defaulting employers under Section 14 of the Employees' Provident Fund Act and prosecutes employers under Section 406/409 of the Indian Penal Code in case they deduct employees share of contribution but do not remit the same to the Fund. During 2002-03, arrears amounting to Rs. 885.99 crore were realised.

Employees' Deposit Linked Insurance Scheme, 1976

Since 1976, the Employees' Deposit Linked Insurance Scheme applies to all factories/establishments. All the employees who are members of the Employees' Provident Fund are required to become members of this scheme. Employers are required to pay contributions to the Insurance Fund at the rate of 0.5 per cent of pay (i.e. basic wages dearness allowance including cash value of food concession, and retaining allowance, if any). During 2002-2003 a sum of Rs. 158.62 crore comprising employers' contribution was deposited. During 2002-2003, 20,871 claims were settled and an amount of Rs. 51.99 crore was disbursed. At the end of 2002-2003, the EPFO had cumulative investments of Rs. 3485.22 crore under this scheme.

Employees' Pension Scheme, 1995

Coverage

Employees' Pension Scheme, 1995, has been introduced w.e.f. 16.11.1995. With the introduction of the Pension Scheme, the erstwhile Family Pension Scheme, 1971 ceased to operate. However, the pensioners who were drawing benefits under the Family Pension Scheme, 1971 will continue to draw Family Pension under the Employees' Pension Scheme, 1995.

Eligibility

Members who are 58 years old and have worked a minimum of ten years' contributory service (including the membership period and with ceased Family Pension Scheme, 1971), shall qualify for superannuation pension. Those members who served less than 10 years shall be eligible for scheme certificate or withdrawal benefit as the case may be.

Benefits under the Scheme

Employees' Pension Scheme, 1995 provides the following benefit package:

- superannuate on attaining the age of 58 years,
- retirement benefit,
- permanent total disablement,
- death during service,
- death after retirement/superannuation/permanent total disablement,
- children pension, and
- orphan pension.

The category break-down of pension claims (all benefits) settled by EPFO during the year 2002-2003 is indicated in the following Table.

Category of Claims	*No. of Claims Settled*
Monthly Pension Benefits	356870
Life Assurance Benefit	3758
Retirement-cum-withdrawal Benefit	1832052
Refunds	20013
Total	**2212693**

Contribution to Pension Fund

The Scheme is financed by transferring 8.33 per cent of the Provident Fund contribution from the employers' share and by contribution approximately 1.16 per cent of basic wages by the Central Government. All accumulations in the ceased Family Pension Fund constitute the corpus of the Pension Fund. During the year

2002-03, Rs. 4787.84 crore were received as Pension Fund contributions, from which Rs. 4387.84 crore were collected from the Employers' Share and Rs. 400 crore were contributed by the Central Government.

Pension Beneficiaries

The beneficiaries of the ceased Family Pension Scheme continue to receive benefits under the new pension scheme. As of March 31, 2003, there were 7,50,657 members, 3,87,752 spouses, 2,90,916 children, 5,808 orphans and 6,537 nominees receiving pensions under the scheme. Total amount disbursed among pensioners during the year was Rs. 995.89 crore, delivered through the nationalised banks and post offices.

Modernisation Programme–Reinventing EPFO

EPFO has its operational presence in over 260 locations throughout the country, employs over 20,000 personnel, and has undertaken a comprehensive Information Technology reform agenda, aimed at creating a country-wide integrated information network. The programme designated as Reinventing-EPF India seeks to achieve the following:

- A unique social security identification number to be allotted to each subscriber. A separate number will also be given to establishments as their business number.
- The subscriber member can go to any of the field offices, access his account and get information, an Anytime-Anywhere service.
- The compliance function will be IT-enabled through a system of intelligence gathering and third party information collection.

The Employees State Insurance Scheme

Coverage

The ESI Act provides for health care and cash benefit payments in the case of sickness, maternity and employment injury. The Act is applicable to non-seasonal factories using power and employing 10 or more persons, and non-power using factories and other establishments employing twenty or more persons. The Act is being implemented area-wise in a phased manner. The ESI Scheme is operated in 678 centres situated in 29 States/Union Territories. As of now, over 78.65 lakh insured persons and about 303.73 lakh beneficiaries are covered under the scheme. The number of factories and establishments covered by the end of the year had gone up to about 2,55,000.

Administration

The ESI scheme is administered by a statutory body called the ESIC, which has members representing employers, employees, central and state governments, the medical profession and the Parliament. The Union Minister for Labour is the Chairman. A Standing Committee comprised of members of the Corporation acts as the executive body for administration of the scheme and is chaired by the Additional Secretary to the Government of India, Ministry of Labour. There are now 21 regional boards and 358 local committees in existence. The Director General (ESIC) is the Chief Executive Officer of the Corporation and is also an ex-officio member of the Corporation. The ESI Corporation, apart from the Headquarters Office located at Delhi, has a number of field offices throughout the country. The Corporation has 23 regional offices, 16 sub-regional and divisional offices, 625 local offices, 299 inspection offices, and 215 pay offices all over the country for administration of the scheme.

Funding and Operation of the Scheme

The ESI Scheme is mainly financed by contributions from employers and employees. The rates of the employers' and the employees' contribution are 4.75 per cent and 1.75 cent respectively. The State Governments' share of the expenditure on the provision of medical care is as high as 12.5 per cent (l/8th within the per capita ceiling). The Corporation has prescribed a ceiling on the shareable expenditure of medical care. From 1st April, 2003, the ceiling on expenditure per insured person family unit has been increased to Rs. 700/- per annum and has been raised to Rs. 750 per annum w.e.f. 1.4.2004. All capital expenditure on construction and maintenance of ESI hospitals and other buildings is borne by the ESI Corporation.

Health Benefits

The scheme provides full medical facilities, from primary health care to super speciality treatment in respect of the insured persons (IPs). The medical care under the scheme is administered by the state governments with Statutory responsibility, except in the National Capital Region of Delhi and NOIDA area in Uttar Pradesh. The Corporation also administers directly the five occupational disease centres-cum general hospitals, one each at Delhi, Pune, Chennai, Kolkata and Nagda (M.P.).

ESI Medical Infrastructure (As on 31.3.2003)

Number of ESI Hospitals	142
Number of ESI Annexes	43
Number of Beds Constructed in ESI Hospitals	23,856
Number of Beds in ESI Annexes	867
Number of Beds Reserved in State Govt. Hospitals	4000
Number of Insurance Medical Practitioners (IMPs)	6812
Number of ESI Dispensaries	1447
Number of Panel Clinics	2651

Achievements of the ESI Corporation for the Year 2002-2003

- The ESI Scheme today provides social protection to 310 lakh beneficiaries through a large network of 142 hospitals, 43 Annexes, 1447 dispensaries, 2651 clinics and 840 local offices.
- During 2002-2003, the Corporation took over ESI hospitals at Hyderabad, Jaipur, Rourkela, Sahibabad, Pune, Chandigarh, Asramam, Bangalore, Ranchi, Patna and Guwahati to develop as model hospitals.
- The ceiling for commutation of partial disablement benefits has been raised from the existing Rs. 10,000 to Rs. 30,000.
- Family photo-identity cards have been issued to about 70 per cent insured persons to check misuse of medical facilities.
- Over six lakh low paid workers drawing wages up to Rs. 40 per day have been exempted from contributing to the ESI Scheme.
- The ceiling on expenditure per insured person family unit has been enhanced to Rs. 750 per annum w.e.f. 1.04.2004.

- The wage ceiling for coverage under the ESI Scheme has been increased from Rs. 6500 to Rs. 7500 w.e.f. 1.04.2004.

Payment of Gratuity Act, 1972

The Payment of Gratuity Act, 1972, applies to factories and other establishments employing ten or more persons. On completion of five years of service, the employees are entitled to payment of gratuity at approximately 15 days wages for every completed year of service or part thereof in excess of six months subject to a maximum of Rs. 3.50 lakh. The current maximum limit is from 24th September, 1997. The wage ceiling for coverage under the Act has since been removed w.e.f. 24.05.1994.

Workmen's Compensation Act, 1923

The Act provides for payment of compensation to workmen and their dependants in case of injury and accident (including certain occupational diseases) arising out of and in the course of employment and resulting in disability or death. The Act applies to railway servants and persons employed in such capacity as is specified in Schedule II of the Act.

Schedule II includes persons employed in factories, mines, plantations, mechanically propelled vehicles, construction works and certain other hazardous occupations. Minimum rates of compensation for permanent total disablement and death have been fixed at Rs. 90,000 and Rs. 80,000 respectively. Maximum amount for death and permanent total disablement can go up to Rs. 4.56 lakh and Rs. 5.48 lakh respectively depending on the age and wages of workmen.

Maternity Benefit Act, 1961

The Maternity Benefit Act, 1961, regulates employment of women in certain establishments for a certain period before and after childbirth and provides for maternity and other benefits. The Act is applicable to mines, factories, circus industry, plantations, shops, and establishments employing ten or more persons, except employees covered under the ESI, 1948. It can be extended to other establishments by the state governments. There is no wage limit for coverage under the Act.

SECTION II

THE UNORGANISED SECTOR WORKERS[1] SOCIAL SECURITY SCHEME, 2004

Short Title, Commencement and Application

(i) This Scheme may be called the Unorganised Sector Workers' Social Security Scheme

(ii) Subject to the provisions of this scheme, self-employed workers without employers have an option to become members of this scheme.

(iii) This Scheme shall apply to all the workers and establishments in the activities listed in the Annexure to the scheme.

Definitions

In this scheme, unless the context otherwise requires:

i. "Authorised officer" refers to any officer authorised by the commissioner for the purpose of the scheme.

ii. "Business number" means the number issued by the Employees Provident Fund Organisation to all establishments/employers for the purpose of uniquely identifying them and for all the transactions under the scheme.

iii. "Commissioner" refers to Central Provident Fund Commissioner appointed under provisions of the Employees' Provident Funds and Miscellaneous Provisions Act, 1952.

iv. "Contributory service" means the period of service rendered by a member for which the contributions to the fund have been received or are receivable.

v. "Designated bank" means any bank or post office that is designated by the Commissioner for the purpose of depositing contributions or drawing pensions for any financial transaction under the scheme.

vi. "Designated hospital" means any hospital designated by the Commissioner for the purpose of hospitalisation under

---

1. Ministry of Labour initiated this scheme in the last (NDA) Government. No further action has been undertaken.

the Universal Health Insurance Scheme or any other appropriate scheme.

vii. "Eligible member" refers to a worker who is eligible to join the Unorganised Sector Workers' Social Security Scheme.

viii. "EPS 95" means Employees Pension Scheme, 1995, established under the Employees Provident Funds and Miscellaneous Provisions Act, 1952.

ix. "Existing Member" refers an existing worker who is a "Member of the Employees' Pension Scheme, 1995."

x. "Facilitator" refers to any person authorised on behalf of this scheme to collect and deposit the contributions from the workers and employers, guide the employers and workers for the purpose of compliance with the provisions of the scheme, and to help them draw the benefits under the scheme.

xi. "Facilitation centre" means the workers' facilitation centres.

xii. "Family" refers to the family of the member, including the member as defined in the Universal Health Insurance Scheme.

xiii. "Filer" refers to a filer authorised and appointed under the provisions of this scheme.

xiv. "Member" refers to an employee who becomes a member of the Unorganised Sector Workers' Social Security Scheme in accordance with the provisions of this Scheme.[2]

xv. "NSSN" means National Social Security Number to be given by the Employees Provident Fund Organisation to Uniquely identify the members.

xvi. "Orphan" refers to a person whose parents are deceased.

---

2. I. A worker shall cease to be a member of Social Security Scheme; from the date of attaining 60 years of age or from the date of vesting admissible benefits under the Scheme, whichever is earlier.

II. A worker drawing pay/income exceeding Rs. 7500 per month at the time of enrolment is not eligible to become a member of the scheme.

III. All workers in the age group of 36-50 are eligible to become members only for a period of five years from the day of launching of the scheme. Thereafter, only the workers who are of the age of 35 years or below on the date of joining the scheme are eligible to become the members of the scheme.

xvii. "POP" means "points of presence," which include bank branches, post offices, depository participant offices and any other location from which electronic connectivity into a central computer system is possible for financial transactions like collection of contributions, payment of benefits, transfer of amount to other POPs or to the fund, etc., under the scheme.

xviii. "Pay" means all remunerations, paid or payable.

xix. "Permanent total disablement" means disablement of a nature that incapacitates a worker for all work which he was capable of performing at the time of disablement, regardless whether such disablement is sustained in the course of employment or otherwise.

xx. "Pension" means the pension payable under the Unorganised Sector Workers' Social Security Scheme.

xxi. "Pension fund" means the pension fund setup under this scheme from the contributions of employers, employees and government towards the pension.

xxii. "Table" means Table appended to this scheme.

xxiii. "Welfare fund" means the fund consisting of contribution from employers, employees and government.

Registration of Members

Registration and Allotment of National Social Security Number (NSSN)

(i) The Commissioner, with the help of worker facilitation centres, facilitators and filers, registers the employers and the members.

(ii) For the purposes of this scheme, the Employees' Provident Fund Organisation will allot an NSSN, which shall be a permanent number all through the worker's life.

Declaration by Persons' taking up Employment after the Pension Fund has been Established

The employer may, before taking any person into employment, ask the person to state in writing whether or not he is a member of the Scheme and, if so require the person to furnish the NSSN.

Options for Joining the Scheme

All workers, including self-employed workers in the age group of 18-50 years, have an option to join the scheme within five years from the date of commencement of the scheme, provided they have an identifiable employer and this employer also contributes to the scheme. Self-employed workers may also join this scheme provided they pay the employers' contribution also.

Resolution of Doubts

If any doubt arises as to whether a worker is entitled to become a member of the Unorganised Sector Workers' Social Security Scheme, the issue shall be referred to the officer authorised in this regard who shall decide the same, provided that an opportunity of being heard shall be given to the employer and worker before passing final order in the matter.

Collection and Recording of Contributors

Unorganised Sector Workers' Social Security Scheme

(i) The Fund will be created out of contributions from:

- (a) the workers in the age group of 18-35 years at a rate of Rs. 50 per month,
- (b) the workers in the age group of 36-50 years at a rate of Rs. 100 per month,
- (c) the employer wherever identifiable, in both age groups at the rate of Rs. 100 per month, and
- (d) the self-employed in the age group of 36-50 years shall contribute the employers share in addition to his/her share.

(ii) The Central Government shall contribute at the rate of 1.16 per cent of monthly wages of enrolled workers, taking as base the average national floor wage as notified by the Central Government.

(iii) The contribution payable under sub-paragraph (2) shall be calculated to the nearest rupee, fifty paise, or more, to be counted as the next higher rupee and fraction of a rupee less than fifty paise to be ignored.

Mode of Payment of Contribution

(i) The employers shall collect the worker contribution from the workers, add their contribution, and then deposit the contribution in the designated branch of the bank or post office/POP in such manner as may be prescribed.

(ii) The workers for whom there is no identifiable employer shall pay the contributions at the designated branch of the bank or post office or POP by submitting his NSSN. He may use the services of Workers Facilitation Centres, facilitators or filers for the purpose.

(iii) The contributions by the employer and the worker under Para 7(1) shall be deposited by the 15th day of every month. Default in such deposit shall attract an interest of Re. 1 per month or part thereof, which shall be deposited by the employer/worker along with the contributions.

(iv) The member who does not deposit contributions for a continuous period of one year shall cease to be a member of the scheme. However, such member can get his membership regularised by depositing the contributions for the gap period along with interest thereon as may be prescribed from time to time.

Unorganised Workers Social Security Scheme Account

The account called the "Unorganised Workers Social Security Scheme Account" shall be opened by the Commissioner in any branch of a designated bank, for depositing contributions by employers, workers, for delivering benefits under the scheme and/or operating for the purpose of administration of the scheme.

Registers, Records, etc.

The Commissioner shall, with the approval of the Board, prescribe the registers and records to be maintained in the form or design of any identity card, token, disc or electronic transfer system for the purpose of identifying, servicing or complying with a request by an employee, his nominee or family member to receive a pension. Other forms/formalities as have to be completed in connection with the award of pension and other benefits or for the continuance thereof are subject to periodic verification as may be considered necessary, or for the purpose of depositing contributions by the workers and employers.

Explanation: The registers and records suggested to be maintained herein are for the purpose of implementing this scheme only. No other register required for any other purpose of the Act will be maintained.

Compliance and Enforcement

Employer to Furnish Particulars of Ownership

Every employer, in relation to a factory or other establishment to which the scheme applies or is applied hereafter, shall furnish to the Commissioner particulars of all the branches and departments, owners, occupiers, directors, partners, managers or any other person or persons who have the ultimate control over the affairs of such factory or establishment. Information as to any change in such particulars must be sent to the Commissioner by registered post within three months of such change.

Duties of Employers

(i) Within three months of the commencement of this scheme, every employer or business shall send to the Commissioner a consolidated return of the workers entitled to become members of the scheme, in electronic or paper form.

(ii) Every employer shall maintain an accounting of the amounts contributed by him to the scheme, if possible, or register himself with the workers facilitation centre, facilitator or filer in his area who will maintain the accounts of such employers for whom it is not possible to maintain any accounts or registers.

(iii) Notwithstanding anything contained in this paragraph, the Commissioner may issue such directions to the employers generally, as it may consider necessary or expedient, for the purpose of implementing the Scheme, and it shall be the duty of every employer to carry out such directions.

(iv) A unique Business number will be issued to each employer by the commissioner or by any other officer authorised on its behalf, which shall be a permanent number and shall be quoted for all the purposes under the scheme.

Explanation: Until such time as the business number is allotted, the employer may use the Permanent Account Number (PAN) issued under the Income Tax Act, 1961.

(v) Every employer shall make a self-declaration about all the relevant facts for the purpose of the scheme and sign a verification, which shall be binding on him. Any false statement, declaration, or verification shall attract the penal provisions under the law.

Punishment for Failure to Submit Returns, etc.

If any person:

(a) deducts or attempts to deduct from the wages or other remuneration of the member, the whole or any part of the employer's contribution; or

(b) fails or refuses to submit any return, statement or other documents required by this scheme or submits false returns, statement or other documents, or makes a false declaration; or

(c) obstructs any Inspector or other official appointed under the Act or this Scheme in the discharge of his duties or fails to produce any record for inspection by such inspector or other officials; or

(d) is guilty of contravention of or non-compliance with any other requirement of this Scheme, he shall be punishable with a penalty which may extend up to Rs. 2000 after giving a reasonable opportunity of being heard.

Provisions under Rule 13 of the Scheme would be applicable after the enactment of the law.

Finance and Investment

Financing the Scheme: The scheme shall be financed with the contributions received from the members, employers, and the Government, as detailed in the Para 7 of this scheme.

The Scheme to be a Fully Funded Pension Scheme

The pension provisioning will be set up as a fully funded pension scheme under sound prudential norms, governance structure and actuarial fairness.

Investment of the Pension Fund Account

(i) All incremental accretions accruing to Unorganised Workers Social Security Scheme Account, including the contributions of the Central Government, shall be transferred to a designated central depository for investment of moneys in accordance with the provisions and guidelines issued by the Government.

(ii) An Advisory Committee of experts and professionals of proven track records in the area investment, social security and banking, will be constituted by the Government which will suggest investment guidelines, broad pattern and options of investment to ensure safe and better returns and growth of the pension fund.

Utilisation of the Unorganised Sector Workers' Welfare Fund

i) An insurance policy to cover accident/death will be purchased from an insurance company.

ii) An appropriate health cover policy shall be purchased to make available the benefits of health coverage to the extent available under the universal health scheme being operated by an insurance company or any such scheme that is purchased for this purpose.

iii) Subject to the provisions of this Scheme, the Fund shall not, except with the prior sanction of the Central Government, be expended for any purpose other than the payments envisaged in this Scheme, for continued payment of Pension, Widow Pension, Disabled Pension, Orphan Pension and premium for insurance and for universal health insurance scheme or any such scheme that covers health insurance.

Administration Account

(i) No more than one per cent of the pension fund shall be spent on administrative expenses, including the collection of contributions, record keeping, maintenance of accounts, investment of the pension fund, compliance and enforcement, and benefit delivery.

(ii) A separate account, called the "Unorganised Workers Pension Fund Administration Account," shall be kept to record all the administrative expenses of the Pension Fund.

Forms of Accounts

The accounts of Unorganised Workers Pension Fund shall be maintained by the Commissioner in such form and in such manner as may be specified by the Central Government.

Audit

The accounts of the Unorganised Workers Pension Fund and the administrative expenses incurred in running this Scheme shall be audited in accordance with the instructions issued by the Central Government, and in consultation with the Comptroller and Auditor-General of India.

Valuation of the Pension Scheme and Review of the Rates of Contributions and Quantum of the Pension and Other Benefits

(i) The Government shall have an annual valuation of the Pension Scheme carried out by an appointed actuary. Responsibility for the annual valuation shall lie with the relevant pension fund.

(ii) The annual valuation will be submitted for validation to an independent panel of three actuaries every third year in order to certify that the pension scheme is fully funded and is sustainable in the long-term (i.e. the income in the present and in future exceed present and future liabilities).

(iii) The Central Government may, at any time, alter the rate of contributions payable under this Scheme or the scale of any benefit admissible under this Scheme, or, the period for which such benefit may be given.

Award and Payment of Benefits

Monthly Member's Pension and other Pension benefits shall be as under:

Monthly Members Pension

For all ages, a Pension Point of 480 will be required to secure a pension of Rs. 500 per month, payable from age 60 for life of Pensioner. For other Pension Points, a proportionate pension will be payable subject to a minimum and a maximum pension.

Contingency of Payment

Superannuation: The Pension, depending on the Pension Point, shall be payable on reaching the age of 60, notwithstanding whether one is still employed/self-employed, for remaining life of the employee.

Exit before 60 Years

Because the pension is based on the Pension Point, If you leave employment before the age of 60, benefits will still be payable after attaining the age of 60 years.

Permanent Disablement

If a worker is permanently disabled, a sum of Rs. 1,00,000/- will be paid from the Personal Accident Policy purchased from an insurance provider and the worker shall receive Pension based on Pension Point on attaining the age of 60 years.

Death before Attaining the Age of 60 Years

If death is due to accident and the money from the Personal Accident Policy is received, the Widow Pension shall commence after the widow turns 60 years old. Such widow pension will be based on Pension Point at the date of death. If the death is not due to accident, the status of the Pension Point shall be determined and paid to the widow for life with immediate effect.

Death during Deferred Period

If death occurs during the non-contributory period, but before attaining the age of 60 years, depending on the Pension Point of the deceased member the pension shall be paid to the widow for life with immediate effect.

Death after Retirement

Fifty per cent of the member's last drawn pension, but not less than Rs. 300 per month, shall be payable to the widow for rest of her lifetime.

Orphan Pension

On death of the member, Orphan Pension shall be payable at the same rate as widow pension till the youngest one reaches age 25. If there is more than one orphan, the Pension amount will be divided equally between two oldest running down to youngest.

Note: Minimum Pension and/or Maximum Pension shall be applicable only in those cases, where member contributes up to age 60.

The calculation of scale of benefits will be as per the Table 1 attached to this Scheme. This Table shall be revised by the Central Government as may be required under the Scheme from time to time.

The member on permanent disablement due to accident is entitled to the insurance amount, or, in the event of accidental death, his nominee is eligible to the sum insured under the insurance policy purchased on his behalf.

Subject to the provisions and alternatives offered under the Unorganised Sector Workers' Social Security Scheme to a particular category of member in the Universal Health Insurance Scheme, five members of the family of the member, including the member, will be eligible for health benefits in designated hospitals.

Explanation: The benefits under the policies purchased from different service providers, including the insurance companies, will be made directly by the insurance company or the service provider.

Payment of Pension

The pension, as admissible under the scheme, shall be paid by the commissioner—or by any authorised officer—through a designated bank, post office or POP (point of presence).

Payment of Insurance Amount

Upon the permanent disability or death of a member, a claim may be submitted along with the policy and other documents to the Insurance Company, which shall be settled by the Insurance Company as per the provisions applicable for such settlement.

Disbursement of Pension and Other Benefits

The Commissioner shall enter into an arrangement for the disbursement of pension and other benefits under this Scheme with disbursing agencies like Post Offices or designated Banks. The commission payable to the disbursing agencies and other charges incidental thereto shall be met from the fund.

Payment of Pension in the Case of a Person Charged with the Offence of Murder

(i) If a person eligible to receive the pension of a deceased member, under paragraph 8, is charged with the offence of murdering the member to receive the pension or money, his claims to receive the pension shall remain suspended till the conclusion of the criminal proceedings instituted against him for such offence.

(ii) If, on conclusion of the criminal proceedings referred to in sub-paragraph (1) above, the person concerned is:

  (a) convicted for the murder or abetting in the murder of the member, he shall be debarred from receiving pension, which shall be payable to other eligible members, if any, of the family of the member; or

  (b) acquitted of the charge of murder or the charge of abetting the murder of the member, pension benefit shall be payable to him from the date of eligibility.

The Central Government shall give directions to the Commissioner on the implementation, monitoring, evaluation and other day to day administrative requirements under the scheme for the purpose of coverage, registration, record keeping, collection of contributions, compliance, finance, investment and benefit delivery.

Miscellaneous

Power to Issue Directions

The Central Government may issue such directions as may be deemed just and proper by it for resolving any difficulty in the disbursement of pension and other benefits, or for resolving any difficulty in the implementation of this Scheme.

Annual Report

The Commissioner shall prepare an Annual Report on the working of the Scheme during the previous financial year and submit to the Central Government before 30th of September or such extended time as the Central Government may allow.

Application of the Provisions of the Employees' Provident Fund Scheme, 1952

In regard to matters for which either there is no provision or there is inadequate provision in this Scheme, the corresponding provisions in the Employees' Provident Fund Scheme, 1952, shall apply.

Information to the Central Government

The Commissioner shall furnish such information to the Central Government from time to time with respect to the income and expenditure from the fund account, as directed by the Central Government.

Interpretation

Where any doubt arises with regard to the interpretation of the provisions of this Scheme, it shall be referred to the Central Government who shall decide the same.

SECTION III

THE EMPLOYMENT GUARANTEE BILL OF 2005

(As passed by Lok Sabha on 23.8.2005)

The problem of employment, specially in the context of the development pattern adopted in India, has been a subject of debate *vis-à-vis* the class of the reform initiated in India nearly over last two decades. The theme of the present book provides an approach different from what the Employment Guarantee Act of 2005 has promised. The details of this Act and its phasing over time and space is not spelt out nor is its pattern and sources of finance. Hence, only few reflections on this Act are attempted here.

This Bill quotes in one place "to provide for the enhancement of the livelihood security of the poor household in rural areas of the country by providing at least one hundred days of guaranteed wage employment in a financial year to every household whose adult members volunteer to do unskilled manual work or matters connected therewith or incidental thereto" whereas in another place, omits the word 'poor household' in the rural area in the same document without any reference to poor households. This shows uncertainty in the selection process in its targeting. The Bill was passed by the Lok Sabha on 23.8.2005 and the Act now may be called the National Rural Employment Guarantee Act, 2005 which extends to the whole of India except the state of Jammu and Kashmir. This Act shall come into force after notification in the Official Gazette by the Central Government and shall be applicable to the whole of the territory to which it extends within a period of five years from the date of enactment of this Act.

The important objectives of the Rural Employment Guarantee Scheme came out to be creation of durable assets and strengthening the livelihood resource base of the rural poor. The focus of the scheme shall be on the following works in their order of priority.

i. Water conservation and water harvesting.

ii. Drought proofing (including aforestation and tree plantation).

iii. Irrigation canals including micro and minor irrigation works.

iv. Provision of irrigation facility to land owned by households belonging to SC and ST or to land beneficiaries of land reforms or that of the beneficiaries under the Indira Awas Yojana of the Government of India.

v. Renovation of traditional water bodies including desilting of tanks.

vi. Land development.

vii. Flood control and protection works including drainage in water logged areas.

viii. Rural connectivity to provide all weather access.

ix. Any other work which may be notified by the Central Government in consultation with the State Government. (Page 13 of the Bill).

All the schemes under this Act shall be funded by the Central Government which shall, by notification, establish the National Employment Guarantee Fund for the purpose of this Act and shall credit by way of grants or loans such sums of money to the National Fund after appropriation made by Parliament by law in this behalf. For implementation of the schemes, the State Government may, by notification, establish the State Employment Guarantee Fund and the amount standing to the credit of the State Fund shall be expanded for the purpose.

The Bill as mentioned here promises to provide at least 100 days of work in a financial year to every household at minimum wage rate which will be decided by the Central/State Government for different schemes; not less than 60 rupees per day for 7 hours work. It will mean an income support to the household with 100 days of wage employment less loss of earning of 100 days which in normal course those persons who are employed received over the year. This means, with the suggested Rs. 60 per day wage rate as minimum wage, 6000 rupees will be the addition to the family provided the people employed in this scheme were unemployed with zero income over these 100 days. This only will give them Rs. 100 per month per capita (with 5 members family). This is not always likely and this fact should be kept in mind. In fact, only when the employed manual workers are doing some remuneration job in the rest of the year and take advantage of the scheme only for their slack time, the scheme is useful. But in that case it is to be regarded as an income support scheme.

The Act also has the provision of payment of unemployment allowance to an applicant for employment under the scheme if it fails to provide employment within fifteen days of his application. However, in the past in similar schemes on Public works, the Planning Commission noted that for giving subsidy of one rupee to a poor in rural areas government has to spend Rs. 3.65 on subsidy i.e., one rupee in the budget become only 27 paisa for the poor in rural areas. This has been often quoted by the Late Prime Minister of India Shri Rajiv Gandhi. Given this finding in the working of the public work programmes when this time the targeted household proposed to cover all (below and above poverty households) the number of poor getting the benefits are likely to be very low and large share of benefits may go to households above the poverty line. This is also the findings of the Poverty Evaluation Organisation of the Planning Commission

Therefore, it should not be regarded as a scheme for generating sustained 'employment' to a totally unemployed person and at best it can be regarded as a 'relief measure or an income support' programme.

In its operation the Bill includes basically a consolidation of a large number of 'ongoing projects' of the Indian Government on Poverty Alleviation and employment generation by public works programme for rural infrastructure. However, most of these individual projects have earned very bad reputation when their benefits have not reached the target groups. Besides, at constant price the employment coefficients of expenditure outlay in all these projects are going down year by year. In aggregation the employment coefficient of most of these schemes over years in the Ninth Plan compared to Eighth Plan went down, as estimates based on the data of the rural development ministry. Further, given the announced policy, and promises by the different wings of the government from time to time and the global movement for more mechanisation and large scale production, this trend of declining employment capacity may accelerate. In this context, what assurance is there that simply by putting the projects under one umbrella, the past experience will not recur? This is specially when we consider that the delivery system of the proposed composite project seems to remain unchanged as before i.e., "the general top down approach of Government Bureaucracy."

In the Mid Term Appraisal of the Tenth Five Year Plan (2002-07), it has been mentioned that Tata Consultancy Services have carried out a study in 2004 of various rural employment schemes including the Maharashtra Rural Employment Guarantee Scheme and it had identified the following flaws in the implementation design of most of these schemes.

- Inflated Schemes
  - Inflated quantity of work, depressed productivity, inflated person day estimates.
- Bogus Registration
  - Registration of non-living persons, minors and medically unfit persons, duplicate and/or proxy registration, fictitious registrations.
- Fraudulent Requisition of Funds
  - False measurement, inflated progress of works, omitting an operation or work item.
- Inflated Muster
  - Ghost workmen, bogus attendance.
- Fraudulent Wage Payment
  - Under payments, dependant fraudulent payments.

The Mid Term Appraisal fortunately suggested a long list of measures which should tackle these issues. It includes building of a large information base and tracking especially all the rural casual manual labours. But as such it seems to be a long 'wish list' when its feasibility regarding enforcement, given a reasonable time coverage, and dealing with a large floating casual labour (who are very mobile and only at times in the rural public works programmes) is questionable. Besides from past experience, the prevalence of corruption and lack of honesty may turn out to be the key constraints in this context. Thus, all these promises are regarded as very open ended, unless they are backed-up by detailed ground work and financial support.

Further, it should be remembered that among the rural manual workers, the unemployment rate as defined by usual status and to some extent also by current daily status is the lowest. The majority of unemployment originates in the educated labour force mostly in self-employed non-agricultural sectors and many new entrants in the labour force in the rural economy. The growth of this sector is much faster than the farm sector. This segment of labour force seeks only white-collar jobs in the government or in a large private corporation, primarily because of the nature of present day education and social environment. This is posing a problem since the corporate sector is experiencing a near jobless growth and looking for only highly trained segment of labour force. As an alternative most of them are going for non-agriculture jobs, like service and small industries. Indeed, a large part of this rural labour force go for non-agriculture, self employed jobs. Along with that there is a growing restriction on the movement of natural persons and a very slow progress on this front in present global negotiations. There is of course a growing opportunity for jobs from outsourcing. However, these numbers run into thousands or lakhs whereas the unemployment touches crores and even in its incremental terms it runs in millions. Hence, we have to find other sources to absorb this growing educated unemployed in India. The enormity of the problem should be realised when more than 8 million young students come out of class 10+ to class 12+. Of them 3 million or more go to labour market for employment.

The present scheme although is designed to cover all rural households (i.e., all adult members of the household), but effectively it covers a part because it works through public work programmes which includes only manual labour as the target. Further, it is of interest to note that at present (NSSO–report 1999-2000) in the public works programme in rural India, only 38.27 per cent of total workers, come from households below the poverty line in the agriculture sector and 25.23 per cent from the non-agriculture sector.[3] The latter segment especially includes as already mentioned, a sizeable number of new entrants to the labour force who are educated (above matriculate) and some of them even have completed 10th to 12th plus but are deprived of a job of their choice because of their lack of skill and vocational training. The organised corporate sector with its capital intensive preference can include only highly technical salaried persons. This trend may increase because of the present government policy often going for large mechanised rural infrastructure programme. Therefore, those educated labour force including the new entrants who also have not got the opportunity of proper vocational training (in most cases because of shortages of capacities in training institutes of 'worth mentioning' with good placement record) are all left out. One should know that the capacity

3. Sastry, N.S. "Estimating Informal Employment and Poverty in India" *Discussion Paper* No. 7 (Table 4.3)/UNDP, India, Council for Social Development (Human Development Resources Centre).

of all the formal training institutes immediately available can be stretched to 1.5 million, at the maximum.

Further, the total educated labour force in the self-employed rural sector almost touches 40 per cent of non-agriculture labour. To enjoy the benefits of the present scheme, therefore, they will have to switch over to manual labour and that only for 100 days, a thought which is not pleasant.

Even this targeted group of manual labour in this scheme (on the basis of past experience in the public works programmes as given by the report by PEO of Planning Commission and often quoted) may cover only 25 per cent or less labour force employed from the below poverty households. This means it is not also a satisfactory poverty reduction programme. It may not also cover eventually even a large section of agriculture manual labour since those for rich firms may not be interested for the 100 days public works manual jobs.

At present, it is very difficult to give a view on the nature of public works in this scheme regarding better delivery, targeting and governance, its relevance to the local conditions in district selection, unless it becomes more transparent in its selection process, its institutional structure and steps against corruption. Same about its funding pattern. However, one can safely say that any scheme supported by large borrowings and fiscal support provide reservations and can be misread as an attempt to create only a vote bank and a source to add opportunities for more corruptions in Bureaucracy.

The above Employment Guarantee Scheme also shows great similarity to an earlier scheme (JPRGY) initiated by the former NDA Government, which has, however, been spelt out in much greater detail in the next Section (Section IV).

SECTION IV

JAI PRAKASH ROZGAR GUARANTEE YOJANA (JPRGY)

The Finance Minister of the earlier (NDA) Government announced in his budget speech 2002-03, that Jai Prakash Rozgar Guarantee Yojana (JPRGY) would be launched to provide guaranteed employment to the unemployed in the most distressed Districts of the country. Accordingly, a Task Force was set up under the Chairmanship of Minister of Rural Development to design the programme. The Task Force further constituted two Sub-Committees to conceptualise and operationalise the Scheme. The combined meetings of the Sub-Committees were held four times under the Chairmanship of Dr. S.P Gupta, Member, Planning Commission. The sub-committees did a detailed exercise to identify the most backward Districts. A number of indicators such as backwardness, SC/ST population, migration, food security, poverty ratio, unemployment etc. were considered for identification of most distressed Districts.

Finally, it was decided that for allotment of the number of the most distressed Districts among the States, poverty ratio as given by (1) the Planning Commission on the basis of NSSO Survey of the year 1999-2000, would be used and that the selection of the Districts within the State would be decided on (2) 1997 Census on the basis of the District-wise percentage of the BPL population as given by the BPL Census of the year 1997.

Allocation of Districts

The JPRGY is proposed to be initially implemented in 130 districts of the country, without excluding any State.

The number of districts to be identified in each State has been determined on the basis of the proportion of the number of BPL persons in the State to the total number of BPL persons in the country, as estimated by the Planning Commission for the year 1999-2000. The proportions so obtained for each State were multiplied by 130, the required number of Districts to be identified under JPGRY, to obtain the initial estimate of number of Districts to be selected in each State. The numbers so obtained for each State have been adjusted slightly to round off and allocate at least one district to every State. The allocation of districts to the newly created States of Uttaranchal, Jharkhand and Chhattisgarh has been obtained by splitting the allocations for Uttar Pradesh, Bihar and Madhya Pradesh respectively in proportion to the number of districts.

Identification of Districts within the States

Since the data generated by the BPL Census 1997 are the latest available for assessing poverty at district level, the percentage of BPL households in each of the districts within the State has been considered the most appropriate indicator for identification of districts within the States. Therefore, the required number of districts in each State were selected, the identifying districts, where percentages of BPL persons (reported by the States based on the BPL Census, 1997) were maximum. The relative position (rank) of the selected districts (in each State) has been compared with the rank of these districts (within the State) obtained with the Task Force (set up by Planning Commission to identify the backward districts) method. The Task Force considered a number of parameters for identification of backward districts. The Members of the Task Force were of the view that agriculture output per worker, agricultural wages and proportion of SC/ST of a district should be the parameters for ranking districts. An exercise to rank districts on an index that assigns equal weights to the above parameters were carried out. However, the SC/ST population considered in this exercise was for the year 1991, wages pertained to the year 1996-1997 and output per agricultural worker pertained to 1990-1993. The districts, which were found common, have been indicated separately. The dependency ratio and the percentage of urban population in the selected districts and the SC/ST population have also been indicated.

Since for Jammu & Kashmir, Sikkim, Tripura and Tamil Nadu, district-wise data of BPL families were not available in the Ministry of Rural Development, these States could be asked to select their most distressed districts according to the number allotted to them on the basis of poverty ratio.

Selection of Blocks within the Selected Districts

In each State, one third of the blocks of the selected districts are to be identified by the State Government as the most backward blocks for the purpose of JPRGY. Each selected district will have at least one such block. For the remaining number of blocks, the State Government will decide how many and which blocks will be selected for which District on the basis of SC/ST population, backwardness and migration.

Each of the UTs will be requested to identify its most backward block for the purpose of the JPRGY.

Wage Employment under the JPRGY

Guarantee

Maharashtra Model cannot be adopted 100 per cent for the JPRGY as legal wage employment guarantee means a huge fund which most of the State Governments can ill-afford. Secondly, as against the whole of the State covered by Maharashtra Model, focus under the JPRGY will be only on the selected most distressed Districts of the State. So far as wage employment is concerned, the JPRGY will be open to all in the Districts who are in need of wage employment and desire to do manual and unskilled work anywhere in the Block. Work will be provided within 15 days of the demand and up to 100 days in a financial year.

Works

The basic idea is that the works meant for wage employment should lead to area improvement, increase in productivity and sustainable employment.

Works to be taken up in the rural areas will be limited to the ones mentioned below in the given priority:

(i) Watershed Development and Development of Water Resources,

(ii) Land Development,

(iii) Horticulture,

(iv) Afforestation,

(v) Road Works,

(vi) Flood Control Measures, and

(vii) Wasteland Development and Agro Forestry.

In the urban areas, they will be limited to basic infrastructure in slums.

Project Approach

In the rural areas, works will be taken up in project mode and the block will be the unit for planning. In the urban areas the slum can be the unit for planning.

Implementation of the Project

The project will be implemented departmentally by the implementing agency which includes NGOs.

Self-Employment under the JPRGY

Guarantee

Those who are unemployed and desirous of self-employment will be provided training, help in project making and financing. Help will also be provided for social mobilisation.

Approach

To supplement efforts of providing wage employment guarantee under the Jai Prakash Rozgar Guarantee Yojana (JPRGY), the Scheme would have a component of Self-employment with a focus on Self Help Groups (SHG) and micro-finance; however, existing channels of institutional finance will be further tapped for implementing under the existing schemes e.g. REGP, PMRY more rigorously.

SHG Route

Most of the backward districts have high level of illiteracy and, as a consequence, lack of awareness and entrepreneurial skill. Therefore, it is envisaged that under the self-employment component, emphasis would be on organising poor families BPL into SHGs, through the process of social mobilisation, their training and capacity building leading to social and economic empowerment. The entry point for the SHG would be thrift. The SHG members would be trained in the concept of self help, conducting group meetings, financial transaction and management of their corpus, conflict resolutions, maintenance of records, skill and entrepreneurship development. For social mobilisation of people the role and capacity of facilitators is very critical. Therefore, besides utilising the services of government department, there would be a provision for involvement of NGOs as facilitators for formation, development and training of SHGs. In areas which do not have presence of good reputed NGOs, the implementing agencies may be permitted to utilise the services of individuals having experience and training in community organisation as Animators/ Community Coordinators. The cost of social mobilisation will be met under the scheme with a maximum permissible amount of Rs. 10,000 per SHG over a period of time (2-3 years) till the SHGs become mature, self-reliant and capable of managing their own affairs. The selection process and mode of payment to NGOs/Animators/ Community Coordinators as facilitator would be same as is done under SGSY.

Individual/Group Entrepreneurs Route

Besides social mobilisation, formation and training of SHGs, the Scheme would have other components, which could supplement the efforts under the on-going self-employment programmes i.e. SGSY, PMRY, REGY etc. These components could be:

- Cost of group formation, wherever possible, and the cost of development including skill development and entrepreneurship training.
- Technical assistance for identification of viable activity, project preparation and financial scrutiny of project: It has been observed in the past that one of the reasons for lack of expected/desired impact of various self employment programme has been the inability to prepare a viable project report which could stand scrutiny of banks/other financial institutions. The Line Departments and development functionaries are not trained for this. Therefore, under this Scheme, there should be a provision to engage experts/ professionals who could assist in identification of viable activity with proper backward and forward linkage and preparation of project report including inputs required for marketing of products. Operational modalities will be worked out by implementing Departments/Ministry etc.
- Once the group is identified and selected for income generating activities/micro enterprise development under the ongoing Self Employment Programmes, the additional expenditure required for imparting skill development training which would include cost of raw materials required for training, boarding and lodging for trainees, honorarium to master craftsmen/master trainer, any other contingency/miscellaneous expenditure would not exceed Rs. 5,000 per trainee. For groups/

individual selected under other Self Employment Programmes (Rural Employment Generation Programme of KVIC, PMRY etc.) the norms for skill development training as prescribed in the respective scheme will be applicable under JPRGY and the required expenditure could be incurred under the Scheme. The assessment regarding technical skills may be made by Line Departments while that of managerial skills may be made by the Bank. Government institutions like engineering colleges/ polytechnics, universities, master craftsmen and NGOs could be utilised for imparting skill development training. The facilities available with private sector industrial units having adequate facilities could also be used for imparting training.

Infrastructure Development

The fund could be utilised for meeting critical gaps in infrastructure related to production, processing, design development, packaging, value addition and diversification projects, marketing infrastructure, etc. for which funds are not available under other programmes. The infrastructure facilities should enable the assisted families in getting sustainable income from their assets. The proposals should emerge out of the specific activities being taken up by the beneficiaries and the location decision should be made by Line Departments/DRDAs, in consultation with bankers and beneficiaries.

Micro-Finance

SHGs organised under the Scheme would be subjected to grading test/evaluation to judge its viability/sustainability as well as credit worthiness. On successful passing of the grading, groups may be assisted with Revolving Fund of Rs. 25,000 to be sanctioned as cash credit by banks, in which Rs. 10,000 would be subsidy component by DRDAs. This would supplement the corpus available with SHGs and could be used for internal loaning to their members for consumption as well as production purpose. The SHGs could also be linked with bank for credit under the NABARD-SHG bank linkage programme.

- SHGs formed under the scheme may be assisted for income generating activities/micro-enterprise development under the ongoing other programmes of self-employment on priority basis as these groups have been already trained. Efforts should be made to involve the private corporate sectors for adopting certain areas/product and assist them in product design, value addition, production/processing technology, maintaining quality standards, developing marketing linkages etc.

- Individual BPL families who are left out and could not be organised into SHG may be identified and assisted for taking up income generating activities under the ongoing self-employment programme.

Operationalisation of the JPRGY

Collector's Role

Overall responsibility of coordination, monitoring and supervision will be of the Collector.

Committee

A committee will be set up to implement project at the district level under the chairmanship of the District Collector. The committee will have maximum number of 10 members and CEO/Project Director as Member Secretary. Half of the members will be drawn from *Zilla Panchayats* and *Panchayat Samitis*, preferably by the members representing project area. Adequate representation will be given to SCs/STs, minorities, NGOs, women organisations.

At the State level, the committee will have Members from the Rural Development Department as well as from the Department of Local Bodies. Development Commissioner will be the Chairman of the committee with Secretary, Rural Development as Member Secretary.

Overall responsibility of the implementation of this Scheme in the rural areas will be of the Ministry of Rural Development and in the urban areas of the Department of Urban Employment and Poverty Alleviation.

The Task Force on the JPRGY will review the implementation of the scheme from time to time.

Perspective Plan

A perspective plan has to be prepared for each selected block on the basis of socio-techno economic survey to be conducted to assess the intensity of unemployment and infrastructure needs on the basis of activity mapping. For this purpose, experts, consultants or institutions from within the State may be engaged and financial provisions for the same may be made.

Project Preparation

Each district will prepare area specific micro-projects to be completed within a maximum period of three years giving details of activities to be taken up, estimated cost of each of the activities and duration of the completion of each activity, alongwith the number of mandays to be generated/number of persons to be employed under each activity. While preparing the project, care will be taken for mobilisation of resources within the project area to sustain the developmental activities/infrastructure created under the project after completion of the project.

Approval of Perspective Plan and Projects

Approval of the Perspective Plan will be at the State level with representatives from the Centre.

Approval of each micro project will be at the district level by the committee set up under the scheme. If necessary, the executing agency will be requested to make a presentation before approval.

Funding Pattern

The programme will be implemented as a centrally sponsored scheme on cost sharing basis between the Centre and the State in the ratio of 80:20 of the cash component. In case of the UTs, the Centre would provide entire (100 per cent) funds under the scheme. Foodgrains will be provided to the States/UTs free of cost.

Allocation of Resources

For wage employment, resources will be provided both in cash and kind. For self-employment it will only be in cash. Sharing of resources for wage employment and of fund for self-employment between the rural areas and the urban areas will be in the ratio of 90:10.

Wages

For wage employment, minimum wages fixed by the State authority shall be paid under the JPRGY both for skilled and unskilled labour. Equal wages shall be paid under the programme to both men and women workers.

Annexures

ANNEXURE I A

Growth of Employment in Rural Areas as per Weekly Status

A. 50th Round (as on 1-1-1994)

Activity	*Numbers (in '000s)*		
	Male	*Female*	*Total*
Employed	180275	85260	265535
Unemployed	5432	2555	7987
Unemployment Rate	(2.93)	(2.91)	(2.92)
Labour Force (LF)	185707	87815	273522
Not in LF	153794	231511	385305
TOTAL	**339501**	**319326**	**658827**

B. 55th Round (as on 1-1-2000)

Activity	*Numbers (in '000s)*			*AAGR* (50th Rd. to 55th Rd.)*		
	Male	*Female*	*Total*	*Male*	*Female*	*Total*
Employed	190755	89427	280183	0.95	0.80	0.90
Unemployed	7855	3535	11389	6.34	5.56	6.09
Unemployment Rate	(3.95)	(3.80)	(3.91)			
Labour Force (LF)	198610	92962	291572	1.13	0.95	1.07
Not in LF	175420	260506	435926	2.22	1.99	2.08
TOTAL	**374030**	**353468**	**727498**	**1.63**	**1.71**	**1.67**

C. 56th Round (as on 1-1-2001)

Activity	*Numbers (in '000s)*			*AAGR* (55th Rd. to 56th Rd.)*		
	Male	*Female*	*Total*	*Male*	*Female*	*Total*
Employed	199561	78012	277574	4.62	-12.76	-0.93
Unemployed	4561	1438	5999	-41.93	-59.32	-47.32
Unemployment Rate	(2.23)	(1.81)	(2.12)			
Labour Force (LF)	204123	79450	283573	2.78	-14.53	-2.74
Not in LF	175994	280053	456047	0.33	7.5	4.62
TOTAL	**380117**	**359503**	**739620**	**1.63**	**1.71**	**1.67**

D. 57th Round (as on 1-1-2002)

Activity	*Numbers (in '000s)*			*AAGR* (56th Rd. to 57th Rd.)*		
	Male	*Female*	*Total*	*Male*	*Female*	*Total*
Employed	202036	88120	290156	1.24	12.96	4.53
Unemployed	5408	2559	7968	18.56	77.99	32.81
Unemployment Rate	(2.61)	(2.82)	(2.67)			
Labour Force (LF)	207444	90679	298123	1.63	14.13	5.13
Not in LF	178858	274963	453821	1.63	-1.82	-0.49
TOTAL	**386302**	**365642**	**751944**	**1.63**	**1.71**	**1.67**

E. 58th Round (as on 1-10-2002)

Activity	*Numbers (in '000s)*			*AAGR* (57th Rd. to 58th Rd.)*			*AAGR* (55th Rd. to 58th Rd.)*		
	Male	*Female*	*Total*	*Male*	*Female*	*Total*	*Male*	*Female*	*Total*
Employed	206843	81099	287942	3.19	-10.48	-1.02	2.99	-3.49	1
Unemployed	5865	1481	7346	11.42	-51.77	-10.26	-10.08	-27.11	-14.74
Unemployment Rate	(2.75)	(1.79)	(2.48)						
Labour Force (LF)	213099	82580	295679	3.65	-11.73	-1.09	2.59	-4.21	0.51
Not in LF	177909	287734	465643	-0.71	6.24	3.49	0.51	3.68	2.43
TOTAL	**391008**	**370314**	**761322**	**1.63**	**1.71**	**1.67**	**1.63**	**1.71**	**1.67**

Note: * AAGR stands for average annual growth rate.
Due to rounding off the figures, total may not necessarily tally.

Source: NSSO.

ANNEXURE I B

Growth of Youth Employment in Rural Areas as per Weekly Status

A. 50th Round (as on 1-1-1994)

Activity	*Numbers (in '000s)*		
	Male	*Female*	*Total*
Employed	64330	30093	94423
Unemployed	3953	1506	5459
Unemployment Rate	(5.79)	(4.77)	(5.47)
Labour Force (LF)	68283	31599	99882
Not in LF	19137	53366	72503
Total	**87420**	**84965**	**172385**

B. 55th Round (as on 1-1-2000)

Activity	*Numbers (in '000s)*			*AAGR* (50th Rd. to 55th Rd.)*		
	Male	*Female*	*Total*	*Male*	*Female*	*Total*
Employed	65923	29801	95724	0.41	-0.16	0.23
Unemployed	5228	2167	7395	4.77	6.25	5.19
Unemployment Rate	(7.35)	(6.79)	(7.17)			
Labour Force (LF)	71151	31937	103088	0.69	0.18	0.53
Not in LF	22473	59310	81783	2.71	1.78	2.03
TOTAL	**93625**	**91246**	**184871**	**1.15**	**1.20**	**1.18**

C. 56th Round (as on 1-1-2001)

Activity	*Numbers (in '000s)*			*AAGR*(55th Rd. to 56th Rd.)*		
	Male	*Female*	*Total*	*Male*	*Female*	*Total*
Employed	69788	25346	95134	5.86	-14.95	-0.62
Unemployed	3496	593	4089	-33.13	-72.62	-44.71
Unemployment Rate	(4.77)	(2.29)	(4.12)			
Labour Force (LF)	73282	25909	99191	3.00	-18.87	-3.78
Not in LF	23988	67734	91722	6.74	14.20	12.15
TOTAL	**97270**	**93643**	**190913**	**3.89**	**2.63**	**3.27**

D. 57th Round (as on 1-1-2002)

Activity	*Numbers (in '000s)*			*AAGR*(56th Rd. to 57th Rd.)*		
	Male	*Female*	*Total*	*Male*	*Female*	*Total*
Employed	70010	30593	100603	0.32	20.70	5.75
Unemployed	3822	1544	5366	9.33	160.20	31.23
Unemployment Rate	(5.18)	(4.81)	(5.07)			
Labour Force (LF)	73832	32102	105934	0.75	23.90	6.80
Not in LF	22215	67802	90017	-7.39	0.10	-1.86
TOTAL	**96047**	**99903**	**195950**	**-1.26**	**6.69**	**2.64**

E. 58th Round (as on 1-10-2002)

Activity	*Numbers (in '000s)*			*AAGR* (57th Rd. to 58th Rd.)*			*AAGR* (55th Rd. to 58th Rd.)*		
	Male	*Female*	*Total*	*Male*	*Female*	*Total*	*Male*	*Female*	*Total*
Employed	71166	23829	94995	2.21	-28.34	-7.36	2.82	-7.81	-0.28
Unemployed	4218	659	4877	14.05	-67.85	-11.96	-7.51	-35.13	-14.05
Unemployment Rate	(5.59)	(2.69)	(4.88)						
Labour Force (LF)	75425	24488	99913	2.89	-30.30	-7.51	2.14	-9.21	-1.13
Not in LF	25455	69572	95027	19.90	3.50	7.49	4.63	5.97	5.61
TOTAL	**100880**	**94060**	**194940**	**6.76**	**-7.72**	**-0.69**	**2.75**	**1.11**	**1.95**

Note: * AAGR stands for average annual growth rate.
Due to rounding off the figures, total may not necessarily tally.

Source: NSSO.

ANNEXURE II A

Growth of Employment in Urban Areas as per Weekly Status

A. 50th Round (as on 1-1-1994)

Activity	*Numbers (in '000s)*		
	Male	*Female*	*Total*
Employed	63340	15433	78773
Unemployed	3471	1443	4914
Unemployment Rate	(5.20)	(8.55)	(5.87)
Labour Force (LF)	66811	16876	83687
Not in LF	57142	94150	151292
TOTAL	**123953**	**111026**	**234979**

B. 55th Round (as on 1-1-2000)

Activity	*Numbers (in '000s)*			*AAGR* (50th Rd. to 55th Rd.)*		
	Male	*Female*	*Total*	*Male*	*Female*	*Total*
Employed	74072	16761	90834	2.64	1.39	2.40
Unemployed	4366	1309	5675	3.90	-1.61	2.43
Unemployment Rate	(5.57)	(7.24)	(5.88)			
Labour Force (LF)	78438	18071	96509	2.71	1.15	2.40
Not in LF	67087	112877	179964	2.71	3.07	2.93
TOTAL	**145525**	**130948**	**276473**	**2.71**	**2.79**	**2.75**

C. 56th Round (as on 1-1-2001)

Activity	*Numbers (in '000s)*			*AAGR*(55th Rd. to 56th Rd.)*		
	Male	*Female*	*Total*	*Male*	*Female*	*Total*
Employed	77574	15748	93323	4.73	-6.04	2.74
Unemployed	3886	673	4559	-10.98	-48.61	-19.67
Unemployment Rate	(4.77)	(4.13)	(4.66)			
Labour Force (LF)	81461	16287	97747	3.85	-9.87	1.28
Not in LF	68008	118313	186322	1.37	4.82	3.53
TOTAL	**149469**	**134600**	**284069**	**2.71**	**2.79**	**2.75**

D. 57th Round (as on 1-1-2002)

Activity	*Numbers (in '000s)*			*AAGR*(56th Rd. to 57th Rd.)*		
	Male	*Female*	*Total*	*Male*	*Female*	*Total*
Employed	83207	15357	98565	7.26	-2.48	5.62
Unemployed	3991	830	4822	2.71	23.35	5.76
Unemployment Rate	(4.57)	(5.13)	(4.66)			
Labour Force (LF)	87352	16187	103540	7.23	-0.61	5.93
Not in LF	66167	122167	188333	-2.71	3.26	1.08
TOTAL	**153519**	**138354**	**291873**	**2.71**	**2.79**	**2.75**

E. 58th Round (as on 1-10-2002)

Activity	*Numbers (in '000s)*			*AAGR* (57th Rd. to 58th Rd.)*			*AAGR* (55th Rd. to 58th Rd.)*		
	Male	*Female*	*Total*	*Male*	*Female*	*Total*	*Male*	*Female*	*Total*
Employed	81917	16666	98583	-2.06	11.52	0.02	3.73	-0.21	3.02
Unemployed	4855	989	5844	29.86	26.24	29.23	3.94	-9.71	1.07
Unemployment Rate	(5.60)	(5.60)	(5.60)						
Labour Force (LF)	86772	17655	104427	-0.88	12.27	1.14	3.74	-0.84	2.91
Not in LF	69857	123583	193440	7.5	1.55	3.63	1.48	3.35	2.66
TOTAL	**156629**	**141238**	**297867**	**2.71**	**2.79**	**2.75**	**2.71**	**2.79**	**2.75**

Note: * AAGR stands for average annual growth rate.
Due to rounding off the figures, total may not necessarily tally.

Source: NSSO.

ANNEXURE II B

Growth of Youth Employment in Urban Areas as per Weekly Status

A. 50th Round (as on 1-1-1994)

Activity	*Numbers (in '000s)*		
	Male	*Female*	*Total*
Employed	21721	4932	26653
Unemployed	2796	1117	3913
Unemployment Rate	(11.40)	(18.46)	(12.80)
Labour Force (LF)	24516	6050	30566
Not in LF	11679	26224	37903
TOTAL	**36195**	**32297**	**68492**

B. 55th Round (as on 1-1-2000)

Activity	*Numbers (in '000s)*			*AAGR* (50th Rd. to 55th Rd.)*		
	Male	*Female*	*Total*	*Male*	*Female*	*Total*
Employed	24573	5065	29638	2.08	0.44	1.79
Unemployed	3470	1005	4475	3.66	-1.75	2.26
Unemployment Rate	(12.38)	(16.56)	(13.12)			
Labour Force (LF)	28029	6070	34099	2.26	0.06	1.84
Not in LF	14337	31467	45804	3.48	3.08	3.21
TOTAL	**42366**	**37538**	**79904**	**2.66**	**2.54**	**2.60**

C. 56th Round (as on 1-1-2001)

Activity	*Numbers (in '000s)*			*AAGR*(55th Rd. to 56th Rd.)*		
	Male	*Female*	*Total*	*Male*	*Female*	*Total*
Employed	26079	4759	30838	6.13	-6.05	4.05
Unemployed	3104	544	3648	-10.55	-45.89	-18.48
Unemployment Rate	(10.64)	(10.26)	(10.58)			
Labour Force (LF)	29166	5302	34468	4.06	-12.66	1.08
Not in LF	15862	33886	49748	10.64	7.69	8.61
TOTAL	**45028**	**39188**	**84216**	**6.28**	**4.40**	**5.40**

D. 57th Round (as on 1-1-2002)

Activity	*Numbers (in '000s)*			*AAGR*(56th Rd. to 57th Rd.)*		
	Male	*Female*	*Total*	*Male*	*Female*	*Total*
Employed	29687	4576	34263	13.83	-3.83	11.11
Unemployed	3206	696	3902	3.28	27.96	6.96
Unemployment Rate	9.75	13.20	10.23			
Labour Force (LF)	32876	5272	38148	12.72	-0.56	10.68
Not in LF	14676	35477	50153	-7.48	4.70	0.81
TOTAL	**47553**	**40750**	**88303**	**5.61**	**3.99**	**4.85**

E. 58th Round (as on 1-10-2002)

Activity	*Numbers (in '000s)*			*AAGR* (57th Rd. to 58th Rd.)*			*AAGR* (55th Rd. to 58th Rd.)*		
	Male	*Female*	*Total*	*Male*	*Female*	*Total*	*Male*	*Female*	*Total*
Employed	29085	5290	34375	-2.70	21.33	0.44	6.32	1.59	5.54
Unemployed	3805	848	4653	25.68	30.19	26.45	3.41	-5.99	1.43
Unemployment Rate	11.57	13.85	11.93						
Labour Force (LF)	32890	6124	39014	0.05	22.10	3.04	5.99	0.32	5.02
Not in LF	15039	35400	50439	3.31	-0.29	0.76	1.75	4.38	3.57
TOTAL	**47928**	**41524**	**89452**	**1.05**	**2.54**	**1.74**	**4.59**	**3.74**	**4.19**

Note: * AAGR stands for average annual growth rate.
Due to rounding off the figures, total may not necessarily tally.

Source: NSSO.

ANNEXURE III A

Growth of Employment in India (Rural and Urban Combined) as per Weekly Status

A. 50th Round (as on 1-1-1994)

Activity	*Numbers (in '000s)*		
	Male	*Female*	*Total*
Employed	243615	100693	344308
Unemployed	8903	3998	12901
Unemployment Rate	(3.53)	(3.82)	(3.61)
Labour Force (LF)	252518	104691	357209
Not in LF	210936	325661	536597
TOTAL	**463454**	**430352**	**893806**

B. 55th Round (as on 1-1-2000)

Activity	*Numbers (in '000s)*			*AAGR* (50th Rd. to 55th Rd.)*		
	Male	*Female*	*Total*	*Male*	*Female*	*Total*
Employed	264827	106188	371017	1.4	0.89	1.25
Unemployed	12221	4844	17064	5.42	3.25	4.77
Unemployment Rate	(4.41)	(4.36)	(4.40)			
Labour Force (LF)	277048	111033	388081	1.56	0.99	1.39
Not in LF	242507	373383	615890	2.35	2.31	2.32
TOTAL	**519555**	**484416**	**1003971**	**1.92**	**1.99**	**1.96**

C. 56th Round (as on 1-1-2001)

Activity	*Numbers (in '000s)*			*AAGR*(55th Rd. to 56th Rd.)*		
	Male	*Female*	*Total*	*Male*	*Female*	*Total*
Employed	277135	93760	370897	4.65	-11.70	-0.03
Unemployed	8447	2111	10558	-30.88	-56.42	-38.13
Unemployment Rate	(2.96)	(2.20)	(2.77)			
Labour Force (LF)	285584	95737	381320	3.08	-13.78	-1.74
Not in LF	244002	398366	642369	0.62	6.69	4.30
TOTAL	**529586**	**494103**	**1023689**	**1.93**	**2.00**	**1.96**

D. 57th Round (as on 1-1-2002)

Activity	*Numbers (in '000s)*			*AAGR*(56th Rd. to 57th Rd.)*		
	Male	*Female*	*Total*	*Male*	*Female*	*Total*
Employed	285243	103477	388721	2.93	10.36	4.81
Unemployed	9399	3389	12790	11.27	60.54	21.14
Unemployment Rate	(3.19)	(3.17)	(3.18)			
Labour Force LF)	294796	106866	401663	3.23	11.62	5.33
Not in LF	245025	397130	642154	0.42	-0.31	-0.03
TOTAL	**539821**	**503996**	**1043817**	**1.93**	**2.00**	**1.97**

E. 58th Round (as on 1-10-2002)

Activity	Numbers (in '000s)			AAGR* (57th Rd. to 58th Rd.)			AAGR* (55th Rd. to 58th Rd.)		
	Male	Female	Total	Male	Female	Total	Male	Female	Total
Employed	288760	97765	386525	1.65	-7.29	-0.75	3.2	-2.96	1.5
Unemployed	10720	2470	13190	19.17	-34.41	4.19	-4.65	-21.72	-8.94
Unemployment Rate	(3.57)	(2.46)	(3.30)						
Labour Force (LF)	299871	100235	400106	2.30	-8.19	-0.52	2.92	-3.65	1.12
Not in LF	247766	411317	659083	1.49	4.79	3.53	0.78	3.58	2.5
TOTAL	**547637**	**511552**	**1059189**	**1.94**	**2.00**	**1.97**	**1.93**	**2**	**1.97**

Note: * AAGR stands for average annual growth rate.
Due to rounding off the figures, total may not necessarily tally.

Source: NSSO.

ANNEXURE III B

Growth of Youth Employment in India
(Rural and Urban Combined) as per Weekly Status

A. 50th Round (as on 1-1-1994)

Activity	Numbers (in '000s)		
	Male	Female	Total
Employed	86051	35025	121076
Unemployed	6749	2623	9372
Unemployment Rate	(7.27)	(6.97)	(7.18)
Labour Force (LF)	92799	37649	130448
Not in LF	30816	79590	110406
TOTAL	**123615**	**117234**	**240849**

B. 55th Round (as on 1-1-2000)

Activity	Numbers (in '000s)			AAGR* (50th Rd. to 55th Rd.)		
	Male	Female	Total	Male	Female	Total
Employed	90496	34866	125362	0.84	-0.08	0.58
Unemployed	8698	3172	11870	4.32	3.22	4.02
Unemployment Rate	(8.77)	(8.35)	(8.65)			
Labour Force (LF)	99180	38007	137187	1.11	0.16	0.84
Not in LF	36810	90777	127587	3.01	2.22	2.44
TOTAL	**135991**	**128784**	**264775**	**1.6**	**1.58**	**1.59**

C. 56th Round (as on 1-1-2001)

Activity	Numbers (in '000s)			AAGR*(55th Rd. to 56th Rd.)		
	Male	Female	Total	Male	Female	Total
Employed	95867	30105	125972	5.94	-13.66	0.49
Unemployed	6600	1137	7737	-24.12	-64.16	-34.82
Unemployment Rate	(6.44)	(3.64)	(5.79)			
Labour Force (LF)	102448	31211	133659	3.30	-17.88	-2.57
Not in LF	39850	101620	141470	8.26	11.94	10.88
TOTAL	**142298**	**132831**	**275129**	**4.64**	**3.14**	**3.91**

D. 57th Round (as on 1-1-2002)

Activity	Numbers (in '000s)			AAGR*(56th Rd. to 57th Rd.)		
	Male	Female	Total	Male	Female	Total
Employed	99697	35169	134866	4.00	16.82	7.06
Unemployed	7028	2240	9268	6.48	97.01	19.79
Unemployment Rate	(6.59)	(5.99)	(6.43)			
Labour Force (LF)	106708	37374	144082	4.16	19.75	7.80
Not in LF	36891	103279	140170	-7.43	1.63	-0.92
TOTAL	**143600**	**140653**	**284253**	**0.91**	**5.89**	**3.32**

E. 58th Round (as on 1-10-2002)

Activity	Numbers (in '000s)			AAGR* (57th Rd. to 58th Rd.)			AAGR* (55th Rd. to 58th Rd.)		
	Male	Female	Total	Male	Female	Total	Male	Female	Total
Employed	100251	29119	129370	0.74	-22.25	-5.40	3.79	-6.34	1.15
Unemployed	8023	1507	9530	19.31	-41.05	3.79	-2.89	-23.71	-7.67
Unemployment Rate	(7.41)	(4.92)	(6.86)						
Labour force (LF)	108315	30612	138927	2.01	-23.36	-4.74	3.26	-7.57	0.46
Not in LF	40494	104972	145466	13.23	2.19	5.07	3.53	5.43	4.88
TOTAL	**148808**	**135584**	**284392**	**4.86**	**-4.78**	**0.07**	**3.33**	**1.89**	**2.63**

Note: * AAGR stands for average annual growth rate.
Due to rounding off the figures, total may not necessarily tally.

Source: NSSO.

ANNEXURE IV A

Growth of Employment in Rural Areas as per Usual Status

A. 50th Round (as on 1-1-1994)

Activity	*Numbers (in '000s)*		
	Male	*Female*	*Total*
Employed	187744	104739	292483
Unemployed	2716	958	3674
Unemployment Rate	(1.43)	(0.91)	(1.24)
Labour Force (LF)	190460	105697	296157
Not in LF	149041	213629	362670
TOTAL	**339501**	**319326**	**658827**

B. 55th Round (as on 1-1-2000)

Activity	*Numbers (in '000s)*			*AAGR* (50th Rd. to 55th Rd.)*		
	Male	*Female*	*Total*	*Male*	*Female*	*Total*
Employed	198610	105687	304297	0.94	0.15	0.66
Unemployed	3366	1060	4427	3.64	1.70	3.16
Unemployment Rate	(1.67)	(0.99)	(1.43)			
Labour Force (LF)	201976	106747	308724	0.98	0.16	0.70
Not in LF	172054	246721	418774	2.42	2.43	2.43
TOTAL	**374030**	**353468**	**727498**	**1.63**	**1.71**	**1.67**

C. 56th Round (as on 1-1-2001)

Activity	*Numbers (in '000s)*			*AAGR*(55th Rd. to 56th Rd.)*		
	Male	*Female*	*Total*	*Male*	*Female*	*Total*
Employed	206784	103177	309961	4.12	-2.37	1.86
Unemployed	3041	360	3400	-9.66	-66.1	-23.18
Unemployment Rate	(1.45)	(0.35)	(1.09)			
Labour Force (LF)	209444	103537	312981	3.7	-3.01	1.38
Not in LF	170673	255966	426639	-0.8	3.75	1.88
TOTAL	**380117**	**359503**	**739620**	**1.63**	**1.71**	**1.67**

D. 57th Round (as on 1-1-2002)

Activity	Numbers (in '000s)			AAGR*(56th Rd. to 57th Rd.)		
	Male	Female	Total	Male	Female	Total
Employed	210921	114812	325732	2	11.28	5.09
Unemployed	2318	1828	4146	-23.78	408.54	21.93
Unemployment Rate	(1.09)	(1.57)	(1.26)			
Labour Force (LF)	213239	116640	329879	1.81	12.66	5.4
Not in LF	173063	249002	422065	1.4	-2.72	-1.07
TOTAL	**386302**	**365642**	**751944**	**1.63**	**1.71**	**1.67**

E. 58th Round (as on 1-10-2002)

Activity	Numbers (in '000s)			AAGR* (57th Rd. to 58th Rd.)			AAGR* (55th Rd. to 58th Rd.)		
	Male	Female	Total	Male	Female	Total	Male	Female	Total
Employed	213490	104058	317549	1.63	-12.29	-3.34	2.66	-0.56	1.56
Unemployed	3128	741	3869	49.14	-70.02	-8.82	-2.63	-12.24	-4.78
Unemployment Rate	(1.44)	(0.71)	(1.20)						
Labour Force (LF)	217009	104799	321808	2.36	-13.3	-3.25	2.64	-0.67	1.52
Not in LF	173999	265515	439514	0.72	8.94	5.55	0.41	2.41	1.77
TOTAL	**391008**	**370314**	**761322**	**1.63**	**1.71**	**1.67**	**1.63**	**1.71**	**1.67**

Note: * AAGR stands for average annual growth rate.
Due to rounding off the figures, total may not necessarily tally.

Source: NSSO.

ANNEXURE IV B

Growth of Youth Employment in Rural Areas as per Usual Status

A. 50th Round (as on 1-1-1994)

Activity	Numbers (in '000s)		
	Male	Female	Total
Employed	67746	37975	105721
Unemployed	2483	714	3197
Unemployment Rate	(3.54)	(1.85)	(2.94)
Labour Force (LF)	70236	38690	108926
Not in LF	17184	46247	63431
TOTAL	**87419.9**	**84936.5**	**172356.4**

B. 55th Round (as on 1-1-2000)

Activity	Numbers (in '000s)			AAGR*(50th Rd. to 55th Rd.)		
	Male	Female	Total	Male	Female	Total
Employed	69392	36466	105858	0.40	-0.67	0.02
Unemployed	3091	1006	4097	3.72	5.88	4.22
Unemployment Rate	(4.27)	(2.68)	(3.73)			
Labour Force (LF)	72454	37474	109928	0.52	-0.53	0.15
Not in LF	21170	53773	74943	3.54	2.54	2.82
TOTAL	**93625**	**91246**	**184871**	**1.15**	**1.20**	**1.18**

C. 56th Round (as on 1-1-2001)

Activity	Numbers (in '000s)			AAGR*(55th Rd. to 56th Rd.)		
	Male	Female	Total	Male	Female	Total
Employed	72935	33057	105992	5.11	-9.35	0.13
Unemployed	2628	375	3003	-14.99	-62.77	-26.70
Unemployment Rate	(3.48)	(1.06)	(2.71)			
Labour Force (LF)	75563	35264	110827	4.29	-5.9	0.82
Not in LF	21707	58378	80085	2.54	8.57	6.86
TOTAL	**97270**	**93643**	**190913**	**3.89**	**2.63**	**3.27**

D. 57th Round (as on 1-1-2002)

Activity	Numbers (in '000s)			AAGR*(56th Rd. to 57th Rd.)		
	Male	Female	Total	Male	Female	Total
Employed	74316	39697	114013	1.89	20.09	7.57
Unemployed	1985	1569	3554	-24.48	318.98	18.35
Unemployment Rate	(2.60)	(3.80)	(3.02)			
Labour Force (LF)	76301	41267	117568	0.98	17.02	6.08
Not in LF	19746	58637	78383	-9.03	0.44	-2.13
TOTAL	**96047**	**99903**	**195950**	**-1.26**	**6.69**	**2.64**

E. 58th Round (as on 1-10-2002)

Activity	Numbers (in '000s)			AAGR* (57th Rd. to 58th Rd.)			AAGR* (55th Rd. to 58th Rd.)		
	Male	Female	Total	Male	Female	Total	Male	Female	Total
Employed	74188	31558	105746	-0.23	-26.36	-9.55	2.46	-5.12	-0.04
Unemployed	2787	535	3322	57.25	-76.21	-8.61	-3.7	-20.54	-7.34
Unemployment Rate	(3.62)	(1.67)	(3.05)						
Labour Force (LF)	76975	32060	109035	1.18	-28.58	-9.56	2.23	-5.52	-0.30
Not in LF	23583	62373	85956	26.71	8.59	13.09	4	5.54	5.11
TOTAL	**100558**	**94433**	**194991**	**6.31**	**-7.23**	**-0.65**	**2.63**	**1.26**	**1.96**

Note: * AAGR stands for average annual growth rate.
Due to rounding off the figures, total may not necessarily tally.

Source: NSSO.

ANNEXURE V A

Growth of Employment in Urban Areas as per Usual Status

A. 50th Round (as on 1-1-1994)

Activity	Numbers (in '000s)		
	Male	Female	Total
Employed	64456	17209	81665
Unemployed	2727	1110	3837
Unemployment Rate	(4.06)	(6.06)	(4.49)
Labour Force (LF)	67183	18319	85502
Not in LF	56771	92818	149588
TOTAL	**123953**	**111026**	**234979**

B. 55th Round (as on 1-1-2000)

Activity	Numbers (in '000s)			AAGR*(50th Rd. to 55th Rd.)		
	Male	Female	Total	Male	Female	Total
Employed	75382	18202	93584	2.64	0.94	2.30
Unemployed	3493	1048	4540	4.21	-0.96	2.84
Unemployment Rate	(4.43)	(5.44)	(4.63)			
Labour Force (LF)	78875	19249	98124	2.71	0.83	2.32
Not in LF	66650	111699	178349	2.71	3.13	2.97
TOTAL	**145525**	**130948**	**276473**	**2.71**	**2.79**	**2.75**

C. 56th Round (as on 1-1-2001)

Activity	*Numbers (in '000s)*			*AAGR*(55th Rd. to 56th Rd.)*		
	Male	*Female*	*Total*	*Male*	*Female*	*Total*
Employed	79368	18844	98212	5.29	3.53	4.95
Unemployed	3288	538	3827	-5.85	-48.61	-15.71
Unemployment Rate	3.98	2.78	3.75			
Labour Force (LF)	82656	19382	102039	4.79	0.69	3.99
Not in LF	66813	115218	182030	0.24	3.15	2.06
TOTAL	**149469**	**134600**	**284069**	**2.71**	**2.79**	**2.75**

D. 57th Round (as on 1-1-2002)

Activity	*Numbers (in '000s)*			*AAGR*(56th Rd. to 57th Rd.)*		
	Male	*Female*	*Total*	*Male*	*Female*	*Total*
Employed	84896	19231	104127	6.96	2.05	6.02
Unemployed	3377	692	4069	2.71	28.49	6.34
Unemployment Rate	(3.83)	(3.47)	(3.76)			
Labour Force (LF)	88273	19923	108196	6.8	2.79	6.03
Not in LF	65246	118431	183677	-2.35	2.79	0.9
TOTAL	**153519**	**138354**	**291873**	**2.71**	**2.79**	**2.75**

E. 58th Round (as on 1-10-2002)

Activity	*Numbers (in '000s)*			*AAGR* (57th Rd. to 58th Rd.)*			*AAGR* (55th Rd. to 58th Rd.)*		
	Male	*Female*	*Total*	*Male*	*Female*	*Total*	*Male*	*Female*	*Total*
Employed	83640	19773	103413	-1.97	3.78	-0.91	3.85	3.06	3.7
Unemployed	3916	989	4904	21.8	60.98	28.26	4.25	-2.08	2.85
Unemployment Rate	4.47	4.76	4.53						
Labour Force (LF)	87556	20762	108318	-1.08	5.65	0.15	3.87	2.79	3.66
Not in LF	69073	120476	189549	7.9	2.31	4.29	1.31	2.79	2.24
TOTAL	**156629**	**141238**	**297867**	**2.71**	**2.79**	**2.75**	**2.71**	**2.79**	**2.75**

Note: * AAGR stands for average annual growth rate.
Due to rounding off the figures, total may not necessarily tally.

Source: NSSO.

ANNEXURE V B

Growth of Youth Employment in Urban Areas as per Usual Status

A. 50th Round (as on 1-1-1994)

Activity	*Numbers (in '000s)*		
	Male	*Female*	*Total*
Employed	22382	5598	27980
Unemployed	2392	990	3382
Unemployment Rate	(9.66)	(15.03)	(10.78)
Labour Force (LF)	24773	6587	31360
Not in LF	11422	25710	37132
TOTAL	**36195**	**32297**	**68492**

B. 55th Round (as on 1-1-2000)

Activity	*Numbers (in '000s)*			*AAGR* (50th Rd. to 55th Rd.)*		
	Male	*Female*	*Total*	*Male*	*Female*	*Total*
Employed	25135	5610	30745	1.95	0.04	1.58
Unemployed	3028	906	3934	4.01	-1.47	2.55
Unemployment Rate	(10.75)	(13.93)	(11.35)			
Labour Force (LF)	28163	6504	34667	2.16	-0.21	1.68
Not in LF	14203	31033	45236	3.70	3.19	3.34
TOTAL	**42366**	**37538**	**79904**	**2.66**	**2.54**	**2.60**

C. 56th Round (as on 1-1-2001)

Activity	*Numbers (in '000s)*			*AAGR*(55th Rd. to 56th Rd.)*		
	Male	*Female*	*Total*	*Male*	*Female*	*Total*
Employed	26851	5685	32536	6.83	1.34	5.83
Unemployed	2742	517	3259	-9.44	-42.95	-17.16
Unemployment Rate	(9.27)	(8.30)	(9.10)			
Labour Force (LF)	29593	6229	35822	5.08	-4.23	3.33
Not in LF	15436	32959	48395	8.68	6.2	6.98
TOTAL	**45028**	**39188**	**84216**	**6.28**	**4.4**	**5.40**

D. 57th Round (as on 1-1-2002)

Activity	Numbers (in '000s)			AAGR*(56th Rd. to 57th Rd.)		
	Male	Female	Total	Male	Female	Total
Employed	30292	5541	35833	12.82	-2.54	10.13
Unemployed	3000	693	3693	9.41	34	13.32
Unemployment Rate	(9.01)	(11.14)	(9.35)			
Labour Force (LF)	33296	6219	39515	12.51	-0.16	10.31
Not in LF	14256	34530	48786	-7.64	4.77	0.81
TOTAL	**47553**	**40750**	**88303**	**5.61**	**3.99**	**4.85**

E. 58th Round (as on 1-10-2002)

Activity	Numbers (in '000s)			AAGR* (57th Rd. to 58th Rd.)			AAGR* (55th Rd. to 58th Rd.)		
	Male	Female	Total	Male	Female	Total	Male	Female	Total
Employed	29840	6636	36476	-1.98	27.2	2.40	6.44	6.3	6.41
Unemployed	3309	871	4180	13.95	35.69	17.96	3.28	-1.43	2.23
Unemployment Rate	(9.98)	(11.60)	(10.28)						
Labour Force (LF)	33165	7508	40673	-0.52	28.54	3.93	6.13	5.35	5.98
Not in LF	14669	34012	48681	3.88	-2	-0.29	1.18	3.39	2.70
TOTAL	**47834**	**41520**	**89354**	**0.79**	**2.53**	**1.59**	**4.51**	**3.73**	**4.15**

Note: * AAGR stands for average annual growth rate.
Due to rounding off the figures, total may not necessarily tally.

Source: NSSO.

ANNEXURE VI A

Growth of Employment in India
(Rural and Urban Combined) as per Usual Status

A. 50th Round (as on 1-1-1994)

Activity	Numbers (in '000s)		
	Male	Female	Total
Employed	252200	121948	374148
Unemployed	5443	2068	7511
Unemployment Rate	(2.11)	(1.67)	(1.97)
Labour Force (LF)	257643	124016	381659
Not in LF	205812	306447	512258
TOTAL	**463454**	**430352**	**893806**

B. 55th Round (as on 1-1-2000)

Activity	*Numbers (in '000s)*			*AAGR* (50th Rd. to 55th Rd.)*		
	Male	*Female*	*Total*	*Male*	*Female*	*Total*
Employed	273992	123889	397881	1.39	0.26	1.03
Unemployed	6859	2108	8967	3.93	0.32	3.0
Unemployment Rate	(2.44)	(1.67)	(2.20)			
Labour Force (LF)	280851	125996	406848	1.45	0.26	1.07
Not in LF	238704	358420	597123	2.5	2.65	2.59
TOTAL	**519555**	**484416**	**1003971**	**1.92**	**1.99**	**1.96**

C. 56th Round (as on 1-1-2001)

Activity	*Numbers (in '000s)*			*AAGR*(55th Rd. to 56th Rd.)*		
	Male	*Female*	*Total*	*Male*	*Female*	*Total*
Employed	286152	122021	408173	4.44	-1.51	2.59
Unemployed	6329	898	7227	-7.73	-57.40	-19.40
Unemployment Rate	(2.17)	(0.73)	(1.74)			
Labour Force (LF)	292100	122919	415020	4.01	-2.44	2.01
Not in LF	237486	371184	608669	-0.51	3.56	1.93
TOTAL	**529586**	**494103**	**1023689**	**1.93**	**2.00**	**1.96**

D. 57th Round (as on 1-1-2002)

Activity	*Numbers (in '000s)*			*AAGR*(56th Rd. to 57th Rd.)*		
	Male	*Female*	*Total*	*Male*	*Female*	*Total*
Employed	295817	134043	429859	3.38	9.85	5.31
Unemployed	5695	2520	8215	-10.02	180.62	13.67
Unemployment Rate	(1.89)	(1.85)	(1.88)			
Labour Force (LF)	301512	136563	438075	3.22	11.10	5.56
Not in LF	238309	367433	605742	0.35	-1.01	-0.48
TOTAL	**539821**	**503996**	**1043817**	**1.93**	**2.00**	**1.97**

E. 58th Round (as on 1-10-2002)

Activity	Numbers (in '000s)			AAGR* (57th Rd. to 58th Rd.)			AAGR* (55th Rd. to 58th Rd.)		
	Male	Female	Total	Male	Female	Total	Male	Female	Total
Employed	297130	123831	420962	0.59	-10.03	-2.75	2.99	-0.02	2.07
Unemployed	7044	1730	8773	32.77	-39.44	9.16	0.97	-6.93	-0.79
Unemployment Rate	(2.31)	(1.38)	(2.04)						
Labour Force (LF)	304565	125561	430126	1.35	-10.59	-2.41	2.99	-0.13	2.04
Not in LF	243072	385991	629063	2.67	6.79	5.17	0.66	2.73	1.91
TOTAL	**547637**	**511552**	**1059189**	**1.94**	**2.00**	**1.97**	**1.93**	**2.00**	**1.97**

Note: * AAGR stands for average annual growth rate.
Due to rounding off the figures, total may not necessarily tally.

Source: NSSO.

ANNEXURE VI B

Growth of Youth Employment in All Areas (Rural and Urban Combined) as per Usual Status

A. 50th Round (as on 1-1-1994)

Activity	Numbers (in '000s)		
	Male	Female	Total
Employed	90128	43573	133701
Unemployed	4875	1704	6579
Unemployment Rate	(5.13)	(3.76)	(4.69)
Labour Force (LF)	95009	45277	140286
Not in LF	28606	71957	100563
TOTAL	**123614.9**	**117233.5**	**240848.4**

B. 55th Round (as on 1-1-2000)

Activity	Numbers (in '000s)			AAGR* (50th Rd. to 55th Rd.)		
	Male	Female	Total	Male	Female	Total
Employed	94527	42076	136603	0.8	-0.58	0.36
Unemployed	6119	1912	8031	3.86	1.94	3.38
Unemployment Rate	(6.08)	(4.35)	(5.55)			
Labour Force (LF)	100617	43978	144595	0.96	-0.48	0.51
Not in LF	35373	84806	120179	3.6	2.78	3.01
TOTAL	**135991**	**128784**	**264775**	**1.6**	**1.58**	**1.59**

C. 56th Round (as on 1-1-2001)

Activity	*Numbers (in '000s)*			*AAGR*(55th Rd. to 56th Rd.)*		
	Male	*Female*	*Total*	*Male*	*Female*	*Total*
Employed	99786	38742	138528	5.56	-7.92	1.41
Unemployed	5370	892	6262	-12.24	-53.35	-22.03
Unemployment Rate	(5.11)	(2.15)	(4.27)			
Labour Force (LF)	105156	41493	146649	4.51	-5.65	1.42
Not in LF	37143	91337	128480	5.00	7.70	6.91
TOTAL	**142298**	**132831**	**275129**	**4.64**	**3.14**	**3.91**

D. 57th Round (as on 1-1-2002)

Activity	*Numbers (in '000s)*			*AAGR*(56th Rd. to 57th Rd.)*		
	Male	*Female*	*Total*	*Male*	*Female*	*Total*
Employed	104608	45238	149846	4.83	16.77	8.17
Unemployed	4985	2262	7247	-7.17	153.59	15.73
Unemployment Rate	(4.55)	(4.76)	(4.61)			
Labour Force (LF)	109597	47486	157083	4.22	14.44	7.11
Not in LF	34002	93167	127169	-8.46	2.00	-1.02
TOTAL	**143600**	**140653**	**284253**	**0.91**	**5.89**	**3.32**

E. 58th Round (as on 1-10-2002)

Activity	*Numbers (in '000s)*			*AAGR* (57th Rd. to 58th Rd.)*			*AAGR* (55th Rd. to 58th Rd.)*		
	Male	*Female*	*Total*	*Male*	*Female*	*Total*	*Male*	*Female*	*Total*
Employed	104028	38194	142222	-0.74	-20.20	-6.73	3.54	-3.46	1.48
Unemployed	6096	1406	7502	30.77	-46.95	4.72	-0.14	-10.58	-2.45
Unemployment Rate	(5.53)	(3.55)	(5.01)						
Labour Force (LF)	110140	39568	149708	0.66	-21.59	-6.21	3.34	-3.77	1.27
Not in LF	38252	96385	134637	17.00	4.63	7.91	2.89	4.76	4.22
TOTAL	**148392**	**135953**	**284345**	**4.47**	**-4.43**	**0.04**	**3.22**	**1.99**	**2.63**

Note: * AAGR stands for average annual growth rate.
Due to rounding off the figures, total may not necessarily tally.

Source: NSSO.

ANNEXURE VII

A Note Highlighting the Salient Features of the Sample Designs of Quinquennial Surveys and Annual Surveys on Consumer Expenditure and Employment-Unemployment in the NSS

Introduction

The quinquennial surveys of the NSSO on household consumer expenditure (CE) and employment-unemployment (EU) are based on relatively large samples in the sense that a sample of 10 households (12 households in 55th round) per selected village/urban block is considered for canvassing the schedules on CE and EU. On the other hand, intervening annual surveys (sometimes such surveys are of six months' duration) consider only a sample of four households per selected village/urban block for data collection. The present note highlights the changes in the sample designs of the two types of surveys carried out during the period 1999-2004.

Surveys Conducted during 1999-2004

During the period 1999-2004, one quinquennial survey and five annual surveys have been conducted. These are:

Quinquennial Survey: NSS 55th Round (July 1999–June 2000)

Annual Survey: NSS 56th–60th Rounds

General Features of the Sample Design for the Two Types of Surveys

A stratified multistage sample design, with villages/urban blocks as the first stage units (FSU) and households as the ultimate stage units (USU), is adopted in both types of surveys. For large FSUs, a sample of segments within the FSU—known as hamlet-groups for rural and sub-blocks for urban—is considered for preparing the frame of USUs. If the survey is oriented towards collecting data on particular type of enterprises (which was the case for NSS 56th and 57th rounds), at the time of selecting hamlet-groups of sub-blocks, the one having maximum concentration of such enterprises is invariably selected for the purpose of listing i.e., for preparing frame on enterprises/households.

Changes in the Sample Design for Two Types of Surveys

Sample design is finalised keeping in view the main subjects of enquiry in any round. The frames for the selection of FSUs vary depending upon whether the survey is focused to collect data on households or enterprises. Normally for the latter cases, the Economic Census frame giving information of number of enterprises/workers at the village/block level, is used for the selection FSUs. The salient features highlighting the changes in the sample designs of NSS 55th to 60th rounds are indicated as follows.

Salient Features of the Sample Designs, NSS 55th to 60th rounds

Aspect	*55th Round (Quin, Survey on CE & EU)*	*56th Round (Unorg. Manufacture & Survey on CE/EU)*	*57th Round (Service Sector Enterprises & Survey on CE/EU)*	*58th Round (Disability, Housing, CE/EU, etc.)*	*59th Round (Land/Livestock Holdings, Survey on Farmers, CE/EU)*	*60th Round (Morbidity & Health Care, EU/CE)*
1	2	3	4	5	6	7
Sampling frame for FSUs.	Rural: List of villages as per 1991 Population census Urban: Latest list of UFS blocks.	Economic Census (ED) 1998 frame mainly used in both rural and urban.	Economic Census (EC) 1998 frame mainly used in both rural and urban.	As in 55th Round	As in 55th Round	As in 55th Round
First-stage strata (for FSU selection).	Rural: Two special strata of relatively smaller and larger villages at the State level. For rest of the villages, each district is a separate stratum. Few smaller districts merged and larger districts split into a number of strata Urban: Strata formed within each NSS Region by grouping towns according to population size classes. Each million plus city formed a separate stratum.	Rural: Sub-strata formed within each district to net adequate number of enterprises. Urban: As above but strata formed within each NSS Region. Each million plus city formed a separate stratum.	Rural/Urban: A special stratum at the State level comprising FSUs having more number of workers engaged in service sector or having at least one big service sector enterprise with a minimum of 200 workers. Remaining FSUs formed general strata. In both rural and urban, strata formed within each NSS Region. Each stratum sub-stratified to net enterprises of different industries.	As in 55th Round. However, urban strata were sub-stratified into two groups: blocks located in slum area (group 1) and rest (group 2).	As in 55th Round	As in 55th Round

Contd. ...

... *Contd.* ...

Aspect	*55th Round (Quin, Survey on CE & EU)*	*56th Round (Unorg. Manufacture & Survey on CE/EU)*	*57th Round (Service Sector Enterprises & Survey on CE/EU)*	*58th Round (Disability, Housing, CE/EU, etc.)*	*59th Round (Land/Livestock Holdings, Survey on Farmers, CE/EU)*	*60th Round (Morbidity & Health Care, EU/CE)*
1	2	3	4	5	6	7
Selection of FSUs.	Rural: Circular systematic sampling (CSS) with probability proportional to population except for stratum of smaller, villages where villages were selected by CSS with equal probability. Urban: CSS with equal probability.	Mostly by CSS with probalility proportional to number of workers as per EC'98 frame.	Mostly by CSS with probalility proportional to number of workers as per EC'98 frame.	Rural: Probability proportional to population with replacement (simple random sampling without replacement i.e., SRSWOR for special stratum of smaller villages). Urban: SRSWOR	As in 58th Round	As in 58th Round
Procedure of selection of households (within selected hamlet-groups/ sub-blocks) for Schedule 10 in quinquennial survey and schedule 1.0 in	Two second-stage strata (SSS) of households (hhs) formed-affluent hhs (SSS1) and remaining hhs (SSS2). 2 hhs from SSS1 and 10 hhs from SSS2 selected by CSS. HHs of SSS2 arranged by means of livelihood	4 hhs selected by CSS from the list of all households after arranging them by means of livelihood code.	As in 56th Round.	Rural: Households grouped into two second-stage strata (SSS): SSS1 those having pucca dwelling structure; SSS2: restUrban: Households grouped into two SSS: SSS1: those having MPCE corresponding to top 10 per cent of urban	Rural: Households grouped into two SSS:SSS1: hhs possessing land >= Y ha (where Y is the cut-off worked at the state level such that top 20 per cent hhs have land >= Y)SSS2:	Rural: Listed households grouped into two second stage strata (SSS): SSS1: hhs possessing land corresponding to bottom 80 per cent of hhs of

Contd. ...

... Contd. ...

Aspect	*55th Round (Quin, Survey on CE & EU)*	*56th Round (Unorg. Manufacture & Survey on CE/EU)*	*57th Round (Service Sector Enterprises & Survey on CE/EU)*	*58th Round (Disability, Housing, CE/EU, etc.)*	*59th Round (Land/Livestock Holdings, Survey on Farmers, CE/EU)*	*60th Round (Morbidity & Health Care, EU/CE)*
1	2	3	4	5	6	7
annual surveys for collecting data on EU.	code X land possessed (for rural)/MPCE (for urban) before sampling.			population in the State; SS2: rest (2 hhs surveyed from each SSS for both rural and urban).	rest Urban: SSS1: hhs having MPCE corresponding to bottom 90 per cent of urban population in the state; SS2: rest(2 hhs surveyed from each SSS for both rural & urban).	the State; SS2: rest Urban: Two SSS as in rural but grouping done in terms of MPCE instead of land possessed (2 hhs surveyed from each SSS for both rural & urban).

ANNEXURE VIII

Growth of Persons Attending Educational Institutions (Usual Status)

Round	*Numbers (in '000s)*		*AAGR (previous rd.)*	
	Age Group 15-29	*All Age Groups*	*Age Group 15-29*	*All Age Groups*
1. Rural Females				
50th	6049	47260		
55th	8990	63978	6.83	5.18
58th	11209	74433	8.36	5.66
2. Rural Males				
50th	15204	75709		
55th	17973	91637	2.83	3.23
58th	20800	99316	5.46	2.97
3. Rural				
50th	21253	122969		
55th	26963	155615	4.05	4.00
58th	32009	173749	6.44	4.09
4. Urban Females				
50th	7024	27201		
55th	8125	32868	2.46	3.20
58th	10211	35168	8.67	2.49
5. Urban Males				
50th	10498	34583		
55th	12805	40893	3.37	2.83
58th	13559	42603	2.10	1.50
6. Urban				
50th	17522	61784		
55th	20930	73760	3.01	3.00
58th	23770	77771	4.74	1.94
7. All India				
50th	38776	184753		
55th	47893	229376	3.58	3.67
58th	55780	251520	5.70	3.41
8. All India (Females)				
50th	13073	74462		
55th	17115	96846	4.59	4.48
58th	21420	109601	8.50	4.60
9. All India (Males)				
50th	25703	110292		
55th	30779	132530	3.05	3.11
58th	34359	141919	4.08	2.52

Source: NSSO.

ANNEXURE IX

Table 1

State-wise Population and Employment Estimates (in '000s) by Usual Status as on 1st January, 1994

	Rural		Urban		Total	
	Population	Employment	Population	Employment	Population	Employment
1. Andhra Pradesh	50453	29068	18671	6995	69123	36063
2. Assam	20808	7170	2727	899	23535	8069
3. Bihar (undivided)	80276	27971	12210	3299	92485	31270
4. Gujarat	28314	13756	15441	5375	43755	19131
5. Haryana	13101	4904	4556	1589	17657	6493
6. Jammu & Kashmir	6329	2891	2011	640	8340	3530
7. Karnataka	32107	16637	14953	5511	47060	22149
8. Kerala	22008	8468	7842	2968	29850	11436
9. Madhya Pradesh (undivided)	53542	26416	16572	5226	70114	31642
10. Maharashtra	50382	25872	33222	11925	83604	37797
11. Orissa	28468	12387	4565	1560	33033	13947
12. Punjab	14779	5804	6565	2237	21343	8042
13. Rajasthan	36363	18189	10874	3659	47236	21848
14. Tamil Nadu	36244	19576	21157	8557	57402	28133
15. Uttar Pradesh (undivided)	118441	44872	29930	9167	148370	54039
16. West Bengal	51612	19468	19694	7139	71306	26606
17. Delhi	948	348	9544	3221	10492	3569
Major States	644175	283796	230532	79968	874707	363765

Source: NSSO.

Table 2

State-wise Population and Employment Estimates (in '000s) by Usual Status as on 1st January, 2000

	Rural		*Urban*		*Total*	
	Population	*Employment*	*Population*	*Employment*	*Population*	*Employment*
1. Andhra Pradesh	54563	29573	20445	7115	75008	36688
2. Assam	22806	7959	3312	1099	26117	9059
3. Bihar (undivided)	92650	31316	14243	3789	106893	35104
4. Gujarat	31156	13989	18313	6318	49469	20307
5. Haryana	14697	5085	5829	1830	20526	6915
6. Jammu & Kashmir	7399	3270	2427	682	9826	3952
7. Karnataka	34420	16763	17433	6380	51853	23143
8. Kerala	23312	9022	8196	3057	31508	12079
9. Madhya Pradesh (undivided)	59742	27601	19521	6227	79264	33828
10. Maharashtra	54862	26553	39702	13737	94563	40290
11. Orissa	30810	13033	5349	1696	36159	14728
12. Punjab	15874	6508	7959	2810	23833	9318
13. Rajasthan	42081	18768	12801	4135	54882	22903
14. Tamil Nadu	35134	18024	26338	10351	61472	28375
15. Uttar Pradesh (undivided)	134583	46431	35517	10797	170100	57228
16. West Bengal	56702	19789	21958	7685	78660	27474
17. Delhi	945	291	12287	4079	13233	4371
Major States	711736	293975	271629	91787	983366	385763

Table 3

State-wise Population and Employment Estimates (in '000s) by Usual Status as on 1st October, 2002

	Rural		Urban		Total	
	Population	Employment	Population	Employment	Population	Employment
1. Andhra Pradesh	56558	28505	21314	7758	77871	36263
2. Assam	23784	9752	3620	1173	27404	10924
3. Bihar (undivided)	98942	32651	15285	4050	114227	36701
4. Gujarat	32553	15495	19802	7505	52354	23000
5. Haryana	15492	5407	6526	1938	22018	7345
6. Jammu & Kashmir	7948	3084	2645	844	10593	3928
7. Karnataka	35536	17448	18703	7107	54239	24555
8. Kerala	23935	9263	8364	2852	32299	12115
9. Madhya Pradesh (undivided)	62819	28708	21043	7049	83862	35758
10. Maharashtra	57046	27953	43080	16026	100126	43978
11. Orissa	31947	14376	5753	1910	37700	16286
12. Punjab	16402	6643	8694	3086	25096	9729
13. Rajasthan	44994	18988	13796	4456	58790	23444
14. Tamil Nadu	34636	17734	29119	11677	63756	29411
15. Uttar Pradesh (undivided)	142699	50230	38415	11064	181114	61294
16. West Bengal	59200	21608	23080	8240	82280	29848
17. Delhi	944	304	13796	4442	14740	4746
Major States	745436	308148	293034	101177	1038470	409325

Table 4

Average Annual Growth Rate (AAGR) of Population and Employment during 1994 to 2000 (50th Rd. to 55th Rd.)

	Rural		*Urban*		*Total*	
	Population	*Employment*	*Population*	*Employment*	*Population*	*Employment*
1. Andhra Pradesh	1.31	0.29	1.52	0.28	1.37	0.29
2. Assam	1.54	1.76	3.29	3.41	1.75	1.95
3. Bihar (undivided)	2.42	1.90	2.60	2.33	2.44	1.95
4. Gujarat	1.61	0.28	2.88	2.73	2.07	1.00
5. Haryana	1.93	0.61	4.19	2.38	2.54	1.06
6. Jammu & Kashmir	2.64	2.08	3.18	1.07	2.77	1.90
7. Karnataka	1.17	0.13	2.59	2.47	1.63	0.73
8. Kerala	0.96	1.06	0.74	0.49	0.90	0.92
9. Madhya Pradesh (undivided)	1.84	0.73	2.77	2.97	2.07	1.12
10. Maharashtra	1.43	0.43	3.01	2.39	2.07	1.07
11. Orissa	1.33	0.85	2.68	1.40	1.52	0.91
12. Punjab	1.20	1.93	3.26	3.87	1.86	2.49
13. Rajasthan	2.46	0.52	2.76	2.06	2.53	0.79
14. Tamil Nadu	-0.52	-1.37	3.72	3.22	1.15	0.14
15. Uttar Pradesh (undivided)	2.15	0.57	2.89	2.77	2.30	0.96
16. West Bengal	1.58	0.27	1.83	1.24	1.65	0.54
17. Delhi	-0.04	-2.94	4.30	4.02	3.94	3.43
Major States	**1.68**	**0.59**	**2.77**	**2.32**	**1.97**	**0.98**

Table 5

Average Annual Growth Rate (AAGR) of Population and Employment during 2000 to 2002 (55th Rd. to 58th Rd.)

	Rural		*Urban*		*Total*	
	Population	*Employment*	*Population*	*Employment*	*Population*	*Employment*
1. Andhra Pradesh	1.31	-1.33	1.52	3.20	1.37	-0.42
2. Assam	1.54	7.66	3.29	2.38	1.76	7.05
3. Bihar (undivided)	2.42	1.53	2.60	2.46	2.44	1.63
4. Gujarat	1.61	3.79	2.88	6.46	2.08	4.63
5. Haryana	1.93	2.25	4.19	2.11	2.58	2.22
6. Jammu & Kashmir	2.64	-2.11	3.18	8.05	2.77	-0.23
7. Karnataka	1.17	1.47	2.59	4.00	1.65	2.18
8. Kerala	0.96	0.96	0.74	-2.49	0.91	0.11
9. Madhya Pradesh (undivided)	1.84	1.44	2.77	4.61	2.07	2.04
10. Maharashtra	1.43	1.89	3.01	5.76	2.10	3.24
11. Orissa	1.33	3.63	2.68	4.42	1.53	3.72
12. Punjab	1.20	0.75	3.26	3.47	1.90	1.58
13. Rajasthan	2.46	0.42	2.76	2.76	2.53	0.85
14. Tamil Nadu	-0.52	-0.59	3.72	4.48	1.34	1.31
15. Uttar Pradesh (undivided)	2.15	2.90	2.89	0.89	2.31	2.53
16. West Bengal	1.58	3.25	1.83	2.57	1.65	3.06
17. Delhi	-0.04	1.59	4.30	3.15	4.00	3.04
Major States	**1.70**	**1.73**	**2.80**	**3.61**	**2.00**	**2.18**

ANNEXURE X

Enrolment Capacities for Vocational Education and Training in Different States and Union Territories

State/Union Territory	*Enrolment Capacity in Vocational Education (+2 Stage)*	*Seating Capacity Under Craftsmen Training Scheme*	*Intake Capacity*
(1)	*(2)*	*(3)*	
1. Andhra Pradesh	94,000	1,09,017	15,775
2. Arunachal Pradesh	200	368	180
3. Assam	25,500	4,620	1,348
4. Bihar	37,600	16912,	4,548
5. Chattisgarh	-	14,320	*
6. Delhi	4,650	10,520	5,237
7. Goa	5,300	2,912	1,190#
8. Gujarat	51,600	73,062	10,414
9. Haryana	43,350	14,617	5,375
10. Himachal Pradesh	4,100	5,301	815
11. Jammu & Kashmir	1,900	4,124	2,850
13. Karnataka	71,350	46,092	36,038
14. Kerala	50,400	57,505	8,190
15. Madhya Pradesh	65,350	21,070	8,470
16. Maharashtra	1,74,000	93,586	34,815
17. Manipur	2,850	540	215
18. Meghalaya	1,000	926	190
19. Mizoram	2,550	294	390
20. Nagaland	800	404	120
21. Orissa	46,200	17,796	4,994
22. Punjab	42,300	15,851	7,265
23. Rajasthan	23,250	10,172	2,973
24. Sikkim	450	140	270
25. Tamil Nadu	1,07,000	81,388	43,754
26. Tripura	600	400	125
27. Uttar Pradesh	1,17,500	47,512	12,450
28. Uttaranchal	-	6,656	
29. West Bengal	1,950	12,304	6130
30. Andaman & Nicobar Islands	150	204	170
31. Chandigarh	2,900	936	640

Contd. ...

... Contd. ...

State/Union Territory	*Enrolment Capacity in Vocational Education (+2 Stage)*	*Seating Capacity Under Craftsmen Training Scheme*	*Intake Capacity*
(1)	*(2)*	*(3)*	
32. Dadra & Nagar Haveli	100	228	-
33. Daman & Diu	250	388	-
34. Lakshadweep	-	96	-
35. Pondicherry	800	1,680	742
All India	**9,72,750**	**6,71,941**	**2,15,675**

Source: Draft Project Implementation Plan of National Programme on Technical and Vocational Education and Training (TVE&T), Department of Secondary and Higher Education, Ministry of Human Resource Development, DGE&T, Ministry of Labour, National Technical Manpower Information System, IAMR.

Note: # includes Daman & Diu, * included in Madhya Pradesh.

ANNEXURE XI

Indicative List of Vocations under Identified Sectors– Reference in Para 8.9 C

Agricultural and Allied Sector

Largely Self Employment and Tied up to Credit Facility.

Dairying; Fish Farming; Fish Processing; Fish seed Production; Floriculture.

Poultry Farming; Sericulture.

Self-employment/wage Employment: Food Preservation; Medicinal and Aromatic Plant Industry; Plant Protection; Seed Production Technology; Vegetable Seed Production, Maintenance of Power Driven Farm Machinery, Soil Testing, Veterinary Assistance and Leather Products.

Construction: While labour saving technology is increasingly used, it is restricted to large complexes and metropolitan areas. Scattered construction activities in small/medium towns is expected to use less of these technologies, and the skill required should include building maintenance services. Vocations for which augmentation of training facilities is required include: Carpentry; Masonry, Plumbing, domestic electrical installation and maintenance; marble cutting and polishing.

Small Scale Manufacturing: Vocations to be tied up with industrial estates, industry clusters; expansion of existing intake capacity in related vocations and entrepreneurial development.

Tertiary Sector: Keeping in view the growth in automobile industry augmenting intake capacity of auto and diesel motor mechanics, denting and painting, two wheeler mechanic, repair and maintenance of household electrical goods, refrigerators, air conditioners, coolers, mobile phones, CD player, assembly and repair of inverters;

Laboratory assistance in diagnostic services; tourism and travel: house keeping, tourist and travel Guides, catering and restaurant management, export-import practices and documentation.

ANNEXURE XII

Summary and Overview of the Report by the Special Group on Targeting 10 Million Employment Opportunity per Year by Planning Commission, Government of India May 2002 (Page 1-17) under Chairmanship of Dr. S.P Gupta, Member Planning Commission

The examination of the major sources of information revealed that the unemployment rate in India has increased significantly since 1993-94 and was above 7.3 per cent in 1999-2000 compared to 6.0 per cent in 1993-94 in Current Daily Status basis. For Scheduled Castes, the corresponding unemployment rates were 9.6 per cent and 8.3 per cent in 1999-2000 and 1993-94 respectively. It is apprehended that now these rates have further increased.

This situation has placed a big challenge before the nation, the policymakers, entrepreneurs and people in general, asking for remedial action. At the same time, increased globalisation, advent of new technology and frontiers of knowledge along with the revival of many traditional technologies and the benefit of increased deregulation and many key economic reforms have opened up, along with several initial challenges, tremendous new opportunities for higher growth and additional job opportunities. Now, in the Tenth Plan it is time to meet the challenges and make use of these new opportunities.

The Group views that to reach the country's development target both in output and employment, in a viable and equitable fashion, several major changes from the past economic policies and launching of innovative pro-employment programmes will be needed in the immediate future-failing which the level of unemployment and also the quality of employment may deteriorate further significantly below the present level.

The deliberation of the group brings out a clear message that if the experiences of the late-nineties are extrapolated i.e., repeated in future, then India is going to face increasingly higher incidence of unemployment, with an ever-increasing gap between the demand for jobs and supply of job opportunities.

On the basis of this ground reality, the Group concluded that for generating the desirable high level of employment, we have to target the unorganised sector, including small and medium enterprises, which also cover a large part of the services sector of the economy, and which have more labour intensiveness in production.

But at the same time it realised that the unorganised sector, to be made viable under the new competitive circumstances, suitable policies and programmes have to be undertaken so that the sectors become more productive and quality conscious. One such policy is to ensure that the rule of level playing field strictly be applied for this sector. For this, appropriate programmes and policies should be devised for suitable reallocation of capital in favour of the labour intensive industries and economising the use of capital in the highly capital intensive organised sector (keeping in view our labour surplus, capital scarce nature of the economy) to boost the growth and to make 8 per cent growth feasible. This may be helped by the fact that the capital efficiency in the unorganised sector is estimated to be much higher than in the organised sector.[1]

To sum up, the employment strategy for the future, to meet the Plan's employment goals is to encourage the use of labour intensive and capital saving technology, in general and to rejuvenate the growth of the unorganised sector in particular, which at present contributes 92 per cent to the country's employment and enjoys more than seven times labour intensity per unit of production, as compared to the organised sector. However, the unorganised sector needs to be made more productive to sustain itself against the domestic and international competition by proper choice of programmes and policies compatible with India's economic reforms and the WTO rules.

There are cases in many of the developed and successful Newly Industrialising Economies, where SMEs are still surviving and with

1. *SIDBI Annual Report* 2002.

given selective incentives, are making substantial contribution to employment, outputs and exports. The focus on the unorganised sector is therefore based not on ideology but on pragmatism when 92 per cent of India's employment and 56 per cent of export and average 46-50 per cent of employment of other emerging countries come from this sector. The group is aware that the organised and unorganised sectors are to co-exist satisfying the different needs of development and growth, as have happened in most of the developed and newly industrialised economies.

The case for encouraging the growth of the organised sector is certainly very strong because of its capacity to invest in major infrastructure projects (in most cases, they are capital intensive) to most needed support to the growth activities of rest of the economy. But it should not be expected to generate employment, because of its capital intensive nature. It has been estimated that because of its low employment base and employment elasticity even if it grows at 30 per cent per annum over a Ten year period, its contribution to total employment will increase hardly by one per cent of the total employment.

The proposed strategy focused on the informal sector however will work only if SME's can produce quality products at competitive prices. All available studies show that the growth and the quality of jobs in the unorganised sector has been very much affected by the absence of timely easy credit, improved technology, better trained workers, good infrastructure, quality consciousness, modern marketing, proper organisation and a synergy with the large organised industries. No reliable data is available as to the flow of total credit going to the unorganised *vis-à-vis* the organised sector. But in a limited way if we look at the outstanding bank credit of scheduled commercial banks, we notice that the flow has increased significantly in favour of the organised sector from 46.2 per cent in 1993-94 to 62.9 per cent in 1999-2000 whereas in the unorganised sector, it fell from 53.8 per cent to 37.1 per cent during the same period. In other words, bank credit grew by 20.5 per cent per annum in organised sector as against 7.5 per cent in the unorganised sector. This is against a marginal increase in the share of the organised sector as a percentage of GDP to the total. *This trend must be reversed.* Similarly, percentage of Net Bank Credit to the total credit going to SSI sector came down from 17.5 per cent in 1998 to 14.2 per cent in 2001 and in 2002 touching 11 per cent of the total. Therefore, a higher allocation of credit is needed to the unorganised sector by reducing say the high transaction cost in the credit market when the capital efficiency in the unorganised sector is expected to be much higher than the organised sector. Besides, all measures should be taken to improve its technology, quality and productivity by better education and vocational training, skill development, organisational changes like cluster development etc. Indeed hardly 5.3 per cent of Indian youths in the labour force in the age group of 19-24 in 1999-2000 are trained in vocational skills through formal training as against nearly 30 per cent in selected LDC's and above 70 per cent in developed countries. Further, because of its comparative advantages for employment generation and high employment elasticity, the employment intensive character of the unorganised sector should be protected by selecting proper labour-intensive technology drawn from all sources including the one from grassroots indigenous levels and proper rules and regulations should be laid down so that benefits of higher growth get translated in the form of increased earnings of the workers. This is needed because traditionally this sector is vulnerable to exploitation.

As has already been mentioned, because the major portion of the poor are in the unorganised sector, a faster growth and productivity in this sector will also reduce poverty. *In the attempt to increase the labour productivity, more emphasis should be on the growth of this sector rather than by substituting labour for capital. Further, to improve the job quality and its security, major changes in legislation will be needed regarding basic social security measures, working conditions, minimum wages and protection of labour interests. They have all been discussed in the main body of the Report.* The report also attempted to identify the activities where there is a major potential of having a large new job opportunities like social forestry, animal husbandry, fishing, horticulture and related areas in agriculture and small and medium industries, construction, tourism, information technology, financial sector, education and health. A major portion of these activities is in the unorganised sector. These sectors also include a large number of self-employeds and artisans.

In many instances, the proposed changes in policies and programmes need not entail any significant additional finance. They would ask for drawn on the knowledge of grassroot enterprises, skills and often the indigenous technologies. This should be further supported by creation of an enabling environment by removing all legislative hurdles and bureaucratic interference. Besides, it is realised that there is a need for launching specific employment generating programmes in some areas where aggregate growth is having little impact.

Care should be taken to avoid programmes or schemes, which generate one time employment only.

The recommended policy changes are spread over a large canvass, covering at one end hi-tech large organised industries and services and at the other end pertaining to those in the small and medium business including even in the tiny industries in the unorganised sector. However, the general message is that the unorganised sector initially will need more support and incentives from the government as compared to the organised sector. The Report ended with the view that most of the education and skill development in the past have been geared to satisfy the need of the organised sector, which provided higher remuneration and better job quality and security. But in future, because of the limit in the absorbing capacity for additional employment in the organised sector, education and skills need to be orientated primarily towards the needs of the unorganised sector like agriculture, small industry, services and self-employed as also the new areas like IT, tourism and financial sectors.

It is however worth mentioning that unless for every programme/ scheme, appropriate delivery systems are developed, most of the above employment generation targets may not materialise. For correcting this gap, among many other necessary measures, the key one is to launch an ambitious civil service renewal programme aimed at strengthening the delivery institutions, district administration and the *panchayats*.

ANNEXURE XIII

Summary Recommendations of Report of the Study Group on Development of Small Scale Enterprises, (Page 4-8) Planning Commission, New Delhi (2001) under Chairmanship of Dr. S.P. Gupta, Member Planning Commission

Some of the important recommendations of the Study Group are :

(a) A three-tier definition of SSEs covering tiny, small and medium sector. Medium sector definition has been brought in for the first time to help SSI units to graduate to medium and then to large scale. Medium scale units (Rs. 1 crore to Rs. 10 crore) would not be provided fiscal and other policy support as available to SSI units. However, these units would be helped by providing credit for technology up-gradation and modernisation from a separate fund.

(b) Need of bringing awareness in small industries sector about WTO implications and its impact on SSI sector, particularly due to bringing more items under OGL as per WTP obligation. Setting up of a new cell in the office of DC (SSI) for matters relating to WTO and its implications on SSI sector.

(c) Need for a single comprehensive law for SSI sector, like Small Business Administration (SBA) Act of United States.

(d) This Study Group has recommended that presently reservation should be continued for SSE sector. However, to enhance exports, the Study Group has recommended that non-SSI units can take up production of reserved items with 30 per cent export obligation to be completed over three years. Presently, this limit is 50 per cent.

(e) The Study Group has recommended to raise investment ceiling from Rs. one crore to Rs. five crore for plant and machinery for export-oriented industries like leather products, garments, hosiery, hand tools, toys, packaging materials, auto components, pharmaceuticals, food processing, etc.

(f) For infrastructure development, the Study Group has recommended a corpus of Rs. 2,000 crore so that adequate infrastructure facilities are available to the SSI sector.

(g) To encourage technocrat entrepreneurs in high-tech industries like electronics, information technology, bio-technology, pharmaceuticals, an Incubation Infrastructure Development Fund with a corpus Rs. 1,000 crore has been recommended by the Study group for setting up of Incubation Centres (ICs) in the Tenth Plan. These ICs would provide all facilities and finance, technical consultancy, etc. to encourage techno-crafts and first generation entrepreneurs to successfully take up production based on recent technologies having potential, but not tried so far. Such incubation centres have been good results in developed countries as well as South East Asian countries.

(h) With a view to encourage large units to make prompt payment to SSI units against deliveries made by SSI units, the Study Group has recommended:

- Lead role of associations as done by CII by issuing a code of ethics on prompt payment to its members.
- Denial of MODVAT credit to defaulters in respect of payment to SSI units for more than 120 days' delay.
- Amendment of Income Tax Act to disallow unpaid SSI bills from business expenditure.
- Strengthening of factoring services.
- Monitoring of implementation of Interest on Delayed Payments to Small Scale and Ancillary Industrial Undertakings Act, 1993, by DC (SSI).

(i) To encourage better linkages between large and medium units, the Study Group has recommended:

- FDI to be encouraged in SSI's for better technology transfer (within the permitted ceiling of equity participation by large scale units in the equity of SSI units).
- Allowing excise exemption on SSI manufactured goods for large units under brand name in urban areas as is presently allowed for rural areas.

(j) The Study group has recommended enactment of Limited Partnership Act to bring in more risk capital in SSI sector and the concept of limited liability. SAMADHAN scheme for one time settlement of dues of sick SSI units so that assets could be reutilised. Sick units to make one time payment including interest not more than double of the credit/loan amount. This would provide an exit route to entrepreneurs of sick units.

(k) To free the SSI sector from rigid and harassing regulatory laws applicable to the SSI sector and to reduce inspectors' visits, the Study Group has recommended a number of measures, like (i) need for single unified Act for small enterprises, (ii) replacement of inspection by self-certification, (iii) simplification of regulatory laws, etc.

(l) To enhance the data base for the SSI sector, the Study Group has recommended (i) conduction of fresh census for SSI sector, (ii) collection of detailed data on clusters, (iii) involvement of SSI associations in the census and other data collection activities.

(m) The Study Group has made a number of recommendations for human resource development of SSI sector which includes inputs like training, skill upgradation, new management practices, etc.

(n) The Study Group has also made a number of recommendations on fiscal and financial measures covering:

- Setting up of targets for tiny and SSI units for credit from banks and FIs under priority sector lending.
- Need for reduction of cost of credit for SSI sector.
- Setting up of more specialised bank branches of SSI sector.
- Measures for strengthening resource support to SIDBI and to make available cheaper resources for on-lending at low interest rates to SSI sector.
- Venture capital for SSIs.
- Setting up of a special venture capital type fund of Rs. 500 crore to be named as *Laghu Udyog Nirman Nidhi* for equity support.
- Standardisation of procedure and simplification of forms by banks.
- Statutory backing to State Level Inter-Institutional Committees (SLIICs).
- Raising of present excise exemption limit from Rs. 50 lakh to Rs. 100 lakh.
- Five per cent notional MODVAT credit to large units buying components, etc. from SSI units.
- Exemption from excise registration and visits of excise inspectors until the turnover reaches a limit of Rs. 50 lakh with a system of self-declaration.
- Extension of Credit Guarantee Fund Scheme with a corpus of Rs. 2,500 crore.

- Allowing additional 10 percentage point abatement over and above the existing rate of abatement under maximum Retail Price (MRP) based assessment to levy excise duty on SSI products. Presently large and small units are allowed 30 to 50 percentage point abatement on MRP for levying excise duty.
- More effective monitoring of credit flow to SSI sector by the Monitoring Committee of Reserve Bank of India.
- To make available credit to SSI sector at a reasonable cost, *viz*, PLR plus three per cent.
- Raising the limit of composite loans from Rs. 10 lakh to Rs. 25 lakh to encourage tiny units to get term loan and working capital from same bank/FI.
- Not to cover all future fixed assets of assisted units for securing its advances.
- Need for restructuring of SFCs.
- Measures to enhance resource support to SIDBI.
- Measures for time-bound disposal of loan applications and easy documentation.

(o) They Study Group has recommended following measures for technology upgradation and modernisation of SSI units:

- Setting up of a Technology Bank for collection and dissemination of Information about technology sources.
- A Technology Up-gradation and Modernisation Fund of Rs. 5,000 crore with an interest subsidy of five per cent.
- Accelerated depreciation on plant and machinery installed for technology up-gradation and modernisation.
- Five per cent custom duty on capital goods with import obligation and five per cent interest subsidy as recommended for technology modernisation.

(p) To provide increased marketing support to the SSI sector, the Study Group has recommended that:

- Statutory backing and continuation of the Price Preference (up to 15 per cent to SSI products) under Government Purchase Programme and Purchase Preference Scheme in respect of 358 items on purchases made by government departments.

- Upto 33 per cent of government purchases may be done from SSI sector on the lines of USA.
- Industry status to all types of consortium industries so that they can avail finance from banks and FIs.
- Subsidisation of participation of SSI units up to 50 per cent in air fare for export related buyer-seller meets.
- Timely release of institutional finance for export orders of SSI units.

Most of these recommendations have been accepted and the SSI Ministry is on implementation.

References

Arora, Sant Lal and Vijay K. Saxena (2003). "Sector-wise Trends of Productivity in India", *IAMR Working Paper* No. 3/2003.

Assaf, George B. (2004). *Too Many with Too Little: The Challenge for India's Development Paradigm*, Konark, New Delhi.

Bhalla, Sheila (2004). *India's Rural Economy: Issues and Evidence*, Institute for Human Development, New Delhi (mimeo)

Chadha, G.K. and P.P. Sahu (2002). "Post-Reform Setbacks in Rural Employment: Issues that Need Further Scrutiny", *Economic and Political Weekly*, Vol. 37, No. 21, May 25-31.

Chandra, Ashoka (1999). "The Role of Training in Productivity: The Objectives of NRF", in M.L. Nandrajob (ed.), *National Renewal Fund: A Look Ahead*, International Labour Organisation, New Delhi

Deshpande, L.K., Alakh N. Sharma, A.K. Karan and S. Sarkar (2003). *Economic Reforms and Labour Market Flexibility*, Institute of Human Development, New Delhi

Dev, S. Mahendra (2004). "Safety Nets for Chronic Poor in India: An Overview", *CPRC-IIPA Working Paper Series* No. 19, Indian Institute of Public Administration, New Delhi and Chronic Poverty Research Centre, Manchester, U.K.

Gaiha, R. (1996). "Do Rural Public Works Influence Agricultural Wages? The Case of the Employment Guarantee Scheme in India", *Oxford Development Studies*, Vol., 25, No. 3

Government of India (2005). *The National Rural Employment Guarantee Bill, 2004*, August 23, New Delhi.

———. (1998). *Planning and Development in India* (Chairman: Dr. S.P. Gupta), Allied Publishers Pvt. Ltd., New Delhi.

Guhan, S. (1995). "Social Security Options for Developing Countries", in Figueiredo, Jose B. and Zafar Shaheed (eds.), *New Approaches to Poverty Analysis and Policy–II*, International Institute for Labour Studies, Geneva.

Gupta, Partha Das (2003). "World Poverty: Cause and Pathways", *The Annual Conference on Developing Economies*, World Bank, May, Bangalore, India.

Gupta, S.P. and K. Venkataraman (ed.) (1992). *Management of Technical Change*, Allied Publishers Ltd.

Gupta, S.P. and V.B. Singh (2000). "Trickle Down Theory Revisited: The Role of Employment and Poverty", Memorial Lecture, *Indian Journal of Labour Economics* Vol. 43 No. 1.

Gupta, S.P. and V.V. Giri (2003). "Employment in the New Economy Order and the Strategy in the Tenth Plan", *V V Giri Memorial Lecture*, Giri Institute of Development Strategy, Lucknow.

Hindustan Times (2005). *Flyover in 36 Hours: Is that Possible*, January 5, New Delhi.

International Labour Organization (2001). *World Employment Report 2001*, Geneva.

———. (2003). "Employment Intensive Investment and Poverty Alleviation: Committees on Technical Co-operation", *Thematic Evaluation Report* GB 286/TC/1, March, Geneva.

Kumar, Anand (2001). "Political Sociology of Poverty in India: Between Politics of Poverty and Poverty of Politics", *CPRC-IIPA Working Paper Series* No. 3, Indian Institute of Public Administration, New Delhi and Chronic Poverty Research Centre, Manchester, U.K.

Mathur, Ashok and P.S. Raikhy (ed.) (2002), *Economic Liberalisation and its Implications for Employment*, Deep & Deep Publication Pvt. Ltd., New Delhi

Mehta, Rajesh and Pooja Agarwal (2002). *WTO Negotiations and Indian Small Scale Industry*, Research and Information System for Developing Countries (RIS), Published jointly with Federation of Indian Micro and Small & Medium Enterprises (FISME), and Office of Development commissioner (SSI), Ministry of Small Scale, 2004.

Min, K.J. (2004). "Victims of Efficiency", *Far Eastern Economic Review*, January 29.

Ministry of Finance (2005). *Economic Survey, 2004-2005*, Govt. of India.

Ministry of Small Scale Industries and Agro & Rural Industries (2004). *Third All India Census of Small Scale Industries (2001-02)*, Government of India,

Nagaraj, R. (2004). "Fall in Organised Manufacturing Employment", *Economic and Political Weekly*, Vol. XXXIX No. 29, July 24.

Nayyar, Rohini (2002). "The Contribution of Public Works and Other Labour-based Infrastructure to Poverty Alleviation: The Indian Experience", *Issues in Employment and Poverty, Discussions Paper* 3, International Labour Office, Geneva.

———. (2004). "Planning for the Development of Backward Districts", *CPRC-IIPA Working Paper Series* No. 23, Indian Institute of Public Administration, New Delhi and Chronic Poverty Research Centre, Manchester, U.K.

NSSO. *Report on Household Consumer Expenditure and Employment: Unemployment Situation in India*, Different Rounds, Ministry of Statistics & Programme Implementation, Government of India, New Delhi.

NSSO (2001). *Employment and Unemployment Situation in India: 1999-2000*, Part-I, p.73, May, Ministry of Statistics & Programme Implementation, Govt. of India.

Papola, T.S. and Alakh N. Sharma (2004). *Employment and Poverty Reduction in India: Policy Perspectives based on Recent ILO Studies*, Paper prepared for ILO, Geneva.

Pant, K.C. (2003). *India's Development Scenario: Next Decade and Beyond*, in Two Volumes, Academic Foundation, New Delhi.

Planning Commission (1951). *First Five Year Plan (1951-56)*, Government of India, New Delhi.

———. (1956). *Second Five Year Plan (1956-61)*, Government of India, New Delhi.

———. (1961). *Third Five Year Plan (1961-66)*, Government of India, New Delhi.

———. (1969). *Fourth Five Year Plan (1969-74)*, Government of India, New Delhi.

———. (1974). *Fifth Five Year Plan (1974-79)*,Government of India, New Delhi.

———. (1980). *Sixth Five Year Plan (1980-85)*, Government of India, New Delhi.

———. (1985). *Seventh Five Year Plan (1985-90)*, Government of India, New Delhi.

———. (1992). *Eight Five Year Plan (1992-97)*, Government of India, New Delhi.

———. (1997). *Ninth Five Year Plan (1997-2002)*, Government of India, New Delhi.

———. (2001). *Report of the Study Group on Development of Small Scale Enterpises*, (Chairman: Dr. S.P. Gupta), March, Government of India, New Delhi.

———. (2002). *Tenth Five Year Plan (2002-07)*, Government of India, New Delhi.

———. (2002). *Special Group on Targeting Ten Million Employment Opportunities Per Year - Employment Generating Growth* (Chairman Dr. S.P. Gupta), Government of India, New Delhi.

———. (2002). *Report of the Committee on India Vision 2020* (under Chairmanship of Dr. S.P. Gupta), Government of India, New Delhi.

Purushotham, P. (2004). *Rural Non-farm Employment*, National Institute of Rural Development, Hyderabad.

Radhakrishna, R., K. Hanumantha Rao, C. Ravi and B. Sambi Reddy (2004). "Chronic Poverty and Malnutrition in India", *CPRC-IIPA Working Paper Series* No. 11, Indian Institute of Public Administration, New Delhi and Chronic Poverty Research Centre, Manchester, U.K.

Rajan, S. Irudaya (2004). "Chronic Poverty among Indian Elderly", *CPRC-IIPA Working Paper Series* No. 17, Indian Institute of Public Administration, New Delhi and Chronic Poverty Research Centre, Manchester, U.K.

Raghavan, K. and Leena Sekhar (ed.) (1995), *Poverty & Employment*, Institute of Applied Manpower Research, New Age International (P) Limited, New Delhi.

Rodrik, Dani and Arvind Subramanian (2004). "From 'Hindu Growth' to Productivity Surge: The Mystery of the Indian Growth Transition", *NBER Working Paper* No. 10376, March, National Bureau of Economic Research (NBER) Program, Massachusetts, U.S.A.

Roy, Prosterman and Jennifer Brown (2004). *Land Tenure Reform in China and India*, May 27-29, Rural Development Institute, New Delhi.

Saachs, Jeffry D. (2005). *Investing in Development–A Practical Plan to Achieve the Millennium Development Goals–Overview*, UN Millennium Project, New York.

Sen, Amartya and Jean Dreze (2004). *The Amartya Sen and Jean Dreze Omnibus:* "Poverty and Famines", "Hunger and Public Action", and "India - Economic Development and Social Opportunity", Oxford University Press.

Sharma, Alakh N. (2004). "Globalisation, Work and Social Exclusion: Emerging Global and Indian Perspective", *Kunda Datar Memorial Lecture*, August 26-27, Gokhale Institute of Politics and Economics, Pune.

Shetty, S.L. (2005) "Saving and Investment Estimates", *Economic and Political Weekly*, Vol.XL No.7, February 12.

Start, Daniel and Craig Johnson (2002). *Diversification, Opportunity and Access: Concepts and Issues in the Study of Rural Livelihoods*, October, Overseas Development Institute, London.

Stiglitz, Joseph E. (2002). Globalisation and its Discontents. Penguin, London.

Sundaram, K. and Suresh D. Tendulkar (2003). "Poverty Among Social and Economic Groups In India in the 1990s", *Working Paper* No. 118, Centre for Development Economics, Delhi School of Economics, Delhi.

Swaminathan, M.S. (2004). "Technological Change in Food Production: Implications for Vulnerable Sections", *CPRC-IIPA Working Paper Series* No. 20, Indian Institute of Public Administration, New Delhi and Chronic Poverty Research Centre, Manchester, U.K.

Thomas, P.V. (2004). "Chronic Poverty in Rural Areas: The Role of Government Policy", *CPRC-IIPA Working Paper Series* No. 16, Indian Institute of Public Administration, New Delhi and Chronic Poverty Research Centre, Manchester, U.K.

United Nations Development Programme (2001). *Human Development Report 2001: Making New Technologies Work for Human Development*, published for UNDP, New York, Oxford, Oxford University Press.

World Bank (2004). *World Development Report: Making Services Work for Poor People*, Washington DC.

U

U

Y

Z

Y

Z

Index

H

I

M